What Your C

Coaching the 5 Practices introduc[es] ...[teach]ers as they plan for orchestrating p[roductive]... ...[m]od[e]l, coaches work collaboratively with teachers as they engage in an inquiry cycle that reinforces the importance of pre-planning, reflection, and encouragement in a productive teacher-coach relationship. This user-friendly model, along with the additional tools, resources, and samples, is a welcome addition to the 5 Practices family!

Latrenda Knighten
President-Elect (2023–2024), NCTM
Curriculum Supervisor, Mathematics, East Baton Rouge
Baton Rouge, LA

What a gem and a "must" for every coach's professional library. In this clearly written and wonderfully focused book, Smith, Yurekli, and Stein begin with a clear vision of "ambitious teaching" that is based on the powerful structure of the 5 Practices, and develop an accessible, example-laden guide to impactful coaching of mathematics. By focusing on the challenges teachers face, coaches are provided with a coherent process for significantly improving how math is taught.

Steve Leinwand
Principal Researcher, American Institutes for Research
Arlington, VA

I love how this book offers explicit guidance on the "how" of coaching for mathematical discourse, deeper conversations, and teaching growth. *Coaching the 5 Practices* offers transformational tips and features that empower both teachers and coaches. I'm excited to begin implementing this user-friendly and much needed coaching model into my practice.

Desiree Y. Harrison
Elementary Instructional Coach, Farmington Public Schools
Farmington, MI

As a 5 Practices math coach, I've eagerly awaited a resource like *Coaching the 5 Practices*. After reading, I promptly incorporated strategies—such as facilitating teachers' reflection and setting clear goals—to enhance my coaching, all while upholding teacher ownership. The inclusion of case studies, coaching conversation scripts, and templates brought the framework to life and enabled me to visualize immediate application. This book is a must-have for all ambitious math coaches!

Mona Iehl
Math Coach, Chicago Math Group
Chicago, IL

This book centers teachers' own thinking on their journeys of instructional improvement, and exudes appreciation for the wisdom of practice. This practical guide for coaching is designed with explicit attention to the parallels between ambitious teaching and coaching. The theories of teaching and learning underlying the coaching model and the model itself are rich and relevant for supporting coaches' and teachers' learning.

Ruth Heaton
Chief Executive Officer, Teachers Development Group
Portland, OR

This book presents a comprehensive coaching model designed for those supporting math teachers who are navigating challenges in implementing the 5 Practices. With its excerpts from authentic coaching conversations, readers can pause, analyze, and reflect to develop their coaching practice. A must-have, practical resource for anyone wondering how to effectively coach teachers in implementing the 5 Practices.

Jennifer Kruger
Director of Mathematics Education Outreach, Center for
Professional Development and Education Reform,
Warner Graduate School of Education and Human Development, University of Rochester
Rochester, NY

Coaching the 5 Practices will be a catalyst for sense-making and deep mathematical learning in the classroom. Smith, Yurekli, and Stein outline a brilliant coaching cycle that focuses on teacher-identified challenges and incorporates video from the lesson to generate the debrief conversation. Coaches and leaders can reflect on challenging coaching scenarios and build an understanding of the tools and processes of planning for an impactful coaching cycle.

Melanie Cifonelli
Director of Mathematics
Syracuse, NY

I wish I had this book when I started coaching! The model and the examples of its use are perfect for new coaches and for those of us who have been coaching for years. It offers clear, actionable steps that help us work on moving teachers to a discourse and thought based mathematics classroom that emphasizes conceptual learning and understanding.

Frederick L. Dillon
Mathematics Educator, Lesley University
Strongsville, OH

The pathway to ambitious teaching is wide and long. This book helps to narrow that pathway by giving you a framework for effective coaching so teachers can shift their instructional practices to follow the 5 Practices. Use these strategies and you will facilitate deep, reflective discussions that will bring insight and relief to a teacher who needs it.

Jon Orr
Mathematics Consultant and Coach
Ontario, Canada

Coaching the 5 Practices

Dedication

This book is dedicated to Victoria Bill, a close colleague, friend, and key member of the team of researchers and practitioners who worked on the project that culminated in this book. Vic passed away before this book was written, but her insights and experiences working with teachers and coaches influenced our thinking and the tools we created to support their work. Vic's passion for improving mathematics teaching and learning, particularly in urban school districts, is well known across the country. We miss her energy, commitment, enthusiasm, and bravery.

Margaret (Peg) Smith | Bilge Yurekli | Mary Kay Stein

Coaching THE 5 PRACTICES

Supporting Mathematics Teachers in Orchestrating Productive Discussions

A JOINT PUBLICATION

CORWIN Mathematics | NCTM NATIONAL COUNCIL OF TEACHERS OF MATHEMATICS

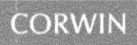

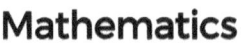

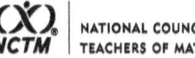

For information:

Corwin
A SAGE Company
2455 Teller Road
Thousand Oaks, California 91320
(800) 233-9936
www.corwin.com

SAGE Publications Ltd.
1 Oliver's Yard
55 City Road
London, EC1Y 1SP
United Kingdom

SAGE Publications India Pvt. Ltd.
Unit No 323-333, Third Floor, F-Block
International Trade Tower Nehru Place
New Delhi – 110 019
India

SAGE Publications Asia-Pacific Pte. Ltd.
18 Cross Street #10-10/11/12
China Square Central
Singapore 048423

Vice President and Editorial Director: Monica Eckman
Associate Director and Publisher, STEM: Erin Null
Senior Editorial Assistant: Nyle De Leon
Production Editor: Tori Mirsadjadi
Copy Editor: Sheree Van Vreede
Typesetter: Integra
Proofreader: Jennifer Grubba
Indexer: Integra
Cover Designer: Rose Storey
Marketing Manager: Margaret O'Connor

Copyright © 2025 by Corwin Press, Inc.

All rights reserved. Except as permitted by U.S. copyright law, no part of this work may be reproduced or distributed in any form or by any means, or stored in a database or retrieval system, without permission in writing from the publisher.

When forms and sample documents appearing in this work are intended for reproduction, they will be marked as such. Reproduction of their use is authorized for educational use by educators, local school sites, and/or noncommercial or nonprofit entities that have purchased the book.

All third party trademarks referenced or depicted herein are included solely for the purpose of illustration and are the property of their respective owners. Reference to these trademarks in no way indicates any relationship with, or endorsement by, the trademark owner.

Printed in the United States of America.

This book is printed on acid-free paper.

24 25 26 27 28 10 9 8 7 6 5 4 3 2 1

DISCLAIMER: This book may direct you to access third-party content via web links, QR codes, or other scannable technologies, which are provided for your reference by the author(s). Corwin makes no guarantee that such third-party content will be available for your use and encourages you to review the terms and conditions of such third-party content. Corwin takes no responsibility and assumes no liability for your use of any third-party content, nor does Corwin approve, sponsor, endorse, verify, or certify such third-party content.

Contents

Preface	xi
Where This Book Comes From	xi
What This Book Is About	xiv
Who This Book Is For	xiv
How to Use This Book	xv
Acknowledgments	xvi
About the Authors	xviii

CHAPTER 1 — A Challenge-Based Approach to Coaching — 1

Power of Organizing Around Challenges	4
Organization and Content	6
Getting Started	8

CHAPTER 2 — An Inquiry Routine for Guiding Coach-Teacher Conversations — 10

Pre-Lesson Conference: Celebration Cakes	13
Considering the Nature of Coach-Teacher Conversations: Analysis	15
Inquiry Routine	17
Guide for Designing Conferences	21
Summary	23

CHAPTER 3 — Preparing for the Lesson — 25

Supporting Teacher Lesson Planning Prior to the Pre-Lesson Conference	26
Setting a Learning Goal and Selecting a High-Level Task	27

Resolving Goals and Selecting Task Issues: Downloading Music	29
Resolving Goals and Selecting Task Issues: Analysis	31
Support for Identifying Goals and Tasks	34
Aligning Tasks and Goals: Analysis	37
Continuing the Lesson Planning Process	39
Summary	40

CHAPTER 4 Preparing for and Engaging in the Pre-Lesson Conference — 42

Preparing for the Pre-Lesson Conference	43
Identifying Challenges	44
Identifying Challenges: Analysis	49
Constructing a Pre-Lesson Conference Plan	50
Constructing a Pre-Lesson Conference Plan: Analysis	51
Engaging in the Pre-Lesson Conference	51
Pre-Lesson Conference: Fractions of Fractions	54
Engaging in the Pre-Lesson Conference: Analysis	57
Summary	61
Looking Ahead	62

CHAPTER 5 Preparing for and Engaging in the Post-Lesson Conference — 64

Preparing for the Post-Lesson Conference	65
Selecting Video Clips	65
Lesson: Tiling a Patio	68
Selecting Video Clips: Analysis	71
Analyzing Video Clips	73
Getting Ready to Plan a Post-Lesson Conference	75
Identifying Focal Noticings and Wonderings: Analysis	77
Constructing a Post-Lesson Conference Plan	79
Constructing a Post-Lesson Conference Plan: Analysis	84

Engaging in the Post-Lesson Conference	90
Post-Lesson Conference: Fractions of Fractions	91
Engaging in the Post-Lesson Conference: Analysis	94
Summary	98

CHAPTER 6   Looking Back and Looking Ahead   101

The Benefits of Our Coaching Model	102
Giving Teachers More Ownership	102
Engaging the Teacher in More of the Thinking	103
Beginning to Implement Our Coaching Model	104
Focusing on the 5 Practices	104
Setting the Expectations	105
Video Recording Lessons	105
Timing of a Coaching Cycle	106
Addressing Teacher Challenges	108
Online Coaching	108
Conclusion	109
Appendices	111
Appendix A: Teacher Challenges Tool	112
Appendix B: Guide for Designing Conferences	116
Appendix C: Task Analysis Guide	139
Appendix D: Goal and Task Identification Guide	140
Appendix E: Lesson Planning Tool	146
Appendix F: Monitoring Tool	147
Appendix G: Pre-Lesson Conference Planning Tool	148
Appendix H: Kyle's Teacher Challenges, Lesson Planning, and Monitoring Tools	149
Appendix I: Emery's Teacher Challenges, Lesson Planning, and Monitoring Tools	157
Appendix J: Coach Jesse's Pre-Lesson Conference Plan	163
Appendix K: Noticing and Wondering Tool	165
Appendix L: Post-Lesson Conference Planning Tool	166

Appendix M: Jamie and Coach Jesse's Noticing and Wondering Tool	167
Appendix N: Coach Jesse's Post-Lesson Conference Plan	168
References	170
Index	174

 Visit the companion website at **https://qrs.ly/7jfli55** for downloadable resources.

Preface

At the heart of the efforts to help students learn mathematics with understanding is the idea of *ambitious teaching*. The goal of ambitious teaching is to ensure that each and every student succeeds in doing high-quality academic work, not simply executing procedures with speed and accuracy. Ambitious teaching also requires attention to equity. Mathematics has long been considered a gatekeeper, limiting opportunities for some while promoting opportunities for others (Martin et al., 2010). These differences are apparent as early as kindergarten, with students of certain racial, ethnic, language, gender, ability, and socioeconomic backgrounds more likely to be in classrooms that focus on procedural aspects of mathematics and/or that underestimate these students' capabilities to engage in high-level problem solving (Aguirre et al., 2017; Turner & Celedón-Pattichis, 2011). Ambitious teaching requires you to challenge these long-standing practices and provide access and opportunity for every student so that they can develop strong positive identities as learners of mathematics (Aguirre et al., 2013).

In ambitious teaching, the teacher engages students in challenging tasks and then observes and listens while students work so that the teacher can provide an appropriate level of support to diverse learners. The work and ideas produced by students then become the vehicle for making key mathematical ideas public and accessible to all students. Encouraging students to share their thinking with the class positions students as valuable resources for learning, helps them to develop positive identities as mathematics doers, and promotes an equitable learning environment. In these ways, organizing discussions around students' ideas becomes critical for successfully enacting ambitious teaching.

> Encouraging students to share their thinking with the class positions students as valuable resources for learning, helps them to develop positive identities as mathematics doers, and promotes an equitable learning environment. In these ways, organizing discussions around students' ideas becomes critical for successfully enacting ambitious teaching.

Where This Book Comes From

More than a decade ago, the National Council of Teachers of Mathematics (NCTM) and Corwin co-published *5 Practices for Orchestrating Productive Mathematics Discussions* (Smith & Stein, 2011, 2018) to guide teachers seeking to improve the quality of mathematics discussions in their classrooms and provide an equitable learning environment for students. The 5 practices is an instructional routine that helps teachers design and implement rigorous lessons that address important mathematical content in ways that build on students thinking. As such, the 5 practices help teachers balance attention both to mathematics and to students. Rather than focusing on in-the-moment responses to students' contributions, the practices instead emphasize the importance of thinking through all aspects of instruction *in advance* of teaching. Careful planning prior to a lesson reduces what teachers need to think about during instruction, allowing them time to listen more actively, question more thoughtfully, and respond in more tailored ways to student thinking. The 5 practices (including Practice Zero) are as follows:

0. Setting Goals and Selecting a Task: Specifying what you want students to learn about mathematics as a result of engaging in a particular lesson and identifying a high-level task that aligns with your goals and provides all students with access (i.e., low floor, high ceiling).

1. Anticipating: Carefully considering the strategies students are likely to use to approach or solve a challenging mathematical task; how to respond to the work that students are likely to produce; and which student strategies are likely to be most useful in addressing the mathematics to be learned.

2. Monitoring: Listening in on what students are saying and observing what they are doing; asking questions to assess what students understand and to advance them toward the goals of the lesson; and keeping track of the approaches that students are using.

3. Selecting: Determining what solution strategies—and what mathematics—will be the focus of the whole-class discussion; choosing particular students to present because of the mathematics available in their responses; and making sure that over time all students have the opportunity to be seen as authors of mathematical ideas.

4. Sequencing: Purposefully ordering the solution strategies that will be presented; making the mathematics accessible to all students; and building a mathematically coherent storyline.

5. Connecting: Asking questions that link different solution strategies; asking questions that make the key ideas that are targeted in the lesson public; and making sure all students are making sense of the ideas.

The 5 practices are sequential as illustrated in Figure 0.1. Practice 0 is the foundation on which the other practices rest, with each successive practice building on the one(s) that preceded it. Successfully engaging in any one of the practices requires having engaged in all the practices that came before it.

Figure 0.1 • Sequencing of the *5 Practices*

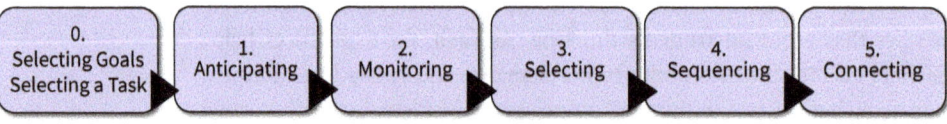

The 5 *Practices* book introduced and illustrated this set of ideas. Using examples of student work and narrative cases of instruction, the book demonstrates how, through planning, teachers can anticipate likely student contributions, prepare responses they might make to them, and make decisions about how to structure students' presentations to further their mathematical agenda for the lesson and to ensure that over time all students' voices were heard.

Since its publication, the 5 *Practices* has become very popular and tens of thousands of teachers have found the practices helpful in their work. The comments from some of the teachers with whom we have worked make salient the ways in which the 5 practices have impacted their teaching:

The 5 practices "makes lesson planning less abstract, and it really helps me anticipate what's going to happen. Instead of just trying to make decisions in the moment, it encourages me to think ahead. It pushes me to really get at the goal and move students toward that goal ..." (Michelle Musumeci, as cited in Smith & Sherin, 2019, p. 9)

"One of the things I have learned is that prior to using the 5 practices, I did not plan enough. I feel like I'm now a prepared teacher and that my students get a well-prepared lesson. The 5 practices gave me a tool that helped me direct my planning towards the goals of the lesson ... I think that the most important part of using the 5 practices is that you really can see what students can do when they are given the opportunity." (Cori Moran, as cited in Smith, Steele, et al., 2020, p. 11)

"I think that working with the 5 practices definitely makes you aware of how often you are leading students, how much you're wanting to control the work, and it really makes you take a step back and value what they have to say ... If you try every day to make it a point to let the students do the explaining, it becomes routine." (Michael Moore, as cited in Smith, Steele, et al., 2020, p. 10)

"Some students present challenging behavior, some are harder workers than others, some have language barriers, some have issues at home that are beyond my comprehension, and some are on grade level, and many are not. But at the end of the day, the work of the 5 practices will bring the largest opportunities for all students to show progress from their current level and will outweigh typical stand and deliver instruction." (Jennifer Mossotti, as cited in Smith & Sherin, 2019, p. 8)

Despite the popularity of and enthusiasm for the 5 *Practices*, however, many teachers have also found that enacting productive discussions in their classrooms remained elusive. In particular, teachers and teacher educators called for videos of teachers enacting the 5 practices so that they could see what they looked like in a real classroom. To address these requests, a three-book series, *The 5 Practices in Practice: Successfully*

Orchestrating Mathematics Discussions, was published focusing on Grades K–5 (Smith, Bill, et al., 2020), Grades 6–8 (Smith & Sherin, 2019), and Grades 9–12 (Smith, Steele, et al., 2020). These books are meant to deepen teachers' understanding of the 5 practices by engaging them in reading, observing, and analyzing episodes of teachers' planning for, enacting, and reflecting on lessons in which they were endeavoring to orchestrate productive discussions.

What This Book Is About

One of the main contributions of the *5 Practices in Practice* series was the identification of specific challenges associated with implementing each of the practices. The *5 Practices in Practice* series not only unpacks what it takes to do each practice well but also helps teachers to use their specific, self-identified challenges as focal points for their own improvement efforts.

In *Coaching the 5 Practices: Supporting Mathematics Teachers in Orchestrating Productive Discussions*, we introduce a coaching model to help teachers address the challenges they face in facilitating discussions. This coaching model provides opportunities for teacher learning through teachers' one-on-one interactions with a coach that focus on the challenges presented in the *5 Practices in Practice* series (see Figure 1.1 in Chapter 1 for a description of the challenges). Prior to a lesson, the coach and teacher jointly plan a lesson that addresses the challenge(s) the teacher is facing. Following the lesson, the coach and teacher reflect on the lesson, with an emphasis on the teacher's efforts to address the challenge. As the coach and the teacher make progress on one challenge, then they move on to the next. This work is neither fast nor shallow. Indeed, ambitious teaching also requires ambitious coaching. Hence, our model aims at coaching that is deep, meaningful, and designed to take place over the course of a quarter, semester, or even an entire school year or more, delivering increased momentum and ongoing impact for the teacher and for students.

Who This Book Is For

Unlike the previous *5 Practices* books that were written primarily for teachers, *Coaching the 5 Practices: Supporting Mathematics Teachers in Orchestrating Productive Discussions* is intended for coaches and other teacher educators, instructional leaders, and professional developers who are committed to providing students with increased opportunities to engage in productive discussions in mathematics classrooms through ambitious teaching. Any education professional working with teachers, however, would likely benefit from the book's tools, guides, and discussions of how to support teachers as they engage students in classroom discussions.

How to Use This Book

You will likely get the most out of this book if you and the teachers with whom you are working are committed to ambitious teaching and have prior experience with the 5 practices. Through thoughtful consideration of the ideas in this book, you will learn much about how to engage teachers in conversations about teaching that surface the challenges they face, elicit their thinking about what it takes to support student learning, and lead to new understandings about how to facilitate productive classroom discussions.

If you, or the teachers with whom you are working, are coming to the 5 practices for the first time, it would be important to take a step back and explore the 5 practices themselves before engaging in the model of coaching presented here. For example, you might begin your work with teachers by organizing a book club around the *5 Practices* (Smith & Stein, 2018), which would give teachers the opportunity to learn about and begin to implement the 5 practices and identify challenges they face in doing this work. With this foundation, you could then begin engaging in the coaching model described herein to support their implementation of the practices and address the specific challenges teachers are facing. As you get into Chapter 1, we'll describe how this book is constructed and what you can expect to encounter as you proceed through the chapters.

We hope this book will be a valuable resource for all education professionals who work with teachers to improve the quality of mathematics instruction.

Margaret (Peg) Smith

Bilge Yurekli

Mary Kay Stein

Acknowledgments

Since the publication of *5 Practices for Orchestrating Productive Mathematics Discussions* (Smith & Stein, 2011) we have worked with teachers and coaches across the country who were committed to improving the quality of mathematics discussions in K–12 classrooms. This book is our attempt to provide coaches and leaders with additional guidance in their efforts to support classroom teachers.

This book would not have been possible without the work and support of several individuals. Specifically, we acknowledge the contributions of the following:

- Our researcher and practitioner colleagues who collaborated with us on the larger coaching project from which this book emerged—Victoria Bill, Richard Correnti, Hillary Henry, Lindsay Clare Matsumura, Christian Schunn, and Eben Witherspoon. Their experiences and insights helped shape the coaching model presented herein.

- The coaches and teachers who graciously welcomed us into their daily work lives and openly shared their professional practice with us. Much of the wisdom portrayed in this book is attributable to what we have learned by observing and listening to them.

- Lisa Correnti, project manager, who made sure that we had a complete and well-organized database to draw on for this book.

- The James S. McDonnell Foundation that funded the *Teacher Change and Teachers as Learners* project, the basis of this book (grant #220020525).

- Erin Null, associate director and publisher for Corwin Mathematics, who supported this work from its inception and provided thoughtful feedback and suggestions throughout the writing process.

- Finally, we would like to thank the anonymous reviewers for their feedback on a draft version of this book. We greatly appreciated their insights and suggestions that enhanced this final product.

Publisher's Acknowledgments

Corwin gratefully acknowledges the contributions of the following reviewers:

Cathy Battles
State Mathematics Consultant Program Manager, University of Missouri
Kansas, MO

Fawn Nguyen
Math Teaching & Learning Specialist, Amplifying Desmos Math
Oak View, CA

Jennifer Rose Novak
Director of Curriculum, Instruction, and Assessment, Howard Public School System
Elkridge, MD

Brendan Scribner
Director of Implementation and Success, Exemplars Mathematics
White River Junction, VT

Jessica Slayton
Director of Mathematics, Metro Nashville Public Schools
Nashville, TN

About the Authors

Margaret (Peg) S. Smith is a professor emerita at University of Pittsburgh. For the past three decades, she has been developing research-based materials for use in the professional development of mathematics teachers. She has co-authored several books, including *5 Practices for Orchestrating Productive Discussions* (with Mary Kay Stein), the middle and high school versions of the *Taking Action* series (with Melissa Boston, Frederick Dillon, Stephen Miller, and Lynn Raith), and *The 5 Practices in Practice: Successfully Orchestrating Mathematics Discussion in Your Classroom* series (with Victoria Bill, Miriam Gameron Sherin, and Michael Steele). In 2006, she received the Chancellor's Distinguished Teaching Award given annually to honor outstanding faculty at the University of Pittsburgh. In 2009, she received the award for Excellence in Teaching in Mathematics Teacher Education from the Association of Mathematics Teacher Educators (AMTE). In April 2019, she received the Lifetime Achievement Award from NCTM.

Bilge Yurekli is a research associate at the University of Pittsburgh's Learning Research and Development Center. She holds a PhD in mathematics education. Her research focuses on mathematics teacher education, at both pre-service and in-service levels, with a specific interest in teacher development of beliefs and practices that is required for high-quality instruction. She has worked with Mary Kay Stein and her multidisciplinary team of researchers on various projects supported by the National Science Foundation (NSF), Institute of Education Sciences (IES), Spencer Foundation, and James S. McDonnell Foundation. Her research has been published in NCTM's *Journal for Research in Mathematics Education* and presented at both national and international research conferences, including those held by NCTM and American Educational Research Association (AERA). Currently, she is working on a project that aims to promote productive struggle in mathematics classrooms.

Mary Kay Stein is professor emerita at the University of Pittsburgh where she held a joint appointment as professor in the School of Education and senior scientist at the Learning Research and Development Center. Her research focuses on the teaching and learning of mathematics in elementary and middle school classrooms with a particular focus on the identification and implementation of high-cognitive-demand instructional tasks. She also examines school- and district-level factors that shape teachers' capacities to maintain high levels of cognitive demand once tasks are launched in the classroom. Her research has been supported by IES, as well as by several private foundations, including the

MacArthur, Spencer, and James S. McDonnell foundations. In addition to co-authoring the *5 Practices* book (with Peg Smith), she has co-authored a book and several articles about district-wide reform. She has given invited addresses to both national and international audiences, including in Beijing, Seoul, Goteborg, Hamburg, Istanbul, Haifa, and Lisbon. She also served as a visiting scholar at Monash University in Melbourne, Australia, in 2012. In 2014, she was named a fellow of the American Educational Research Association.

CHAPTER 1

A Challenge-Based Approach to Coaching

Coaching is one of the fastest growing forms of professional development across the United States (Darling-Hammond et al., 2009). Many districts have turned to instructional coaching to provide intensive one-on-one support to teachers as they grapple with planning and enacting lessons that are aligned with ambitious teaching. Indeed, one in four schools now has a mathematics coach (Hill & Papay, 2022). Although the number of studies that have focused on the effectiveness of coaching programs is small, research has found that coaching can lead to positive changes in mathematics teachers' knowledge, beliefs, instructional practices, and student achievement (e.g., Campbell & Malkus, 2011; Chapin, 1994; Kraft & Hill, 2020).

Research suggests that mathematics coaching is highly personal and idiosyncratic, with coaches' practice varying significantly from school to school and district to district (e.g., Coburn & Russell, 2008). This variety is due—in part—to the wide range of coaching materials available in the marketplace to which coaches can refer to guide their practice. For example, *Coaching for Equity* (Aguilar, 2020) provides advice on ways in which coaches can help teachers surface their implicit biases. A popular coaching model, *Cognitive Coaching: Developing Self-Directed Learners and Leaders* (Costa & Garmston, 2015), provides guidance for coaches to plan conversations that aim to support the cognitive development of teachers, including teacher values, beliefs, and identities. *Instructional Coaching: A Partnership Approach to Improving Instruction* (Knight, 2007) focuses on how coaches can help teachers improve their instruction through a variety of activities (e.g., building an emotional connection, observing and modeling classroom lessons, and collaboratively exploring data).

Resources specifically designed for *mathematics* coaches are also available. For example, Content Focused Coaching (West & Cameron, 2013; West & Staub, 2003) guides coaches of individuals or groups of teachers to plan, teach, and reflect on mathematics lessons. *Everything You Need for Mathematics Coaching* (McGatha et al., 2018) offers a plethora of tools to help busy coaches support mathematics teachers.

What is missing from this body of work is a coaching model designed to address the specific challenges teachers face as they are learning to support productive mathematics discussions. To address this gap, our coaching model creates opportunities for teacher learning through one-on-one coach–teacher interactions that focus on the challenges teachers encounter when engaging in the *5 Practices for Orchestrating Productive Mathematics Discussions* (Smith & Stein, 2011, 2018). As mentioned in the Preface, the 5 practices are a set of instructional practices intended to help teachers plan and enact productive mathematics discussions that build on student thinking. The 5 practices (including Practice Zero) are *Setting Goals and Selecting a Task, Anticipating, Monitoring, Selecting, Sequencing,* and *Connecting*. The challenges associated with the 5 practices and described in the *5 Practices in Practice* series (e.g., Smith & Sherin, 2019) are central to our coaching model, providing the focus for coach–teacher conversations. Each of these challenges, along with their descriptions, are given in Figure 1.1.

Figure 1.1 • Teacher challenges associated with each of the *5 Practices*

	TEACHER CHALLENGE	DESCRIPTION
1. GOALS AND TASKS	(1) Identifying learning goals	Goal needs to focus on what students will learn as a result of engaging in the task, not on what students will do. Clarity on goals sets the stage for everything else!
	(2) Identifying a doing-mathematics task	While doing-mathematics tasks provide the greatest opportunities for student learning, they are not readily available in some textbooks. Teachers may need to adapt an existing task, find a task in another resource, or create a task.
	(3) Ensuring alignment between task and goals	Even with learning goals specified, teachers may select a task that does not allow students to make progress on those particular goals.
	(4) Launching a task to ensure student access	Teachers need to provide access to the context and the mathematics in the launch but not so much that the mathematical demands are reduced and key ideas are given away.
2. ANTICIPATING	(5) Moving beyond the way *you* solve a problem	Teachers often feel limited by their own experience. They know how to solve a task but may not have access to the array of strategies that students are likely to use.
	(6) Being prepared to help students who cannot get started on a task	Teachers need to be prepared to provide support to students who do not know how to begin work on the task so that they can make progress without being told exactly what to do and how.
	(7) Creating questions that move students toward the mathematical goals	The questions teachers ask need to be driven by the mathematical goals of the lesson. The focus needs to be on ensuring that students understand the key mathematical ideas, not just on producing a solution to the task.

	TEACHER CHALLENGE	DESCRIPTION
3. MONITORING	(8) Trying to understand what students are thinking	Students do not always articulate their thinking clearly. It can be quite demanding for teachers, in the moment, to figure out what a student means or is trying to say. This requires teachers to listen carefully to what students are saying and to ask questions that help them better explain what they are thinking.
	(9) Keeping track of group progress—which groups you visited and what you left them to work on	As teachers are running from group to group, providing support, they need to be able to keep track of what each group is doing and what they left students to work on. Also, it is important for a teacher to return to a group in order to determine whether the advancing question given to them helped them make progress.
	(10) Involving all members of a group	All individuals in the group need to be challenged to answer assessing and advancing questions. For individuals to benefit from the thinking of their peers, they need to be held accountable for listening to and adding on, repeating and summarizing what others are saying.
4. SELECTING AND SEQUENCING	(11) Selecting only solutions that are most relevant to learning goals	Teachers need to select a limited number of solutions that will help achieve the mathematical goals of the lesson. Sharing solutions that are not directly relevant can take a discussion off track, and sharing too many solutions (even if they are relevant) can lead to student disengagement.
	(12) Expanding beyond the usual student presenters	Teachers often select students who are articulate and on whom they can count for a coherent explanation. Teachers need to look for opportunities to position each and every student as a presenter and help students develop their ability to explain their thinking.
	(13) Deciding what work to share when the majority of students were not able to solve the task and your initial goal no longer seems obtainable	Teachers may on occasion find that the task was too challenging for most students and that they were not able to engage as intended. This situation requires the teacher to modify her initial plan and determine how to focus the discussion so students can make progress.
	(14) Moving forward when a key strategy is not produced by students	In planning the lesson, a teacher may determine that a particular strategy is critical to accomplishing the lesson goals. If the success of a lesson hinges on the availability of a particular strategy, then the teacher needs to be prepared to introduce the strategy through some means.
	(15) Determining how to sequence incorrect and/or incomplete solutions	Teachers often choose not to share work that is not complete and correct for fear that students will remember incorrect methods. Sharing solutions that highlight key errors in a domain can provide all students with an opportunity to analyze why a particular approach does not work. Sharing incomplete or partial solutions can provide all students with the opportunity to consider how such work can be connected to more robust solutions.

(Continued)

Figure 1.1 (*Continued*)

	TEACHER CHALLENGE	DESCRIPTION
5. CONNECTING	(16) Keeping the entire class engaged and accountable during individual presentations	Often, the sharing of solutions turns into a show and tell or a dialogue between the teacher and the presenter. The rest of the class needs to be held accountable for understanding and making sense of the solutions that are presented.
	(17) Ensuring key mathematical ideas are made public and remain the focus	It is possible to have students share and discuss a lot of interesting solutions and never get to the point of the lesson. It is critical that the key mathematical ideas that are being targeted in the lesson are explicitly discussed.
	(18) Making sure that you do not take over the discussion and do the explaining	As students are presenting their solutions, the teacher needs to ask questions that engage the presenters and the rest of the class in explaining and making sense of the solutions. There is a temptation for the teacher to take over and tell the students what they need to know. When this happens, opportunities for learning are diminished. Remember whoever is doing the talking is doing the thinking!
	(19) Running out of time	Teachers may not have enough time to conduct the whole class discussion the way they had planned it. In such cases it is important to come up with a Plan B that provides some closure to the lesson but does not turn into telling.

Source: From *The 5 Practices in Practice: Successfully Orchestrating Mathematics Discussions in Your Middle School Classroom* by M. S. Smith and M. G. Sherin, 2019, Corwin. Note that, in their work on *5 Practices in Practice*, the authors found the identification of challenges to be most meaningful when they considered *Selecting* and *Sequencing* practices together.

Power of Organizing Around Challenges

The teacher challenges associated with the 5 practices have been identified over the past decade from conversations with teachers, coaches, and professional developers, as well as from classroom observations. They have been further verified through surveys of 1,200 teachers in which each of the 19 challenges was selected by a subset of teachers. Although some challenges were identified more frequently than others (e.g., Challenges 10 and 16), every teacher—even those who were not familiar with the 5 practices—identified at least one of the challenges as something they struggled with in their teaching.

The challenges serve three purposes for our coaching model. First, they signal what is important. To ensure teacher engagement in the most critical aspects of ambitious teaching, we constrain the issues that are addressed during the coach–teacher conversations to a subset of 19 challenges shown in Figure 1.1. By asking teachers to identify the specific challenges with which they are struggling, we argue, coaches ensure that coach–teacher conversations will be devoted to issues that are at the heart of what matters most in achieving a rigorous and equitable learning environment.

Second, the challenges explicate what is entailed in doing each practice well. For example, as shown in Figure 1.1, the practices of *Selecting and Sequencing* are further specified by five challenges, starting with "*Selecting only solutions that are most relevant to learning goals.*" Although this challenge often receives primary consideration in coach–teacher conversations, the subsequent challenges identify an array of additional features that must be attended to if the practice is to be done well. The challenge of "*Expanding beyond the usual student presenters*" keeps equity issues on teachers' and coaches' radar screens while working on this practice. Attending to the challenge "*Moving forward with the lesson when a key strategy is not produced by students*" further unpacks this practice to include being prepared to introduce the key strategy through some means.

Third, when coaches use the challenges with the 5 practices to guide their work with teachers, they provide learning opportunities for teachers paralleling the learning opportunities that cognitively challenging tasks provide for students. We conceptualize the effort that teachers expend when working on challenges regarding the *5 Practices* as a process similar to the effort students expend when they work on challenging tasks in the classroom (Yurekli & Stein, in press). As a key element of ambitious teaching, engaging students with challenging tasks is necessary for the development of meaningful learning because it provides students with opportunities to struggle with important mathematical ideas and relationships (Hiebert & Grouws, 2007).

In terms of teacher learning, we argue that engaging teachers in their own instructional challenges is a process necessary to improve their learning. Coach–teacher conversations create more opportunities to learn when teachers question and reflect critically on their practices rather than just discussing *what* to do next (Witherspoon et al., 2021). In our coaching model, we aim to engage teachers in specific challenges that teachers must reason their way through as they make sense of what they should do to resolve them. Coaches who implemented our model have stated the advantages of focusing on challenges:

> *You can ask a teacher, "What do you find challenging about teaching mathematics?" It's almost like they don't know what they don't know .... I feel like the teacher challenges [associated with the 5 practices] opened the door. I absolutely loved that because it gave me some insight into what the teachers saw as a challenge.* (Coach Drew)

> *So sometimes you ask teachers, "What is it you want to work on?" And you get broad amorphous answers. You might even have a teacher say, "I want to work on the debrief." I love that in those [teacher] challenges, though, we're really fine-tuning from the start. We're picking a thread from the debrief. "What about that is challenging?"* (Coach Shawn)

> *I think that the most helpful part for me was focusing on the teacher challenges .... It just helped us to get a lot more specific. Because*

previously, it was like, "Well, this is happening and I don't really know how to tell you how to fix it. I can show you. I can do a model lesson in your room of me doing it." But the teacher challenges [associated with the 5 practices] was just super helpful to kind of lay that out and make it very specific feedback for them. (Coach Avery)

As illustrated in the above quotations, using challenges to organize your work can bring a deeper level of specificity to your interactions with teachers. Although there may be some value in discussing challenges in general (e.g., in Professional Learning Communities), our model calls for surfacing and addressing challenges within one-on-one coaching conversations that we believe are a more powerful catalyst for teacher learning.

Organization and Content

In subsequent chapters, we will dive into the details of coaching conversations and describe the specifics of our coaching model. In Chapter 2, we will introduce a routine that guides coach–teacher conversations while planning for and reflecting on a lesson. In Chapters 3 through 5, we will provide details regarding the activities in which coaches and teachers engage and the tools and guides that support their work—with an emphasis on the importance of preparation for coaching activities. We conclude the book with Chapter 6, which summarizes the key features of our coaching model that differentiate it from others and provides guidance on how to begin implementing our model (e.g., what you need to explain to the teacher before the coaching starts, how to plan the timing of a cycle, how often you should engage in a cycle with a teacher). We also interweave in these chapters the voices of our coaches who speak from their experiences in using the model.

Throughout the book, you will find examples that illustrate coaching the 5 practices. Most examples are based on the data and artifacts (e.g., tasks, lesson plans, coaching conversations) we collected from a group of eight coaches and the 16 teachers with whom they worked during the 2021–2022 school year. Each coach and teacher has been given a pseudonym. Coaches will be distinguished from teachers by the inclusion of title "Coach" in front of their first names (e.g., Coach Avery). The coaches and teachers worked in different contexts (urban, suburban, and rural), grade levels (3–8), and geographic regions in the United States (East, South, West, Mid-West). Although the examples are drawn from elementary and middle school contexts, the ideas represented in these examples transcend grade levels. The examples highlight what coaches did in their efforts to support teachers who were trying to improve the quality of discussions in their classrooms and how teachers responded to their efforts. The examples are not intended to be exemplars to be copied but opportunities for analysis, reflection, discussion, and learning.

Across the chapters, you will have the opportunity to actively engage in three types of activities: *Stop and Consider* questions (reflection), *Analyzing*

Coaching (analysis), and *Putting into Practice* (implementation). The Stop and Consider questions give you the opportunity to think about what a coach should do in a particular situation. Analyzing Coaching activities engage you in examining aspects of a coach's planning for and enactment of coach–teacher conversations. Putting into Practice provides you with the opportunity to try out the ideas, tools, and guides discussed in a chapter into your own coaching practice.

As you engage in these activities, we encourage you to keep a journal to write down your responses to questions that are posed and make note of questions that you have. You also may want to keep a record of your experiences in implementing the *Putting into Practice* recommendations. Such a journal can be helpful in reflecting from time to time on how your work and thinking about coaching is evolving and improving.

 **STOP AND CONSIDER**

Imagine that you are coaching a sixth-grade teacher who decided to use the Max's Dog Food task (Figure 1.2) as the basis for a lesson on fraction division.

- How would you prepare for a coach–teacher conversation to plan this lesson?

- What questions would you ask the teacher?

- What points would you hope to make?

CHAPTER 1 | A Challenge-Based Approach to Coaching

Figure 1.2 • The Max's Dog Food task

> Dog food is sold in a $12\frac{1}{2}$-pound bag. My dog, Max, eats a $\frac{3}{4}$-pound serving every day. How many servings of dog food are in the bag?
>
> Draw a picture, construct a number line, or make a table to explain your solution.

Source: Institute for Learning at the University of Pittsburgh (2016; as cited in Smith & Stein, 2018).

Getting Started

Before you begin to engage in the coaching model described in this book, you need to address several things. In the list that follows, we provide some thoughts about how to get started in your work.

1. If you are a first-time coach, if you are in a new school, or if there are new teachers with whom you will be working, you need to build trusting relationships with them. Teachers need to believe that you have a vested interest in their success and the success of their students and that you will do whatever you can to support them in their work. Although it is beyond the scope of this book to offer specific suggestions for how to go about building this trust, the following online resources can help you get started:

   - Learning Forward's Tools for Learning Schools article "Teacher-coach relationships" by Joellen Killion, Cindy Harrison, Chris Bryan, and Heather Clifton: https://bit.ly/48to3hd

   - Knowles Teacher Initiative's Kaleidoscope article "Building Relationships as an Instructional Coach" https://bit.ly/3uISO3E

   - ASCD's article "How Good Coaches Build Alliance with Teachers" https://bit.ly/3wsr580

2. If the teachers you are coaching are not familiar with the 5 practices for orchestrating productive mathematics discussion, you might consider creating an opportunity for teachers to learn about them. As we suggested in the Preface, you might organize a book club (either face-to-face or virtually) around the *5 Practices* (Smith & Stein, 2018) to give teachers the opportunity to learn about and begin to implement the 5 practices and identify challenges they face in doing this work. Alternatively, you might host a few sessions in which you introduce the 5 practices and engage teachers in some activities from the *5 Practices in Practice*

series (e.g., Smith & Sherin, 2019). Teachers could then engage in analyzing instruction, which might spark interest in implementing the 5 practices.

3. Carefully consider who you might coach. Which teachers seem most open to new learning, collaboration, and reflection? What about the teachers who are resistant to coaching? In *Moments in Mathematics Coaching*, Woleck (2010) provides some guidance for making these decisions and advice on how to engage all teachers in opportunities to learn.

As you continue to read this book, we encourage you to think about how you can use the coaching model in your work and, if you are currently working with teachers, who might be willing to engage in this process with you. We will provide additional details on implementing the model (e.g., the amount of time involved in and frequency of a cycle, the importance of video recording a lesson) in Chapter 6, once you have the whole picture of what is involved in the model.

CHAPTER 2
An Inquiry Routine for Guiding Coach–Teacher Conversations

Coach Taylor will be meeting Joey, a teacher whom he is coaching, to discuss an upcoming lesson based on the Max's Dog Food task (see Figure 1.2). In thinking about past conversations with Joey, Coach Taylor realizes that, as a coach, he often does too much of the talking and perhaps too much of the thinking. Coach Taylor is struggling to figure out how to engage Joey in a meaningful conversation that both honors Joey's thinking yet presses him to consider in more depth what he and his students will do during the lesson.

Have you ever found yourself in a situation similar to the one Coach Taylor is facing? In this chapter, we introduce a routine for guiding coaching conversations in ways that make the teacher's thinking more central to the discussion. First, we will explain where these coaching conversations will take place in our coaching model. Then, we will engage you in the analysis of a coach–teacher conversation to identify what an effective coaching conversation looks like. Finally, we will introduce a route for structuring conversations with teachers.

The interactions between a coach and a teacher in our coaching model are organized by cycles, which is similar to other coaching models (e.g., Costa & Garmston, 2016; West & Staub, 2003). As shown in Figure 2.1, a coaching cycle includes three phases: pre-lesson, lesson, and post-lesson. The *pre-lesson* phase includes preparation activities for an upcoming lesson and a pre-lesson conference. This phase is followed by the *lesson* phase in which the lesson is enacted and video-recorded by the teacher and (if possible) observed by the coach. The cycle is completed with the *post-lesson* phase, which includes the teacher and coach reflections on the video recording of the enacted lesson and a post-lesson conference.

The most critical part of a coaching cycle is the coach–teacher conversations that take place in the pre-lesson and post-lesson phases (i.e., pre-lesson conference and post-lesson conference, respectively). The goal of these conversations is to help teachers think deeply about their practices and make decisions to ensure that all students have the opportunity to learn mathematics with understanding through participating in rich

> The most critical part of a coaching cycle is the coach–teacher conversations that take place in the pre-lesson and post-lesson phases.

Figure 2.1 • Phases of a coaching cycle

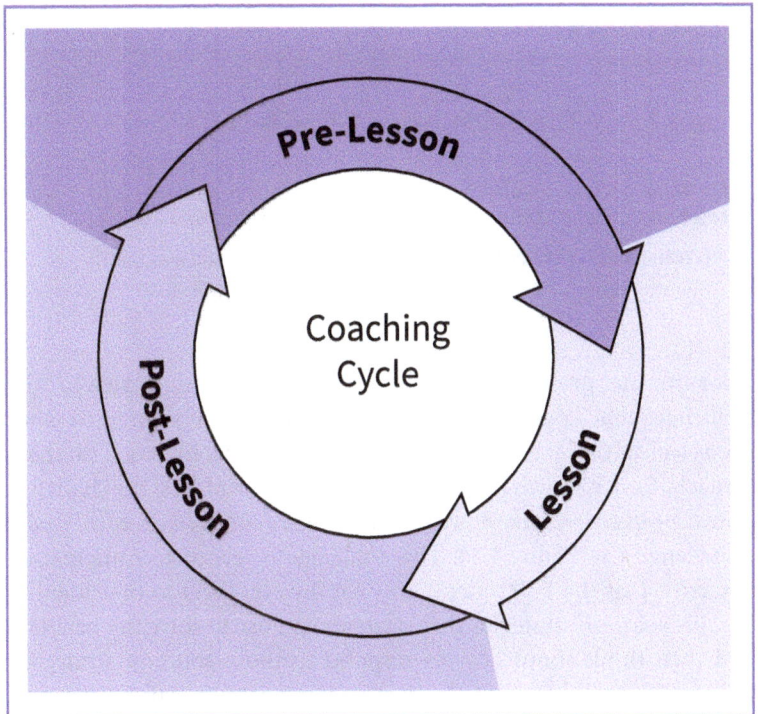

mathematical discussions. To achieve this goal, coaches help teachers grapple with their specific challenges (see Figure 1.1 in Chapter 1 for a list of challenges associated with the 5 practices). Through this process, teachers have the opportunity to rethink current practices and look for alternative instructional practices to address their challenges. In this chapter, we will introduce our inquiry routine. This routine will provide structure for planning and enacting coaching conversations that engage teachers in grappling with and addressing their challenges with the 5 practices.

Before we get into the details of our inquiry routine, let's drop in on an actual conversation between a coach and a teacher to get us warmed up. In this pre-lesson conference, Coach Shawn is helping Logan prepare for a fourth-grade lesson on subtracting a mixed number from a whole number. Logan has selected the Celebration Cakes task shown in Figure 2.2 as the basis for the lesson. Because the students had not been taught how to solve this type of problem, Logan expected that they would have difficulty solving this task and wanted to be as prepared as possible. Together, Logan and Coach Shawn identified three inter-related learning goals for the students: (1) realizing that you can't subtract a fraction from the whole number without renaming the whole number, (2) understanding that whole numbers can be partitioned into equal-sized pieces, and (3) understanding that, when subtracting a fraction a/b from 1, 1 should be converted into a fraction with the same denominator of b.

Figure 2.2 • The Celebration Cakes task

> Mr. Wane decided to make some cakes for his fourth-grade class to celebrate the end of the school year. He made 5 cakes for his class.
>
> Mr. Wane and his students ate $3\frac{2}{6}$ cakes. How much cake was left?

Prior to the pre-lesson conference, Coach Shawn reviewed the challenges that Logan had previously indicated she wanted to work on, as well as the lesson materials Logan had prepared. Based on these artifacts, Coach Shawn planned a conversation to address the challenge *"Creating questions that move students toward the mathematical goals"* (Challenge 7 in Figure 1.1). This challenge is related to Anticipating (practice 1 of the 5 practices) and requires teachers to first identify specific solution strategies that students can use to solve the problem and then think about how to respond to those solution strategies. The goal is to ensure that the teacher is prepared to surface student thinking through *assessing* questions and move student thinking forward through *advancing* questions (Smith & Stein, 2018).

Analyzing Coaching 2.1
Considering the nature of coach–teacher conversations

The following transcript is an excerpt from the pre-lesson conference between Logan and Coach Shawn. We join the conversation as Coach Shawn asks Logan to share how she will help the students reach the second learning goal—*understanding that whole numbers can be partitioned into equal-sized pieces*. As you read the transcript, consider these two questions and record your responses in your journal:

1. How does the coach help the teacher create questions that will support students' efforts to reach the goals of the lesson?

2. How productive do you think this conversation was in helping Logan address the identified teacher challenge? Why?

Pre-Lesson Conference: Celebration Cakes

1	Coach:	With our second goal, "*understanding that whole numbers can be partitioned into*
2		*equal-sized pieces*," how do you think you are going to move students toward this goal?
3		Let's say a student may understand that initial goal "*you can't subtract the fraction*
4		*from the whole number without renaming the whole number*" but not this second goal.
5		*(Coach Shawn writes the following)*
6		

$$5 - 3\frac{2}{6}$$

7	Logan:	This is where I really struggled to think of those advancing questions. Like, how do you
8		prompt that without just totally giving it away?
9	Coach:	Mm-hmm (affirmative).
10	Logan:	Yes. ... So, I think, those kids are going to need the models because if they can't
11		subtract the fraction from the whole number, we're going to have to have something
12		else to help us.
13	Coach:	I think that's true. What I'm potentially envisioning is like, they get to that hurdle of,
14		"Okay, yes, I need to rename." So then they're like, "Cool. I make 5 wholes into 4
15		wholes, then I come over here to the fraction ..." and that's where the understanding
16		kind of hits a wall, potentially. And I do feel like the prompt, "Can you model what's
17		going on in this situation?" is almost advancing them because they're going to be
18		forced, they'll draw their 5 cakes probably, take away 3, and then be faced with the $\frac{2}{6}$.
19		*(Coach Shawn draws the following)*
20		
21	Logan:	So then they're going to have to split one of the cakes. Like this ... *(Logan draws the*
22		*following)*
23		
24	Coach:	Yeah ...
25	Logan:	Then, I wonder if we can help them get to that understanding of "this whole number
26		has been renamed."
27	Coach:	Yes.
28	Logan:	Bridging it to our model like, "None of the whole numbers are cut into pieces. Where
29		are the ones that are cut into pieces? Where do those go?" Well, "Those have to go
30		back over here to the fractions."

31	Coach:	Mm-hmm (affirmative). Yeah, I can totally envision a student being successful
32		modeling this, but then struggling with the understanding that "what you did was you
33		actually renamed that whole."
34	Logan:	So asking like, "You couldn't look at this as one whole to take $\frac{2}{6}$ from. ... How did you
35		have to change it?"
36	Coach:	Exactly. Yep.
37	Logan:	So, they would say, "I had to split it into $\frac{1}{6}$'s for that to equal one whole. You have to
38		look at all 6 of those pieces."
39	Coach:	Yeah. I'm looking at the kind of strategy we want to see from them and trying to
40		connect it to that model. I think, if we hit on what you said. ... Once they've done this
41		and you ask, "What actually happened here? What happened here?" So, "I split a whole
42		into 6 equal pieces" would be the optimal response. Yeah?
43	Logan:	Mm-hmm (affirmative).
44	Coach:	And you would ask, "Why $\frac{1}{6}$'s?" which would move them to the third goal.
45	Logan:	Mm-hmm (affirmative). And then, "Now there are 6 pieces in one whole, can we name
46		our whole number using a fraction?"
47	Coach:	There we go. Yes. To me, that gets us to that second understanding, *understanding that*
48		*whole numbers can be partitioned into equal-sized pieces*. And moves to the third
49		understanding that *1 whole should be converted into a fraction with the same*
50		*denominator as the fraction you are subtracting from it*. It's almost understanding that
51		whole numbers can be partitioned and renamed and how to do it.
52	Logan:	Mm-hmm (affirmative).
53	Coach:	Great. So, we have advancing questions for this first solution strategy, for students
54		who use a model. What about the second solution strategy? This is what you anticipated
55		*(Coach Shawn points to the following solution)*, that students might use the standard
56		algorithm but fail to rename the whole number and bring down the $\frac{2}{6}$.
57		

$$\text{Bringing fraction down}$$
$$\begin{array}{r} 5 \\ -3\frac{2}{6} \\ \hline 2\frac{2}{6} \end{array}$$

58	Logan:	Mm-hmm (affirmative).
59	Coach:	Yeah, what would you ask them to get to the point of actually doing the renaming and
60		understanding why that is possible?
61	Logan:	I'm not sure. Some kind of question to get them to look at the missing value and realize
62		there's nothing above it. "Does anything look strange? What could that mean?"
63	Coach:	So, I feel like, in that line of questioning, we push them to the place of "I've got to do
64		something else." A realization that "my initial strategy isn't sufficient here." Now,
65		we're getting them to renaming. Okay. Here, I'm wondering if you could ask them,
66		"Okay, if we were subtracting whole numbers and we get to this spot and we can't
67		move forward, what do we do?"
68	Logan:	Yes, and that's where like the bridge of like, "We have to borrow."
69	Coach:	You mean regrouping?
70	Logan:	Yeah, like, "We have to regroup."
71	Coach:	Yeah, "What does this look like with this whole number and mixed number?" I like that

72		bridge. And when they know, "Oh, we can *borrow*," you might ask, "So how's that
73		going to look in fractions?" Does it feel like, with this line of questioning, we've teased
74		out that second goal?
75	Logan:	Yes, I think so. When I ask them, "Well, I don't have a 10 to *bring over*. So what am I
76		going to bring over in this situation?", they will have to split one whole from the 5 into $\frac{1}{6}$'s,
77		just like the students using the first strategy. So it would look like this: *(Logan*
78		*writes the following solution)*
79		

$$\begin{array}{r} 4\frac{6}{6} \\ - 3\frac{2}{6} \\ \hline 1\frac{4}{6} \end{array}$$

80	Coach:	Exactly. And this way, we are not telling them bringing down $\frac{2}{6}$ is wrong, we are helping
81		them realize their mistake. Then, we can move them toward our goal of understanding,
82		"Okay, I can partition a whole number to create a fraction and I have to use the same
83		denominator as the fraction I already have to make a new fraction."
84	Logan:	Mm-hmm (affirmative).
85	Coach:	Okay. So, in looking at your goals for this lesson and kind of looking over your
86		questions, how do you feel like this line of questioning might support student learning?
87	Logan:	I think this is going to be more of the "why," the more conceptual, like what needs to
88		happen and why, and less, "What did you do?" Less of a show and tell of what they
89		actually did. Even in the conversations, like sharing with each other, "I did this
90		because …"
91	Coach:	It also feels like we're getting closer to valuing the levels of understanding that students
92		might be at. I feel like, even at the very start, we were appreciating "Okay, if a student
93		gets to this point, even if they had a roadblock, they've understood something
94		significant about what we're doing" versus like, "Well, they couldn't get started."
95	Logan:	Yeah.
96	Coach:	Okay, I'm interested in seeing those questions in action and kind of how that feels in
97		making adjustments to your practice.

Considering the Nature of Coach–Teacher Conversations: Analysis

As mentioned in the *Pre-Lesson Conference: Celebration Cakes* transcript, Logan and Coach Shawn were working on the challenge "*Creating questions that move students toward the mathematical goals.*" To help teachers reduce the pressure of asking tailored questions on the fly during the lesson, creating questions in response to anticipated solution strategies *prior* to the lesson is critical. In the *5 Practices in*

Practice, Smith and Sherin (2019) explain the importance of addressing this challenge:

> *It is important to note that while the teacher establishes specific learning goals for the lesson, students will be at different places in their learning based on their prior knowledge and experiences. Therefore, students are asked questions that help them make progress toward the goals based on their current understanding.* (p. 62)

Coaches help teachers support individual students' efforts to reach the goals of the lesson by assisting them in creating advancing questions. In the *Pre-Lesson Conference: Celebration Cakes* transcript, you might have noticed several things that Coach Shawn did to help Logan address the challenge of creating advancing questions to help students move toward understanding the lesson goals, especially the second goal: *Understanding that whole numbers can be partitioned into equal-sized pieces.* For one thing, Coach Shawn begins the conference by asking questions, the answers to which reveal how Logan is thinking about the challenge. Coach Shawn learns that Logan is not confident in her ability to create tailored questions (lines 7–8); the coach also learns that the teacher has a student solution strategy in mind (using models) that could help students think through the task (lines 10–12). Although Logan doesn't specify what student work would look like when they use modeling, Coach Shawn uses this teacher-suggested idea to engage Logan in grappling with her challenge. Starting at line 13, the coach helps the teacher think more deeply about what it might look like when students use a model (in this case, drawings) to solve the Celebration Cakes task. In this way, the coach is building the conversation on the thinking that the teacher produced (as opposed to introducing something new that might be harder for the teacher to relate to).

You might also have noticed that the coach's questioning focused on the identification of advancing questions that the teacher could use to move students toward the second learning goal (lines 16–17; lines 34–35; lines 41–42; line 44). Importantly, these questions were constructed in the context of specific student solution strategies. Thus, the teacher is set up to learn that constructing "advancing questions" needs to occur in response to what students are thinking and doing (or to the teacher's anticipation of what they might do).

Finally, you may have noticed that Coach Shawn was more directive in the discussion of the second solution strategy than in the first one. When discussing students' use of the standard algorithm, Logan cannot come up with a way to support students who are stuck because "you cannot subtract a fraction from a whole number," so the coach steps in and suggests that the teacher might want to revisit what the students already know about regrouping in the context of whole-number subtraction (starting on line 63). As they talk through student responses, the teacher works with the coach in identifying questions specific to what students might say and do. As a result, the coach is not "telling" the teacher what to do as much as providing an alternative pathway for the teacher to consider in resolving her challenge.

Overall, Coach Shawn provided opportunities for Logan to think about how she could move the students toward the learning goals of the lesson without "just totally giving it away" (line 8). By the end of the conference, Logan was equipped with specific questions to ask based on what students might produce or where they might be struggling as they engage with the Celebration Cakes task. Although the focus of the conversation was on *advancing questions*, the conversation included prompts to get students talking about what they were doing and why. As such, student thinking was "on the table" providing grist for the development of advancing questions. At the end of the conference, Logan seems more confident about what questions to ask and when.

You might have also noticed that Logan and Coach Shawn did not discuss *why* the use of assessing and advancing questions is important for supporting students' development of conceptual understanding and *how* Logan might create and use them productively in future lessons. By focusing Logan's attention on the rationale for using assessing and advancing questions, Coach Shawn would have helped the teacher extract a general practice to be applied in the context of other lessons when appropriate. However, this is sometimes easier said than done. You may run out of time or just feel that talking about one more thing is just too much. As a coach, it is important to see the benefit of moving beyond specific instances and of making sure at some point in your work with a teacher you raise the discussion to a more general level.

Inquiry Routine

One way to look at what Coach Shawn did to support Logan's efforts to create questions that advanced the goals of the lesson is that she engaged in the inquiry routine. We developed our *inquiry routine* by drawing parallels between coaching and ambitious teaching. In ambitious mathematics teaching, teachers build instruction on student thinking by surfacing students' mathematical ideas and responding in ways to advance their thinking toward the key mathematical idea that is targeted in the lesson (National Council of Teachers of Mathematics [NCTM], 2014). This process allows students to make connections between new and existing mathematical ideas, which is important for their learning of mathematics with understanding (Hiebert & Carpenter, 1992).

Similarly, we argue, coach–teacher conversations that support teacher learning with understanding should build on teacher thinking. This means coaches should elicit and respond to teacher thinking in ways that will help teachers connect new information to their existing knowledge. Our coaching model, therefore, uses an inquiry routine for coach–teacher conversations that build on teacher thinking. The coaches with whom we have worked have found this routine helped them be less directive with teachers. As Coach Hunter commented:

> *[The inquiry routine] has helped me with being a little bit more hands-off and not being the driver of trying to make the change happen. We know, just like with kids, when people come to their own "Aha!" moments, chances are it's going to go the distance, it's not going to be a one-and-done.*

Our inquiry routine comprises four coaching moves:

1. *Invite*
2. *Rehearse*
3. *Suggest*
4. *Generalize*

The first move is to **Invite** the teacher to explain what they might do (in a pre-lesson conference) or could have done (in a post-lesson conference) to resolve a specific challenge that is under discussion. The invitation allows you to assess where the teacher's current thinking or understanding is with respect to the challenge so that you can respond effectively. For example, in the *Pre-Lesson Conference: Celebration Cakes*, Coach Shawn poses a question about Logan's plans to move students toward an understanding of whole numbers as fractions (lines 1–4), which is related to the challenge they are discussing. As seen in lines 7–8, this invitation helps surface the fact that Logan has been struggling to come up with questions to move students toward this learning goal without "giving it away" and guiding student thinking too much.

The second coaching move in our inquiry routine is to **Rehearse** how a teaching action would play out in the classroom by considering possible student responses or reactions. The rehearsal provides the opportunity to think through a particular strand of reasoning in a hypothetical situation and helps the teacher specify what they would do or say if this or that occurred in the classroom. For example, in the *Pre-Lesson Conference: Celebration Cakes*, Coach Shawn draws what student representation would look like when they use models to show their thinking (line 20). Logan is then prompted to engage in a rehearsal with Coach Shawn of how students are expected to respond to the questions she created and what questions she would ask next to move students toward the goal of the lesson (lines 34–45). Through this rehearsal, Logan could make sense of the questions she is going to use in the lesson and how these questions will help her address the particular challenge she and her coach are discussing.

The next coaching move in our inquiry routine is to **Suggest** specific ideas for a teacher's consideration. As you invite a teacher to explain their plans regarding a challenge, it can become evident that the teacher is still struggling with that challenge without any progress toward resolution. It is possible that after a rehearsal, the teacher might also decide that their "solution" will not help them with a particular challenge. In such cases, as a coach, you can make suggestions to help the teacher move forward.

Even though suggestions represent a more directive stance on the part of the coach, coach suggestions should not be confused with the coach "telling" the teacher what to do and how to do it to improve teaching. Coach telling can be problematic because it doesn't provide the teacher with opportunities to grapple with challenges to develop their own understanding. Without these opportunities, teachers will be more likely to depend on their coaches to continue telling them what to do. More importantly, when coaches tell teachers what to do, teachers can be reluctant to change their practices since coach telling takes away teacher ownership of the ideas to improve their practices.

> When coaches tell teachers what to do, teachers can be reluctant to change their practices since coach telling takes away teacher ownership of the ideas to improve their practices.

Contrary to coach telling, the suggestions we have in mind provide alternative pathways for a teacher to consider in resolving the challenge under discussion. This approach will help you build coaching on teacher's thinking and ensure that the teacher has the opportunity to make sense of the ideas you offer. Moreover, since the teacher will be keeping the ownership of decision-making, they will more likely take up your suggestions. For example, in the *Pre-Lesson Conference: Celebration Cakes*, once it appears that Logan has difficulty creating advancing questions, Coach Shawn suggests questions (lines 66–67) that Logan could ask students who come up with the second solution strategy (line 57). Following this suggestion, Coach Shawn asks Logan to explain whether these questions would help her address the challenge (lines 73–74), allowing Logan to make her own decision about the questions Coach Shawn is suggesting. As a result, Logan unpacks the reasoning for her decision (lines 75–79), which provides evidence for Coach Shawn that shows Logan is not blindly following her coach but making sense of the coach-suggested ideas.

The final coaching move in our inquiry routine is to **Generalize** specific actions that a teacher decides to use in one lesson to deal with a challenge. The generalization allows you to push a teacher's thinking in ways that go beyond the particulars of the lesson under discussion so that they can extract a general practice to be applied across different lessons and classrooms. For example, in the *Pre-Lesson Conference: Celebration Cakes*, Coach Shawn could have asked Logan, "What are you going to do in future lessons to create questions that move student thinking toward the goal of the lesson?" This question would lead Logan to think about anticipating specific student solution strategies to the tasks she will use in future lessons so that she can plan advancing questions for each solution strategy. Although Coach Shawn poses a question (lines 85–86) that allows Logan to recognize the importance of teacher questioning in supporting student learning with understanding (lines 87–90), we argue that this won't help Logan extract a practice (i.e., planning questions for anticipated solution strategies to advance student thinking) that could be generalized.

As we learned from Coach Shawn, it was initially difficult to get to generalization in conversations with a teacher, but it was something she came to recognize and work on in subsequent cycles. The takeaway here is that, when a teacher is asked to consider the implications of a practice beyond a single lesson, they will more likely recognize that improving instruction is more than just enhancing an individual lesson.

> When a teacher is asked to consider the implications of a practice beyond a single lesson, they will be more likely to recognize that improving instruction is more than just enhancing an individual lesson.

⏸ STOP AND CONSIDER

Think about a conversation regarding a mathematics lesson that you had with one of your teachers recently. This conversation could have been about planning for an upcoming lesson or a discussion on a completed lesson. Reflect on the conversation by writing down some notes in your journal.

Do you think you built the conversation on the teacher's thinking?

- If your answer is yes, which of the coaching moves from the inquiry routine (**Invite, Rehearse, Suggest,** and **Generalize**) did you use? How did those coaching moves help you support the teacher's learning?

- If your answer is no, what would you have done differently to build the conversation on the teacher's thinking? Which of the coaching moves from the inquiry routine (**Invite, Suggest, Rehearse,** and **Generalize**) would have helped you achieve that?

- In the future, which parts of the inquiry routine do you think you should pay more attention to so that you can build coaching conversations on teachers' thinking?

Guide for Designing Conferences

We created the *Guide for Designing Conferences* (Appendix B) that you can refer to as you plan your coaching conversations with teachers. The Guide for Designing Conferences can serve as a resource for determining how to engage the teacher in a discussion of the focal challenge. There are three columns in the Guide for Designing Conferences: The first column identifies challenges with the 5 practices, the second column provides suggestions on how to address each challenge through the use of the inquiry routine, and the third column provides a rationale regarding the importance of addressing the identified challenge.

Now, imagine that you were coaching a sixth-grade teacher who decided to use the Max's Dog Food task (Figure 1.2) as the basis for a lesson on fraction division. The teacher has anticipated solution strategies that students might use and prepared assessing and advancing questions for each solution strategy, but the advancing questions they are planning to ask students are not likely to move students toward the goals of the lesson. In the Guide for Designing Conferences in Appendix B, you find *"Creating questions that move students toward the mathematical goals"* (Figure 2.3) and plan to follow the coaching moves in the second column:

- **Invite** the teacher to explain how their advancing questions will move students toward the goals of the lesson.

- Engage the teacher in **rehearsing** possible actions they could take to move students toward the goals of the lesson.

- If the teacher is unsure about what advancing questions will move students toward the lesson goals, then make a **suggestion** about what they might say or do.

- You might also push for a **generalization** by asking the teacher what they will do to create questions that move students toward the goals of a lesson in the future and how these questions will support student learning.

The third column of the Guide for Designing Conferences could be used as your rationale—why the teacher challenge you are raising is an important one to consider.

Figure 2.3 • A section of the Guide for Designing Conferences from Appendix B

IDENTIFY THE CHALLENGE	ADDRESS THE CHALLENGE	GUIDING RATIONALE(S)
7. Creating questions that move students toward the goals of the lesson.	ii. **Invite the teacher** to explain how their advancing questions will move students toward the goals of the lesson. • *You indicated that after you had the student explain the number line they had created, you would ask them if they could solve the problem another way. What is it you hope to learn from having a student produce a second solution strategy? How will this help you get to the key mathematical ideas you have targeted in the lesson?*	Engaging students with high-level tasks doesn't guarantee that they will learn the mathematics behind the task and achieve the learning goal. Successfully solving the task or making progress toward a "correct" solution doesn't mean that students understand what they are doing and why.

IDENTIFY THE CHALLENGE	ADDRESS THE CHALLENGE	GUIDING RATIONALE(S)

	ii. **Engage the teacher in rehearsing** possible actions the teacher could take to move students toward the goals of the lesson.
	
	• *You indicated that you had 3 goals for the lesson:*
	  – *When you find "how many ___ are in ___?" you are doing division. That is, in a ÷ b you are trying to find how many times b is contained in a.*
	  – *When dividing by a fraction, the remainder is expressed as a fraction of the divisor.*
	  – *Division situations can be represented in different ways and connections can be made between symbolic, physical, pictorial, and contextual representations.*
	
	• *Let's work on the second goal. What question(s) can you ask the students who produced the number line in order to focus on this goal?*
	
	iii. If the teacher is unsure about what advancing question will move students toward the lesson goals, then **make a suggestion** about what they might say or do.
	
	• *You want the students to understand that the ½ pound that is left over needs be represented as a fraction of a serving. Suppose I ask, "You had ½ lb. left after 16 servings. What part of a serving is this? Can you use your number line to investigate the relationship between pounds and servings?" What might you learn from asking this question? How is this different from the question you initially planned to ask?*
	
	iv. Push for a **generalization**. Ask the teacher what they will do to create questions that move students toward the goals of a lesson in the future and how these questions will support student learning.
		To move students toward the goals of the lesson, teachers should create assessing and advancing questions that are guided by the goals of the lesson. Although assessing questions are used to surface student thinking and understand where students are, advancing questions move students from where they are to the learning goal. When planning the lesson, teachers can create these questions for each of the correct and incorrect anticipated solution strategies.
		
		By creating assessing and advancing questions ahead of time, you will be prepared to respond to and support student thinking and, as a result, ensure that students don't just produce correct solutions to the task but also understand the key mathematical ideas you targeted.

Summary

Research on coaching has identified a tension that coaches often experience during coach–teacher conversations (e.g., Heineke, 2013; Hu & Veen, 2020; Ippolito, 2010; Saclarides & Lubienski, 2020). On the one hand, while trying to be responsive to teacher knowledge and expertise, coaches might allow teachers to take over the conversation without any attention to the most critical aspects of instruction to be improved. On the other hand, while trying to help the teacher deal with the issues they are facing in their teaching, coaches might be too directive and use telling without any connection to teacher knowledge or experience. Either way, these types of coaching conversations will offer teachers limited opportunities to grapple with the challenging aspects of their practices that are important for improving their learning.

We argue that coaching conversations should help teachers connect new information to their existing knowledge and develop meaningful learning of new ideas and practices. Therefore, more important than coaching being responsive or directive is ensuring that coaching conversations *build on teacher thinking*. Toward that end, we designed an inquiry routine that consists of **Invite, Rehearse, Suggest,** and **Generalize** moves that can guide the planning and enacting of coaching conversations.

Implementing the inquiry routine is not going to be straightforward until you get some practice with using it. First, although we argue that every conversation with teachers should begin with an **Invite**, the other moves in the routine don't have to occur in the given order, nor occur at all, because the flow of every conversation will depend on the teacher's responses. For example, when you **invite** a teacher to share their ideas regarding what they would have done differently to address a teacher challenge that they experienced in an enacted lesson, they might provide a well-reasoned answer to sufficiently resolve the challenge. Then, you might choose to move on to **Generalize** to ensure that the teacher can extract a practice to be used in the future. In another scenario, the teacher's response might not be enough to build on the conversation. Then, you might need to use another **invitation** to help them think a little deeper or move on to a **suggestion** for them to consider. Either way, the goal of this routine is to equip you with the tools to make teacher thinking explicit and respond to it in ways to make connections to new ideas. To fully participate in the inquiry routine, teachers need to feel secure. As Coach Avery noted:

> I do think that by wording things in that flow in that (inquiry routine) structure, I think you are giving them information in a way that is easy to hear. You're not criticizing. You're not saying, "You're doing this wrong, let's fix it." I think that right there lowers the anxiety around a coaching cycle. I think that that sequence helped keep the anxiety low. It kept the focus on what the students were doing.

The next chapters will provide additional guidance on planning for the pre-and post-lesson conferences. At this point, we want you to become familiar with the inquiry routine and think about what it can help you achieve.

The goal of the inquiry routine is to equip you with the tools to make teacher thinking explicit and respond to it in ways to make connections to new ideas.

CHAPTER 3
Preparing for the Lesson

This chapter, and the one that follows, focuses on the pre-lesson phase of the coaching cycle. As shown in Figure 3.1, as a coach, you have three activities in this phase of the cycle to work through: Preparing for the Lesson, Planning for the Pre-Lesson Conference, and Engaging in the Pre-Lesson Conference. The first activity, *Preparing for the Lesson*, is discussed herein; the remaining two activities are discussed in Chapter 4.

Figure 3.1 • Pre-lesson phase of a coaching cycle

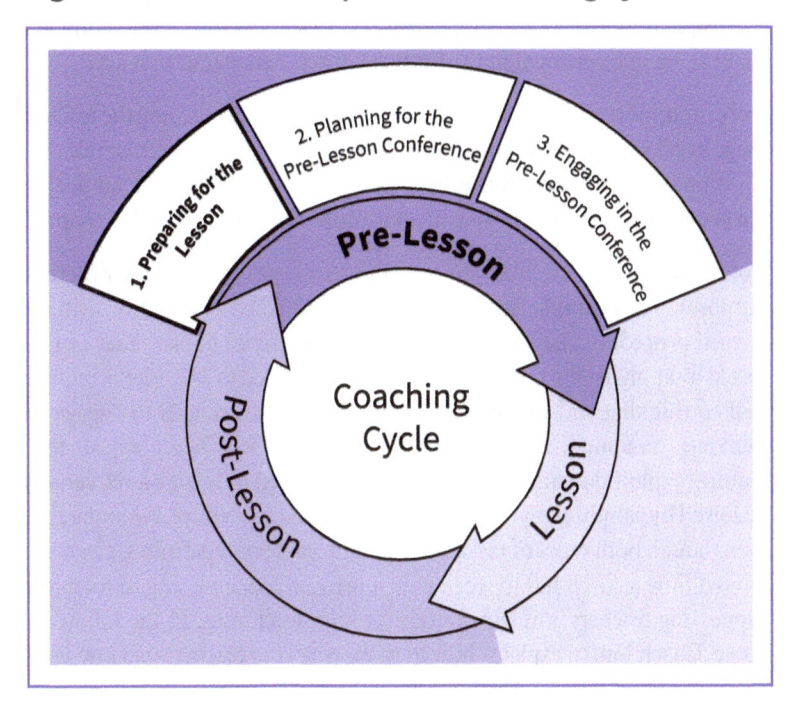

As we discussed in Chapter 1, the challenges a teacher identifies are used to guide your coaching work and to provide learning opportunities for the teacher. Thus, before you and the teacher with whom you will be working get started on a coaching cycle, you need to ask the teacher to reflect on the challenges that they are facing in teaching. Toward that end, you should give the teacher the Teacher Challenges Tool (Appendix A) and ask them to identify up to five challenges and, for each identified challenge, to briefly describe how the challenge plays out in their classroom. Although teachers' responses to the Teacher Challenges Tool will be a valuable resource in designing the pre-lesson conference (the focus of Chapter 4), knowing teachers' perceptions of their challenges early in your relationship will give you insights into their teaching practice and help you plan conversations that will support the teacher in developing strategies for addressing the challenges they are facing.

Supporting Teacher Lesson Planning Prior to the Pre-Lesson Conference

Stigler and Hiebert (1999, p. 156) describe lesson planning as a "premier teaching skill"—one that has a significant impact on the quality of instruction and on students' opportunities to learn mathematics with understanding. Good planning for a lesson "shoulders much of the burden" of teaching by limiting the number of decisions teachers have to make during the lesson. Teachers then have more time to listen to what students are saying, ask questions more thoughtfully, and respond in more tailored ways to student thinking. As noted in earlier *5 Practices* books, because discussions are challenging to implement in the moment, teacher preparation is key.

You can support a teacher's planning process both by (1) helping the teacher make key decisions about the lesson *prior* to the pre-lesson conference and (2) supporting how the teacher refines and revises the lesson plan *during* the pre-lesson conference. We will address the first of these in this chapter.

Note that teachers are likely to use different types of tasks for different purposes. For example, if a teacher wants students to practice using a learned procedure, they will most likely assign a series of tasks that can be solved by applying the procedure. Such tasks, referred to as *low level*, require limited thinking and reasoning. If a teacher wants students to engage in thinking, reasoning, and problem-solving, they will select a task that requires exploration and effort. Such tasks, referred to as *high level*, cannot be solved by simply applying a previously learned procedure. We argue that even though both types of tasks should be in teachers' repertoires, given the limited time a coach has to work with a teacher, coaching should focus on supporting teachers' implementation of high-level tasks. In the following quote, Coach Jordan explains how to make it clear to teachers that low-level tasks are not ones they need to work on together:

> Given the limited time a coach has to work with a teacher, coaching should focus on supporting teachers' implementation of high-level tasks.

> Maybe that—[a procedural task]—is not the task on which I'm gonna engage with you as a coach. Maybe that's not where my focus lies. Yes, students need to practice procedures. Yes, this is a great goal, great task for doing that. Go ahead and do it. But, is there a task for

us to work on together that asks students to think and reason? Not that it would be wasting our time [to work on procedural tasks], but I don't think it would have the impact that we could have in a coaching cycle which takes up so much time. I think, we would have low impact by choosing this [procedural] task.

Therefore, the teacher must engage in Practice 0 (i.e., setting a learning goal and selecting a high-level task) before engaging in the pre-lesson conference. The practice of identifying an appropriate goal and task prior to the pre-lesson conference provides the foundation on which the *5 Practices* are built. There is no point in digging into other practices unless you have established a sound basis for the lesson. As Coach Robin commented, "If we aren't really clear on what we want kids to come away with, why would we do any of the other practices, because it's all built on that." Several of our coaches also noted that not attending to Practice 0 before the pre-lesson conference "eats up" valuable time during the conference and makes it more difficult to address other challenges a teacher may be facing.

Setting a Learning Goal and Selecting a High-Level Task

The teacher should identify the learning goal and select the high-level task without assistance from you, as it will help you diagnose where the teacher is in their capacity to accomplish this very important activity. You may want to make the Task Analysis Guide (TAG) (see Appendix C) available to teachers as they decide on the task that will be the focus of the lesson. The TAG specifies a set of characteristics of low-level tasks (i.e., *memorization* and *procedures without connections*) and high-level tasks (i.e., *procedures with connections* and *doing mathematics*) and can, over time, help teachers develop the capacity to differentiate between tasks that provide the opportunity to think and reason compared with those that do not.

Teachers often have a difficult time identifying a learning goal, selecting a high-level task, and ensuring alignment between tasks and goals (Challenges 1–3 on the Teacher Challenges Tool, Appendix A), yet these are seldom challenges they identify when completing the tool. For example, in our survey of 1,200 teachers from Grades 3–12, only 3 percent or less of teachers at each grade band (i.e., 3–5, 6–8, 9–12) indicated that "*Identifying learning goals*" was an issue for them. In fact, it was the least often selected of any of the challenges. Nevertheless, our experience in working with teachers and coaches suggests that identifying learning goals is actually a challenge for many teachers. Why is there a mismatch? Most teachers are accustomed to stating goals in terms of performance or what "students will be able to do" as a result of engaging in a particular lesson (e.g., students will be able to find the slope of a line given any two points) rather than what students will learn and understand about mathematics (e.g., students will understand that the slope is the ratio of the vertical change [rise] to the horizontal change [run] between any two points on the line). As a result, when asked to identify a learning goal, teachers describe a performance goal, not fully understanding the distinction between the two. Coach Jesse encountered this when working with one of her teachers. She commented:

> *I realized the teacher was looking at more of a performance goal, like what students were going to do rather than the learning part of it. I kind of facilitated, "Let's look at the goals," and then the teacher realized, "I don't know what the goal is." The teacher was struggling because they had been teaching for a long time and were still having a hard time identifying the learning goal. I shared with them, it's actually really hard and it's something many of us still need practice with.*

Once the teacher has identified a goal, selected a task, and shared them with you, you can engage the teacher in a back-and-forth set of exchanges in which you invite the teacher to unpack the learning goals as needed and make suggestions about the task until you feel that the goal and task have the potential to engage students in grappling with key mathematical ideas.

Collaboration between you and the teacher about the goal and task can be conducted virtually or face to face. Communicating virtually will provide both you and the teacher with the opportunity to respond when it is convenient to do so, to have time to think before responding, and lessen the need to find a mutually agreeable time to meet. Communicating face to face, however, has the advantage of being more expedient—the goal and task can be negotiated during a prearranged meeting time without extending over several days. You can make the decision with individual teachers based on their schedules and preferences.

In Analyzing Coaching 3.1, we ask you to consider the discussion regarding goals and tasks that took place between Coach Parker and an eighth-grade teacher, Morgan, who was preparing a lesson on systems of equations for his Algebra 1 class. Morgan and Coach Parker decided to meet a week before the lesson so they could discuss the goal and task that Morgan had identified, as shown in Figure 3.2.

Figure 3.2 • Goal and task identified by Morgan

Goal
To find the point of intersection of two linear functions

Downloading Music Task
You are trying to decide which service you should use to download music. TUNE IN charges 99¢ for each song you download plus an $8.00-per-month membership charge. NOTEABLE charges 50¢ for each song you download plus a $12.00-per-month membership charge. How many songs would you have to download in a month before NOTEABLE is a better deal?

Source (Task): Adapted from *The 5 Practices in Practice: Successfully Orchestrating Mathematics Discussions in Your Middle School Classroom* (p. 23) by M. S. Smith and M. G. Sherin, 2019, Corwin.

> ### ▶ Analyzing Coaching 3.1
> *Resolving Goal and Task Issues*
>
> Prior to the meeting, Morgan completed the Teacher Challenges Tool and sent the goal and task he identified to Coach Parker. Although Morgan had identified several challenges he was facing, none of them had to do with setting goals and selecting a high-level task. As you read the transcript from the meeting between Coach Parker and Morgan, consider the following questions and record your responses in your journal:
>
> 1. What stands out to you in this dialogue?
> 2. To what extent was Coach Parker able to elicit and build on Morgan's thinking?
> 3. What impact do you think such a brief discussion might have had on Morgan?

Resolving Goals and Selecting Task Issues: Downloading Music

1	*Coach:*	Let's start by talking about your goal for the lesson. What do you want students to
2		learn as a result of engaging in the lesson on systems of equations you will be teaching
3		next week?
4	*Morgan:*	I want them to learn how to find the point of intersection of two linear equations.
5	*Coach:*	What is it you want them to know and understand about the point of intersection?
6	*Morgan:*	I want them to know how to find the point of intersection using tables and graphs.
7	*Coach:*	You are focusing on what you want students to do and how they might do it, which is
8		fine. But you need to be clear not just about what you want them to do, but about what
9		understanding you want students to have as a result of engaging in this lesson. What is it
10		you want them to understand about the point of intersection?
11	*Morgan:*	I want them to know what the point of intersection represents.
12	*Coach:*	Okay, let's unpack that. What does the point of intersection represent?
13	*Morgan:*	It's where the two equations have the same x and y values, and the point makes both
14		equations true. In this task, the point of intersection is when the two music plans cost
15		the same for the same number of songs.
16	*Coach:*	With this level of specificity, you will be able to determine not only whether or not
17		students can find the solution to the system but also what the solution means in the
18		context of the problem. You indicated that you wanted students to solve the system
19		using tables and graphs. Is there something specific you would want them to notice in
20		the table or on the graph?
21	*Morgan:*	I want students to notice that on the graph the point of intersection is where the two
22		lines cross. In the table, I want them to notice that the point of intersection is where the
23		y values for both equations are the same for one x value.
24	*Coach:*	Let's summarize what we have so far. You want students to understand that (1) the
25		point of intersection represents where the two equations have the same x and y values
26		and the point makes both equations true; (2) on the graph the point of intersection is
27		where the two lines cross; and (3) in the table the point of intersection is where the

28		y values for both equations are the same for one x value. How are these goals similar to
29		or different from the goal you started with?
30	Morgan:	Well, these goals really get at what the point of intersection means and how it shows
31		up in a table and graph. It is more than just getting the right answer. It is being able to
32		make sense of the answer and see how you would find it using different
33		representations.
34	Coach:	Exactly! So, you are planning to use the Downloading Music task for this lesson?
35	Morgan:	Yes. I thought students would find it interesting because they all like to download
36		music.
37	Coach:	How would you classify the task using the Task Analysis Guide? *(Coach Parker*
38		*hands Morgan the guide [Appendix C] and waits for Morgan to respond.)*
39	Morgan:	I think it would be high level—doing mathematics. There are different ways to solve it
40		and they can choose a strategy that makes sense to them.
41	Coach:	You indicated earlier that you wanted them to use tables and graphs to solve the task.
42		Can they also use substitution or elimination? Will they have any technology available
43		like a graphing calculator or Desmos?
44	Morgan:	We haven't done the algebraic methods yet and I wasn't planning on having them use
45		technology. I will give them graph paper and a ruler.
46	Coach:	Have you solved the task yet?
47	Morgan:	Not yet, but I will.
48	Coach:	Let's take a few minutes now and work on it. *(Coach Parker waits a few minutes and*
49		*notices that Morgan is using substitution to find the point of intersection and is*
50		*frowning.)* Why the frown?
51	Morgan:	I didn't realize the numbers were so messy. *(Morgan points to his solution.)* This is
52		going to be really hard for my students to do with a table or graph.
53		

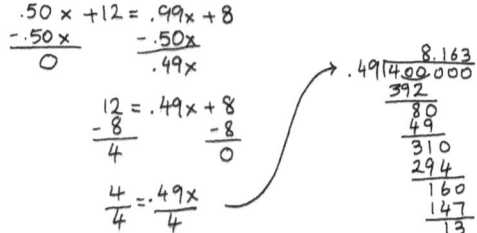

$$.50x + 12 = .99x + 8$$
$$\underline{-.50x} \quad \underline{-.50x}$$
$$0 \quad .49x$$

$$12 = .49x + 8$$
$$\underline{-8} \quad \underline{-8}$$
$$4 \quad 0$$

$$\frac{4}{4} = \frac{.49x}{4}$$

$$.49 \overline{) 400.000} \quad \begin{array}{r} 8.163 \\ \hline \end{array}$$
$$\underline{392}$$
$$80$$
$$\underline{49}$$
$$310$$
$$\underline{294}$$
$$160$$
$$\underline{147}$$
$$13$$

54	Coach:	I agree. The 99¢ per download for TUNE IN is going to make it really challenging to
55		graph the equations by hand and it will make it harder to see the rate of change in the
56		table. The point of intersection is actually (8.163, 16.082). I am wondering what you
57		think about changing 99¢ to $1.00?
58	Morgan:	I think that makes sense.
59	Coach:	Changing 99¢ to $1.00 will make the task more accessible to students and make it
60		possible for them to *see* what you want them to see with the strategies they will have
61		access to. I am wondering, what do you think about adding a sentence to the task that
62		asks the students to explain their reasoning?
63	Morgan:	I like that idea. This way they will have to do more than just give an answer. They will
64		have to explain how they arrived at the conclusion they reached and why it makes
65		sense.
66	Coach:	You initially said that you thought the task was high level. Do you think the changes
67		we made in the task change the level of the task?
68	Morgan:	I am now not sure the task was high level before we made the changes. The strategies
69		that my students had access to would not make solving the task possible. And if

70		students did know substitution, it was the most likely thing to do in the task given the
71		numbers. So this would not require much decision-making!
72	Coach:	Great. So, the next step is to anticipate how you think students will solve the task and
73		what difficulties they may face in so doing. Be sure to use your monitoring chart so
74		you can create assessing and advancing questions for each possible solution strategy
75		that will give insights into students' thinking and the progress they are making in
76		understanding the goals for the lesson.

Resolving Goals and Selecting Task Issues: Analysis

Many things might have stood out to you in this dialogue, and we will discuss a few of them. First, you may have noticed that Morgan selected a performance goal and a low-level task, although he had not identified goals and tasks as challenges. As we mentioned, this is not uncommon and speaks to the need to talk with a teacher about goals and tasks whether they have identified them as problematic or not. As a result, the discussion focused on Coach Parker's efforts to support Morgan's closer examination of the goal and task in an effort to help him see the limitations in both.

The second thing you may have noticed is that Coach Parker was prepared for the conversation with Morgan. Based on how the discussion unfolded, we can infer that prior to the meeting the coach most likely (1) gave serious thought to what could be learned about mathematics from engaging in a task on systems of equations; (2) solved the task prior to the meeting and noted that the point of intersection would be nearly impossible to determine without algebraic methods or technology, but that knowledge of and access to either or both would make the task less challenging; and (3) considered possible ways to modify the task so as to increase the level of thinking and reasoning required to solve it. Thinking through the goal and task—both what they were and what they could become—prior to the meeting limited the number of decisions Coach Parker had to make on the fly. In this way, a coach planning for a meeting or conference is much like a teacher planning for a lesson—the work you do in advance improves the quality of the interaction.

The third thing you may have noted is that Coach Parker asked a lot of questions (i.e., lines 1–3; 5; 9–10; 12; 19–20; 28–29; 34; 37; 42–43; 46; 50; 56–57; 61–62; 66–67). Why did the coach ask so many questions? Answering this requires a discussion of the second question: To what extent was Coach Parker able to elicit and build on Morgan's thinking? As we described in Chapter 2, coach–teacher conversations that support teacher learning should build on teacher thinking. Throughout the conversation, Coach Parker asked questions to first elicit Morgan's thinking and to then build on Morgan's responses by continuing to press for more detail. Coach Parker began the discussion by inviting Morgan to explain what he wanted students to learn as a result of engaging in the lesson about solving a system of equations. Although Morgan had submitted the goal to Coach Parker prior to the meeting, asking him to explain it got the goal "on the table" (line 4) so it could be further discussed. The subsequent questions, "What is it you want students to understand about the point of intersection?" (lines 9–10); "What does the point of intersection represent?" (line 12); and "Is there something specific you would want them to notice in the table and on the graph?" (lines 19–20), pressed Morgan to move beyond his procedural goal (finding the point of intersection) and to focus on what he wanted students to understand about mathematics from engaging in the task (i.e., a learning goal). As a result of the questioning by Coach Parker, Morgan articulated a set of specific goals, which the coach summarized (lines 24–28), and explained how these goals differed from the initial goal (lines 30–33).

Coach Parker continued the conversation with a discussion of the task by confirming that the lesson would be built around the Downloading Music task and asking Morgan to evaluate the task using the Task Analysis Guide (line 37). The coach did not argue with Morgan's classification of the task as high level but asked what technology and algebraic strategies would be available or accessible to students (lines 42–43). As Morgan responded that students had not learned algebraic methods and technology wouldn't be available to the students (lines 44–45), it became clear to Coach Parker that it would be difficult for students to find the point of intersection. Thus, the coach asked Morgan to solve the task in order to help him realize the numbers are difficult to work with. Through his work on the task, Morgan in fact came to realize that the task would be difficult to solve using tables or graphs—the two strategies students had available to them. Such difficulty has the risk of pushing students unnecessarily into frustration and missing the mathematical goal because they're lost in the weeds of a tedious procedure. At this point, Coach Parker made two suggestions: "What do you think about changing 99¢ to $1.00"? (lines 56–57) and "What do you think about adding a sentence to the task that asks the students to explain their reasoning?" (lines 61–62). Although the coach provided a rationale for the first suggested change (lines 59–61) that Morgan thought made sense, Morgan not only liked the second suggested change but also explained why he thought the change would be helpful (lines 63–65). The final question for Morgan, to consider whether the changes to the task changed the level of the task (lines 66–67), led him to realize that the original task was probably not high level and the reason why.

You may have noted that Coach Parker used two of the moves from the inquiry routine that we described in Chapter 2. Specifically, the questions that the coach asked were *invitations* to the teacher to share their thinking and the *suggestions* that the coach made helped the teacher recognize how the changes could improve the task. Coach Parker did not engage Morgan in a rehearsal. Rehearsals are not generally relevant in discussions regarding goal and task identification because setting goals and selecting tasks does not involve any interaction with students. In addition, the coach did not press Morgan to generalize the features of high-level tasks and learning goals beyond the specific lesson. Although by asking Morgan to compare the original goal and task with the revised versions that emerged through their conversation, Coach Parker pushed Morgan to think about the differences between learning and performance goals, as well as between high- and low-level tasks, these differences were not made explicit enough to achieve *generalization*. Similarly, Coach Parker's use of the TAG (Appendix C), which listed characteristics of tasks with varying levels of cognitive demand, provided Morgan with a tool that is applicable to any task and could be useful in selecting tasks for subsequent lessons, but Coach Parker did not press Morgan to consider how he was going to make use of this tool in the future. You may want to be explicit with teachers that (1) they should use the TAG in making decisions about the tasks as the tasks will form the basis of a lesson and that (2) every effort should be made to select a task that would be characterized as high level.

The inquiry routine can be a helpful tool in any conversation with a teacher, not just in those that focus on challenges the teacher identified or in ones that take place during pre- or post-lesson conferences. As we discussed in Chapter 2, a coach needs to decide which moves from the routine (i.e., **invite, rehearse, suggest,** and **generalize**) will be most useful in a particular situation, as Coach Parker did in this instance.

The conversation left Morgan with a revised goal that focused on student learning and could serve to guide his decision-making during the lesson (e.g., the questions he would ask students, the solutions that he would select to share during the whole-class discussion) and a revised task that had the potential to engage students in not only finding the point of intersection but also in thinking about what the point of intersection actually means and how it shows up in a table and in a graph. What is perhaps most critical is that Morgan played a central role in both revisions and had ownership of the final products.

Coach Parker could have simply told Morgan that the goal was procedural and the task was low level and offered suggestions on both. But, even though "telling" solves the short-term problem, it is not a long-term solution for it does not connect to the teacher's thinking, nor does it help the teacher evaluate the difference between where they started and where they ended up. As we discussed in Chapter 2, simply telling a teacher what to do creates dependence on the coach.

Support for Identifying Goals and Tasks

As mentioned, the identification of goals and tasks can be challenging for teachers, as it was for Morgan. The Teacher Challenges Tool (see Appendix A) describes specific challenges related to setting goals and selecting tasks (Challenges 1–3). In our work, we have found that these challenges manifest themselves in several different ways. Specifically, a teacher may experience four possible scenarios for the challenges regarding goal and task identification:

   a. a teacher might select a low-level task and a performance goal,
   b. a teacher might select a low-level task and a learning goal,
   c. a teacher might select a high-level task and a performance goal (or no goal), and
   d. a teacher might not select a task or establish a learning goal.

The Goal and Task Identification Guide (Appendix D) is a resource that will help inform your discussion with a teacher about their lesson goal and the task they plan to use to accomplish the goal. The guide follows the same format as the Guide for Designing Conferences (Appendix B) discussed in Chapter 2. Each of the four scenarios related to goals and tasks is identified in the first column, examples of how you might implement the inquiry routine (i.e., *invite*, *suggest*, and *generalize*) to probe these challenges are found in the second column, and the guiding rationale that makes salient why addressing this challenge is important to student learning is found in the third column. An example from the Goal and Task Identification Guide, based on the Max's Dog Food task, can be found in Figure 3.3. This example provides ideas regarding how you might structure a conversation around the challenge of selecting a high-level task and establishing a learning goal.

Figure 3.3 • Example from the Goal and Task Identification Guide

IDENTIFY THE CHALLENGE	ADDRESS THE CHALLENGE	GUIDING RATIONALE(S)
d. Identified a topic, unit, or standard but has not selected a task or established a learning goal.	i. **Invite the teacher** to consider a high-level task (or tasks) that would fit with the identified topic, unit, or standard and what students could learn from engaging in such a task. • *You indicated that you wanted to use a task that involves the division of fractions, specifically a mixed number divided by a proper fraction. Here are two examples that you might consider:*	**Learning goals** for students set the stage for everything else. When a teacher knows what they want their students to learn, they are better equipped to make downstream decisions (e.g., deciding how to advance a student's thinking during small group work; selecting which student responses to publicly share during the final phase of the lesson).

IDENTIFY THE CHALLENGE	ADDRESS THE CHALLENGE	GUIDING RATIONALE(S)
	Task 1 Max's Dog Food	Learning goals that are about what a teacher wants their students to understand are critical for the design of lessons in which students engage in high cognitive demand tasks. Performance goals, on the other hand, focus on procedures that lead to correct answers without providing insight into the underlying concepts or meaning.
	• Dog food is sold in a $12\frac{1}{2}$ pound bag. My dog, Max, eats $\frac{3}{4}$ of a pound of dog food every day. How many servings of dog food are in the bag?	
	• Draw a picture, construct a number line, or make a table to help explain your solution.	
	Task 2 The Pizza Party	Student engagement with **high-level tasks** is a necessary condition for students' opportunity to develop thinking, reasoning, and problem-solving skills; to experience mathematics as something that is meaningful and that they can make sense of; and to build understanding of important mathematics ideas and concepts, including the learning goal of the lesson.
	• You ordered pizza for your birthday party. When the party was over, you still had $4\frac{5}{6}$ pizzas left over. Your mother decided to freeze the remaining pizza. She put $\frac{2}{3}$ of a pizza (one serving) in each freezer bag. How many servings would your mother be able to freeze?	
	• Draw a picture, construct a number line, or make a table to help explain your solution.	Alignment matters! A high-level task without a learning goal often leads to lessons that fail to live up to their potential; a low-level task that is paired with a learning goal will not set into motion the kinds of thinking and reasoning that students must engage in in order to achieve the goal of the lesson.
	You could change the numbers and the context to what you think would work best for your students but think about the general structure of the problems.	
	• How could students solve a problem of this type?	
	• What prior knowledge would students need to solve a task like this?	
	• What might students learn about fraction division from engaging in this task?	

(Continued)

Figure 3.3 (*Continued*)

IDENTIFY THE CHALLENGE	ADDRESS THE CHALLENGE	GUIDING RATIONALE(S)
	ii. If the teacher is unsure about what students would learn from engaging in such a task, **make a suggestion** regarding possible learning goals: • *Here are some things that students could learn from engaging in a task such as the Max's Dog Food or the Pizza Party. For each goal, consider how students' work on the task could help you accomplish each goal.* – *When you find "how many ____ are in ____ ?" you are doing division. That is, in a ÷ b you are trying to find how many times b is contained in a.* – *When dividing by a fraction the remainder is expressed as a fraction of the divisor.* – *Division situations can be represented in different ways and connections can be made between symbolic, physical, pictorial, and contextual representations.* iii. Push for **generalization**. Ask the teacher to consider how high-level tasks, and the alignment of goals and tasks, can support student learning during the lesson.	

Source (Task 1): Adapted from the Institute for Learning at the University of Pittsburgh (2016; as cited in Smith & Stein, 2018).

Source (Task 2): Adapted from *Making Sense of Mathematics for Teaching Grades 6–8: (Unifying Topics for an Understanding of Functions, Statistics, and Probability)* by E. C. Nolan, J. K. Dixon, G. J. Roy, and J. Andreasen (2016; as cited in Smith & Sherin, 2019), Solution Tree Press.

In Analyzing Coaching 3.2, we ask you to put yourself in the role of the coach and consider how you would plan for a conversation with a teacher about the goal and task shown in Figure 3.4. (Although the task originally appeared in Grade 5 curricular materials, it is now consistent with most standards for Grade 6.)

Figure 3.4 • Area of a right triangle goal and task

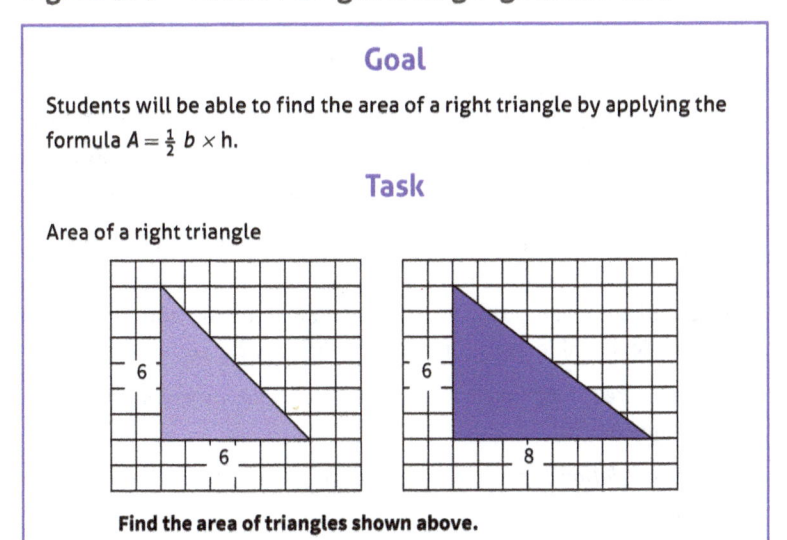

Goal

Students will be able to find the area of a right triangle by applying the formula $A = \frac{1}{2} b \times h$.

Task

Area of a right triangle

[Two right triangles on grid. First triangle: base 6, height 6. Second triangle: base 8, height 6.]

Find the area of triangles shown above.

Source: Adapted from *Everyday Mathematics. Fifth Grade: Teacher's Resource Package* by University of Chicago School Mathematics Project, 2007, Wright Group/McGraw-Hill.

▶ Analyzing Coaching 3.2
Aligning Tasks and Goals

Imagine a sixth-grade teacher has sent you the goal statement and task shown in Figure 3.4. Drawing on the Task Analysis Guide (Appendix C), the Goal and Task Identification Guide (Appendix D), and/or any other resource you have access to, use the following questions to create a plan for a conversation with the teacher. Record your plan in your journal.

1. What do you notice about the task and goal statement?
2. In what ways might the goal statement and task be revised?
3. What questions could you ask the teacher to help them see the limitations of the current goal and task?

Aligning Tasks and Goals: Analysis

The first thing you may have noticed is that the teacher has identified a performance goal and selected a low-level task. The goal focuses on what students will do, not on what they will understand about mathematics as a result of engaging in the task. As stated, students need to know only how to plug the numbers for base and height into the formula (i.e., Area $= \frac{1}{2} b \times h$).

The Common Core State Standards for Mathematics (CCSSM) for Grade 6 states that students should find the areas of right triangles by relating the right triangles to rectangles and then use these relationships to develop and discuss formulas for areas of triangles (National Governors Association Center for Best Practices & Council of Chief State School Officers, 2010, p. 40). Hence, students are given the opportunity to develop their own formulas rather than simply being asked to apply a formula created by someone else.

Drawing on the statement in CCSSM, the goal could be revised to focus on the relationship between the area of a rectangle and the area of a right triangle and the relationship between the area, length, and width of a right triangle. Possible goals (Smith et al., 2017, p. 21) could include:

- *The area of a triangle is $\frac{1}{2}$ of its length times its width (or base times height).*

- *The relationship between area, length, and width of a triangle can be generalized to a formula.*

- *There are several equivalent ways of writing the formula for the area of a triangle (e.g., $A = \frac{1}{2} (l \times w); A = \frac{1}{2} l \times w; A = l \times \frac{1}{2} w$), and each can be related to a physical model.*

You might want to begin a discussion of the goal and task by asking the teacher where this lesson falls in a unit of study and what students have worked on prior to the lesson they are currently planning. If students have already learned the formula for finding the area of a right triangle, you might suggest the teacher consider a lesson that builds on that knowledge rather than just asking students to practice substituting values. As we discussed earlier in the chapter, you want to communicate that students may need practice but that this may not be the best type of lesson for the two of you to collaborate on. Therefore, either the teacher will need to go back to the drawing board or you will need to work with the teacher to identify a task that would be appropriate.

If the teacher indicates that this is an introductory lesson, you might begin by asking the teacher what they want students to learn about the area of a right triangle. If the teacher says "the formula," you might then ask a series of questions such as: "What do you want them to understand about the formula?" "What other areas do they already know how to find?" "How is the area of a right triangle related to the areas of other shapes?" If the teacher cannot answer any of these questions, you could suggest one of the goals you have created and ask them how this goal compares with the original goal and why the difference might matter. In this way, you are engaging the teacher in analyzing the two goals, abstracting the differences between them, and considering the implications of the differences. As such, the teacher is not just encouraged to replace their current goal with your goal but to make sense of why they might want to reconsider their goal.

The task as it is presented in Figure 3.4 is low level. All the criteria in the TAG (Appendix C) for procedures without connections apply to this task. Although the right triangle is on a grid, the grid is not needed since the length and width are given. The task could be revised by:

1. removing the labels on the diagram that specify the length and width of the triangle,

2. inviting students to construct a formula for the area of a triangle instead of telling students what to do and how, and

3. giving students objects to manipulate, such as several copies of the diagram so they can cut out the triangles and manipulate them on grid paper.

Once students have worked with specific right triangles, the teacher could ask them to generalize a formula for any right triangle. In your discussion with the teacher, you could begin by asking how they could change the task so that students would have to determine the area without using the formula. If the teacher isn't sure about what to change, you could provide copies of the task without numbers and a pair of scissors and ask the teacher to explore what they could do to determine the area. If the teacher is still unsure about how to proceed, you can make two copies of the purple triangle or draw a rectangle with the purple triangle as $\frac{1}{2}$ of its area and ask the teacher what they notice. This approach will likely help the teacher realize how opening the task up and providing resources for students to draw on could facilitate student exploration.

Continuing the Lesson Planning Process

Once a learning goal and a high-level task have been identified, the next step for the teacher is to continue with the lesson planning process. Two tools can support the teacher as they continue to think through an upcoming lesson: The Lesson Planning Tool (Appendix E) and the Monitoring Tool (Appendix F). The *Lesson Planning Tool*, adapted from "Thinking Through a Lesson Protocol: A Key for Successfully Implementing High-Level Tasks" by Smith et al. (2008), provides a template for explicating key aspects of a lesson, including but not limited to the 5 practices. In addition to asking teachers to identify a learning goal, high-level task, anticipated student solutions, and a plan for selecting and sequencing solutions, the Lesson Planning Tool also asks teachers to consider other questions such as how they will launch the lesson to ensure student access, what tools and resources will be available, and what they will take as evidence that students are achieving the lesson goals. This tool is intended to support the teacher in thinking through the lesson prior to ever setting foot in the classroom.

The *Monitoring Tool* (Smith & Stein, 2018), referred to in the Lesson Planning Tool, provides a template for recording solution strategies that a teacher anticipates and the *assessing* and *advancing* questions that they can ask students who produce them. Assessing questions are intended to make students' thinking visible, ensuring that the teacher understands what the students did and why they did it. Advancing questions are intended to move students beyond where they currently are, toward the goal of the lesson. These components of the Monitoring Tool are constructed prior to the lesson. During the lesson, the teacher can use the Monitoring Tool to keep track of the students or groups that produce specific strategies, record additional strategies that were not anticipated, and specify an order in which specific strategies will be shared during the whole-group discussion and who will present them. In addition, the Monitoring Tool can serve as a reminder of the solutions that the teacher is looking for and the questions that could be asked when interacting with students.

A teacher should complete the Monitoring Tool and the Lesson Planning Tool on their own before the pre-lesson conference and submit them to you for review. These completed tools, along with the Teacher Challenges Tool, provide the fodder for planning the pre-lesson conference.

Summary

The goals teachers set and the tasks they identify influence what students learn about mathematics. The goals need to be specific enough to guide the teacher's decision-making (e.g., what task to select, what questions to ask, what solutions to discuss) and to support reflection after the lesson (e.g., what evidence is there that students learned what was intended, what could be done differently). As Hiebert and colleagues (2007) noted:

> *Without explicit learning goals, it is difficult to know what counts as evidence of students' learning, how students' learning can be linked to particular instructional activities, and how to revise instruction to facilitate students' learning more effectively. Formulating clear, explicit learning goals sets the stage for everything else.* (p. 51)

Formulating clear, explicit learning goals is the first step in planning a lesson. Then, teachers need to identify tasks that are aligned with the learning goals. However, different tasks provide different learning opportunities. Specifically, students who have opportunities to engage in tasks that require thinking and reasoning (i.e., high-level tasks) on a regular basis have greater learning gains than do students who routinely engage with tasks that focus on the application of procedures (i.e., low-level tasks; e.g., Boaler & Staples, 2008; Stein & Lane, 1996; Stigler & Hiebert, 2004).

Although identifying goals and tasks is critical to students' opportunities to learn, many teachers struggle in this area. Therefore, support from the coach in this area can make a difference in the trajectory of a lesson. The activities in this chapter (Analyzing Coaching 3.1 and 3.2) focus on the teacher's identification of a performance goal and low-level task. However, a coach should always discuss the goal and task with the teacher even if they don't fit one of the four scenarios we described. For example, if a teacher uses an existing lesson plan with an established learning goal and a *doing mathematics* task that has the potential to achieve this goal, the coach needs to determine what the teacher understands about the lesson. You should **invite** the teacher to explain what they want students to learn (e.g., a conversation similar to the one between Morgan and Coach Parker) and how they see the task helping them accomplish the goal. Using a lesson prepared by someone else does not guarantee that the lesson will be successful, regardless of how well-planned the lesson is.

In the next chapter, we discuss planning for and conducting the pre-lesson conference. The coach can begin planning for the conference once the Teacher Challenges Tool (Appendix A) has been completed, the goal and task have been set, and other lesson materials (e.g., Lesson Planning Tool, Monitoring Tool) have been prepared. These materials will be critical resources the coach will draw on in determining the focus of the conference.

Putting into Practice

PROVIDING FEEDBACK ON A GOAL AND TASK

Ask a teacher with whom you work to provide you with the goal for an upcoming lesson that you will be observing and the task they will be using as the basis for the lesson and set a time to meet to discuss them. Prior to the meeting, outline a conversation and think about how you can use the relevant parts of the inquiry routine—**Invite, Suggest,** and **Generalize**—to uncover the teacher's thinking about what they are trying to accomplish and the task they have selected. During the conversation with the teacher, probe them for more specificity if they provide a surface-level response. Be ready to make a suggestion if the teacher is not sure how to respond. You may want to consult the Goal and Task Identification Guide (Appendix D) and the Task Analysis Guide (Appendix C) as you prepare for the conversation.

Following the meeting, reflect on the conversation by writing down some notes in your journal. What did you learn about the teacher's understanding? What surprised you? To what extent did using the inquiry routine result in a different conversation than the ones you have previously had with the teacher?

CHAPTER 4
Preparing for and Engaging in the Pre-Lesson Conference

In this chapter, we continue to discuss the pre-lesson phase of the coaching cycle, shifting our focus from Preparing for the Lesson (Figure 4.1, Activity 1) to *Planning for* and *Engaging in the Pre-Lesson Conference* (Figure 4.1, Activities 2 and 3). As we indicated in Chapter 2, the most critical part of a coaching cycle is the coach–teacher conversations that take place in the pre-lesson and post-lesson conferences. Herein we discuss what the coach must do to prepare for and conduct the pre-lesson conference.

Figure 4.1 • Pre-lesson phase of a coaching cycle

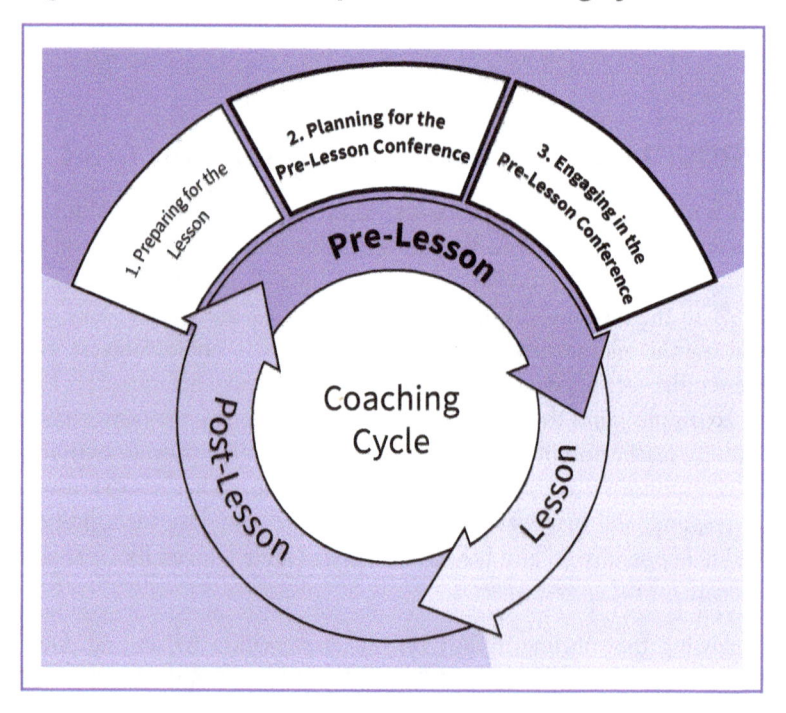

The purpose of the pre-lesson conference is to help teachers think deeply about the lesson they are about to teach—what they want students to learn and what they will do to support student learning in ways that honor and build on students' thinking. Through the pre-lesson conference conversations, teachers will have the opportunity to rethink and refine their current instructional practices in ways that give each and every student the opportunity to learn mathematics with understanding. The challenges with which a teacher is grappling become the grist for the conversation.

Establishing the focus of the pre-lesson conference is a major task to be performed by the coach, and it can be difficult for two reasons. First, when determining the challenges to address in a pre-lesson conversation, you need to attend to both the teacher's perceived needs and your view of what the teacher needs to address—which might be different from what the teacher identified. Second, there will be more challenges than you will be able to work on with the teacher during one meeting so you will have to decide which challenge(s) will be the most helpful at that moment in time. Each of these is discussed in the following sections.

Preparing for the Pre-Lesson Conference

As we indicated in Chapter 3, in Activity 1 in the coaching cycle, you and the teacher discussed the goal and task that would serve as the basis for an upcoming lesson. The teacher then continued with lesson planning by completing the Lesson Planning Tool (Appendix E) and the Monitoring Tool (Appendix F) on their own and submitted these tools to you. These completed tools, along with the Teacher Challenges Tool (Appendix A), will be essential resources in designing the pre-lesson conference. A review of these documents will help you determine which challenge(s) to focus on during the conference. The challenges you chose may be ones that the teacher has explicitly identified on the Teacher Challenges Tool. You might also choose challenges that you infer to be problematic for the teacher based on your review of the teacher's lesson materials (e.g., the teacher has provided no details on the strategies they have anticipated, the teacher plans to ask for volunteers to share their work during the whole class discussion, the teacher plans to show the students the strategy they want them to use).

Although it is important for you to pay close attention to the challenges that the teacher has identified, it is equally important to spot any evidence of other challenges that the teacher seems to be facing but has not identified yet. When teachers have a voice in determining what they need to work on, they are more likely to persevere through difficult moments and engage deeply with the challenging work of improving their instruction (Atteberry & Bryk, 2011; Olson & Barrett, 2004). However, when deciding what challenges to discuss is based solely on teacher input, one runs "the risk of ignoring coaches' intended role as more accomplished others, and thus a key aspect of the rationale for one-on-one coaching" (Kochmanski & Cobb, 2023, p. 439). Furthermore, having teachers alone determine the focus of coaching assumes that teachers can identify their most pressing challenges based on self-assessments of their current practices and their knowledge of the *5 Practices*. Research, however, suggests that this is often not the case (e.g., Beisiegel et al., 2018; Cohen, 1990; Kraft & Hill, 2020; Saclarides & Lubienski, 2020). Thus, our model asks the coach to attend to the challenges identified by their teachers, while not ignoring what they consider to be critical areas for improvement for their teachers.

Identifying Challenges

Let's use an example to illustrate the decision-making involved in determining what challenges to address in a pre-lesson conference. Imagine that you are the coach working with Kyle, a seventh-grade teacher who is working on a ratios and proportions unit. The goals Kyle has identified and the task he has selected are shown in Figure 4.2. Kyle has also completed the Teacher Challenges, the Lesson Planning, and Monitoring Tools, which you can find in Appendix H.

Figure 4.2 • Kyle's goals and task

Goals

- Students will understand that equivalent ratios represent mixtures with the same taste.
- Students will understand that to compare different mixtures/ratios, you need a common basis for comparison.
- Students will understand that different strategies and models can be used to accurately compare the same set of ratios.

Mixing Juice Task

Every year, the Grade 7 students at Langston Hughes School go on an outdoor education camping trip. During the week-long trip, students study nature and participate in recreational activities. Everyone pitches in with the cooking and cleanup.

This year Arvin and Mariah were in charge of making orange juice for the campers. They plan to make juice by mixing water and frozen orange juice concentrate. To find the mixture that would taste the best, they decided to test some mixes.

Mix A	Mix C
2 cups concentrate	1 cup concentrate
3 cups water	2 cups water
Mix B	**Mix D**
5 cups concentrate	3 cups concentrate
9 cups water	5 cups water

1. Which recipe will make juice that is the most "orangey"? Explain.
2. Which recipe will make juice that is the least "orangey"? Explain.

Source (Task): From *Connected Mathematics 3: Comparing and Scaling* by G. Lappan, J. Fey, G. Fitzgerald, S. Friel, and E. Phillips, 2014, Pearson.

In reviewing the materials a teacher has submitted, we recommend that you use the following questions when selecting challenges as the focus of the pre-lesson conference:

1. What challenges has the teacher identified?
2. To what extent has the teacher addressed any of these challenges in the lesson materials?
3. Are there other challenges evident in the materials that go beyond what the teacher has identified?
4. Which subset of challenges—if addressed—are likely to give the teacher the most traction during instruction?

We will walk through each question as we review the materials that Kyle submitted.

1. *What challenges has the teacher identified?*

As you see in Kyle's Teacher Challenges Tool, he identified five challenges:

- Challenge 4. *Launching a task to ensure student access,*
- Challenge 6. *Being prepared to help students who cannot get started,*
- Challenge 9. *Keeping track of group progress,*
- Challenge 10. *Involving all members of a group,* and
- Challenge 12. *Expanding beyond the usual student presenters.*

In the last column of the Teacher Challenges Tool, Kyle also briefly explained how each challenge plays out in his classroom. Since every teacher experiences these challenges in different ways, the information Kyle provided is important in that the coach has an idea about Kyle's perspective.

2. *To what extent has the teacher addressed any of these challenges in the lesson materials?*

Kyle provided some description of his launch in his lesson plan—"I will introduce the task through a PowerPoint and give each student a handout with the task on it"—but provided no insight into what he will do to make sure students understand the context (e.g., What is orange juice concentrate?), the language used in the task (e.g., What does *orangey* mean?), and what is expected of students (e.g., What product will they create?). Even though Kyle's PowerPoint may address these points, you would need to ask more questions about the details of the plan to determine whether it is sufficient to be sure all students have access to the task.

The lesson materials do not specifically address any of the other challenges. Although Kyle has indicated that students often struggle to get started, he has not listed "can't get started" on the monitoring tool or provided specific questions that could be asked to help struggling students make progress. Regarding Challenges 9 and 10, we know that students will be working in groups, but we have no idea how Kyle plans to track what they are doing or involve all students in a discussion. Finally, we know that Kyle plans to select work from the groups to share, but we don't know how the presenters will be selected and if Kyle intends to move beyond the usual presenters.

> To be clear, just because something isn't in the lesson plan doesn't mean that the teacher hasn't considered it. In fact, providing sufficient detail to address all of these challenges would be impractical and exhausting for the teacher.

To be clear, just because something isn't in the lesson plan doesn't mean that the teacher hasn't considered it. In fact, providing sufficient detail to address all of these challenges would be impractical and exhausting for the teacher. The only way you are going to learn enough about some of these issues is to ask questions about them during the pre-lesson conference.

3. *Are there other challenges evident in the materials that go beyond what the teacher has identified?*

Kyle has listed the names of strategies that he thinks students will use to solve the task (e.g., finding a common denominator, drawing a picture, finding unit rate, using a double number line). However, it is not clear that Kyle actually used these strategies to solve the task. This might make us wonder whether Kyle moved beyond the way he solved the problem (Challenge 5). For example, the common denominator needed to solve this task would be 840 not 90; it is not clear what a double-number line or picture would look like; the scaling-up strategy is not mentioned at all; although if the recipes are scaled up to have the same number of cups of water, each recipe could have 90 cups of water. Asking Kyle to detail the solutions he expects students to produce can better prepare him to support students as they work, to make decisions about which solutions will be presented in the class, and to make use of specific solutions to highlight the lesson goals.

4. *Which subset of challenges—if addressed—are likely to give the teacher the most traction during instruction?*

After reviewing the materials that Kyle submitted, along with the challenges he identified, we decided that addressing Challenges 4 and 6 (both of which Kyle identified) would give him the most traction during instruction. In addition, since we found evidence in Kyle's documents that he might be struggling with Challenge 5, we might want Kyle to provide more detail on the solution strategies he is expecting students to use.

When you review the teacher's documents with these four questions in mind, how do you decide what to focus on during the pre-lesson conference? Here are a few things to consider:

- Be judicious in the challenges you choose to work on during the conference. You can't address every challenge the teacher seems to be facing in one conference. It would take more time than you are likely to have, and it would be overwhelming—both for you and your teacher. Remember, each coaching cycle is just one step toward improving instruction. Two or three challenges are probably the most you could hope to address in one meeting. We decided to focus on three challenges in our discussion with Kyle.

> Remember, each coaching cycle is just one step toward improving instruction.

- You need to decide which challenges are likely to be most helpful in enacting a 5 practices lesson. Selecting challenges that relate to early practices (e.g., goals and tasks, anticipating) may have a greater impact on a lesson than working on later practices (e.g., selecting, sequencing, connecting), especially if earlier practices have not already been discussed. For example, focusing on *expanding beyond the usual presenters* may not be productive when you are still struggling to *construct a launch that ensures that all students have access to the task*. For our discussion with Kyle, we selected Challenges 4. *Launching the task* and 6. *Helping students who can't get started* since these two challenges are directly related to ensuring that students understand and can enter the task. If these two challenges aren't addressed early on in preparation for a lesson, it is not clear that focusing on any of the other challenges makes sense.

- Select at least one challenge that the teacher has identified, but don't hesitate to also choose one that you have identified. In your meeting with Kyle, you may want to discuss Challenge 5. *Moving beyond the way you solve a problem*. Although Kyle did not identify this challenge, it would be helpful to understand what he expects students to do and to clarify the strategies that might be most useful in accomplishing the goals he has set. Being clear on what students are likely to do will help Kyle in monitoring, selecting, sequencing, and connecting.

Note that different coaches—looking at the same set of materials—may make different decisions about which challenges to focus on during the pre-lesson conference. These decisions coaches make are based not only on the materials submitted by the teacher but also on their work with and knowledge of the teachers. Our suggestions regarding the focus of the conversation with Kyle are based solely on the materials he provided, not on what we know about Kyle's teaching nor on his relationship with the coach.

We used Kyle's case to walk through a review of the documents he submitted and determined what challenges we wanted to work on in the pre-lesson conference and why we made those decisions. In Analyzing

Coaching 4.1, you will review the materials that Emery, a fifth-grade teacher who is working with students on fraction multiplication, prepared for an upcoming lesson. We ask you to consider why Emery's coach, Coach Rowan, selected a particular challenge to discuss and what the coach hoped would emerge from their conversation with Emery around this challenge. The goals and the task Emery has identified are shown in Figure 4.3 and the Teacher Challenges, Lesson Planning, and Monitoring Tools can be found in Appendix I.

Figure 4.3 • Emery's goals and task

Goals

Students will be able to:

- Use strategies that make sense to them to multiply whole numbers by a fraction.
- Decide when and how to use mathematical tools, pictures, and models to solve problems.
- Use strategies that make sense to them to solve real-world problems using fractions and whole numbers.

Cookie Servings Task

There are 3 cookies in a serving.

1. How many cookies are in 5 servings?
2. How many cookies are in $\frac{1}{2}$ of a serving?
3. How many cookies are in $\frac{2}{3}$ of a serving?

⏸ STOP AND CONSIDER

Before you engage in the following activity, review Emery's materials in Appendix I and decide what you would choose to work on during the pre-lesson conference if you were Emery's coach. Provide a justification for your decision in your journal.

> ## ▶ Analyzing Coaching 4.1
> *Identifying Challenges*
>
> Coach Rowan decided to work on Challenge 5. *Moving beyond the way you solve a problem* in the pre-lesson conference with Emery. In your journal, respond to the following questions:
>
> 1. Why do you think the coach selected this challenge?
> 2. What do you think the coach wanted as an outcome of the conference? What specifically do you think the coach will want to see and hear from the teacher?

Identifying Challenges: Analysis

As we indicated earlier in the book, the 5 practices are sequential. That is, each successive practice builds on the one(s) that preceded it (see Figure 0.1 in the Preface). Successfully engaging in any one of the practices requires having engaged in all the practices that came before it. Coach Rowan may have selected Challenge 5. *Moving beyond the way you solved the problem* because *Anticipating* (Practice 1) is the foundation on which the remaining practices are built. Without a clear understanding of the strategies that students might use in solving the task, it would be difficult to help students move toward the mathematical goal of the lesson.

Emery acknowledged that she was "struggling to find and fully understand" the identified strategies. Therefore, it is likely that she would be open to exploring the strategies in order to understand mathematics at a deeper level. More clarity about specific strategies will help Emery with asking more targeted questions to assess and advance students' thinking. The questions that are currently on Emery's Monitoring Tool are too general to help uncover student thinking or to advance them toward the goals of the lesson. In addition, specifying the student strategies will facilitate Emery's thinking about selecting and sequencing these strategies, and what errors or partially formed conceptions might be worth sharing in the class.

Coach Rowan would likely want to see Emery produce solutions to the task during the pre-lesson conference using the different strategies she named (i.e., models, number line, and repeated addition) and to create questions for students that are tied to specific strategies. The coach might also want to engage the teacher in a discussion regarding how the strategies connect to each other and to the goals of the lesson. With all of this support, Emery should leave the conference with more confidence about the upcoming lesson and her ability to support student learning. (You may have noticed that listing strategies students might use to solve a task without indicating how the strategy would be used is the same issue we noted in our review of Kyle's materials and is very common among teachers.)

Identifying the challenges on which to focus is a critical first step in planning for a pre-lesson conference. Both Kyle's and Emery's cases illustrate how you can make informed decisions to guide your planning. Now, we will move on to describing in detail how you can prepare for a conversation that addresses the challenges you identified.

Constructing a Pre-Lesson Conference Plan

Once you identify challenges to discuss during the pre-lesson conference, you can begin to plan how you will facilitate the conversation, using the inquiry routine we presented in Chapter 2—*Invite, Rehearse, Suggest,* and *Generalize*. We created the Pre-Lesson Conference Planning Tool (Appendix G) for you to use as you plan a conversation to address each teacher challenge that will be the focus of the pre-lesson conference. The first column of this tool asks you to identify the challenge (i.e., **what** seems to be the challenge) that you have noted. The second column of this tool indicates **how** you will address the challenge. The third column of the tool asks you what addressing this challenge will accomplish (i.e., **why** this is important more broadly).

The Guide for Designing Conferences (Appendix B) can serve as a resource for determining how to engage the teacher in a discussion of the focal challenge. Each of the three columns in the Guide for Designing Conferences corresponds to the same column number in the Pre-Lesson Conference Planning Tool (Appendix G): The first column identifies the specific challenge, the second column provides suggestions on how to address the challenge, and the third column provides a rationale regarding the importance of addressing the identified challenge. In Analyzing Coaching 4.2, you will plan a pre-lesson conference using the Pre-Lesson Conference Planning Tool and the Guide for Designing Conferences.

▶ Analyzing Coaching 4.2
Constructing a Pre-Lesson Conference Plan

As Emery's coach, you have reviewed the materials that Emery has prepared and identified Challenge 5. *Moving beyond the way you solved the problem* as the focus of the pre-lesson conference. Complete the Pre-Lesson Conference Planning Tool (Appendix G) and decide how you will use the inquiry routine (*Invite, Rehearse, Suggest,* and *Generalize*) to engage Emery in a conversation about this challenge.

Constructing a Pre-Lesson Conference Plan: Analysis

There are many different ways to approach the pre-lesson conference with Emery, but the key to the conversation will be engaging Emery in producing solutions using different strategies. The *invite* might acknowledge that Emery had listed several different strategies for solving the task (i.e., models, number line, repeated addition) and ask her to use these strategies in solving the task.

If Emery cannot solve the task using one or more of the strategies, you might ***suggest*** specific strategies and ask questions about them. For example, you might begin by saying, "Let's think about a visual representation." Then, ask a set of questions that would help Emery produce the strategy: "How could you represent one serving of cookies?" "Since one serving is 3 cookies, how could you show $\frac{2}{3}$ of a serving?" "How many cookies or parts of a cookie are in $\frac{2}{3}$ of a serving?" "How could a solution using this strategy help you achieve the lesson goals?"

At this point, to make the discussion more concrete, you might engage Emery in a ***rehearsal***. For a particular strategy that Emery has produced, you can ask, "What questions could you pose to a student who produced this strategy to assess their thinking and move them toward the goals of the lesson?" (You may have noticed that we provided a suggestion before engaging Emery in a rehearsal. It makes sense in this situation to do so since otherwise there would be nothing to rehearse. This is another example of using the routine flexibly as needed based on where the teacher is in their thinking.)

At the conclusion of the pre-lesson conference, you might ask Emery to ***generalize*** by asking her to explain what she would do in the future to come up with different solution strategies that students might use to solve a problem. To ensure that Emery is making sense of the importance of addressing this challenge, you might also ask how solving the problem in different ways in advance of the lesson can help her prepare to support student learning during the lesson.

Constructing a pre-lesson conference plan will prepare you to engage in a productive coaching conversation and limit the decisions you will need to make during the pre-lesson conference. In the following section, we provide an excerpt from a pre-lesson conference and ask you to consider how the conversation supported the teacher in addressing the challenge they faced and how the pre-lesson conference plan supported the coach in navigating the conversation.

Engaging in the Pre-Lesson Conference

Once you have planned a pre-lesson conference, you are ready to engage the teacher in discussing the upcoming lesson and put your plan into action. In Analyzing Coaching 4.3, you will explore the conversation that took place between Jamie, a fifth-grade teacher working on a multiplication with fractions lesson, and Coach Jesse. Prior to planning the lesson, Jamie met with Coach Jesse to discuss the goals and task he had selected. After some discussion, they agreed on the goal and task shown in Figure 4.4.

Figure 4.4 • Jamie's goals and task

Goals

As a result of engaging in the lesson, students will understand:

1. How to visually represent a fractional part of a fractional quantity and name the fraction of a whole it represents.
2. When multiplying two fractions, both of which are less than 1, the product will be less than either factor.
3. When multiplying a fraction by a fraction, multiplying the numerators together gets the numerator of the product and multiplying the denominators together gets the denominator of the product.

Fractions of Fractions Task

For each problem, use the fraction bar to show your solution, then write your equation.

1. If $\frac{1}{4}$ of the shaded part is striped, how much of the bar is striped? Equation_____

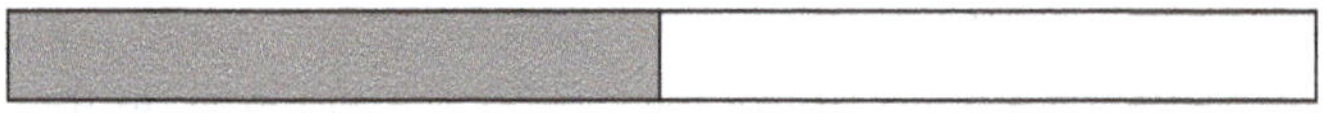

2. If $\frac{1}{5}$ of the shaded part is striped, how much of the bar is striped? Equation_____

3. If $\frac{1}{8}$ of the shaded part is striped, how much of the bar is striped? Equation_____

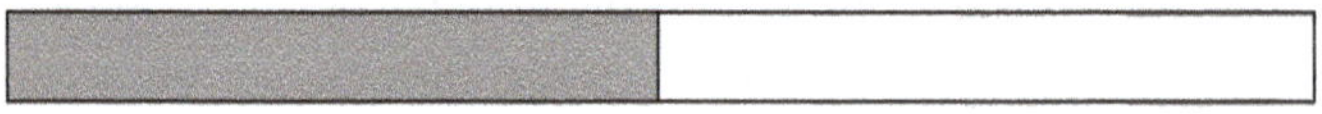

4. If $\frac{1}{2}$ of the shaded part is striped, how much of the bar is striped? Equation_____

5. If $\frac{1}{4}$ of the shaded part is striped, how much of the bar is striped? Equation_____

> 6. If $\frac{1}{3}$ of the shaded part is striped, how much of the bar is striped? Equation_____
>
> 7. If $\frac{1}{6}$ of the shaded part is striped, how much of the bar is striped? Equation_____
>
> 8. $\frac{1}{2}$ of a fraction bar is shaded, and $\frac{1}{6}$ of the shaded part is striped. Without finding out exactly how much of the bar is striped, is more or less than $\frac{1}{2}$ of the bar striped? How do you know?
>
> 9. $\frac{1}{3}$ of a fraction bar is shaded, and $\frac{1}{8}$ of the shaded part is striped. Without finding out exactly how much of the bar is striped, is more or less than $\frac{1}{3}$ of the bar striped? How do you know?

Source: From *Investigations 3, Grade 5, Unit 7 Races, Arrays, and Grids* (p. 444–445) by TERC, 2017, Pearson.

Coach Jesse prepared for the pre-lesson conference by reviewing the Teacher Challenges Tool that Jamie had completed and by reviewing the Monitoring and Lesson Planning Tools he shared. Jamie described three challenges he was facing: *Involving all members of a group* (Challenge 10), *Determining how to sequence incorrect and/or incomplete solutions* (Challenge 15), and *Running out of time* (Challenge 19). Coach Jesse decided to focus on Challenge 10 because she had been in Jamie's classroom several times and noted that Jamie tended to talk to individual students rather than to the whole group, and Jamie seemed to have a clear sense of what the problem was, as he explained on the teacher challenges tool:

> *There are always students who want to/will do most of the work. In addition, there are some students who will not immediately participate, possibly due to not having an entry into the task. I know that there are times where I can do better with making sure that everyone in a group is participating equally, and that everyone is held accountable for listening to, adding on, repeating, and summarizing what others in their group are saying.*

Additionally, in reviewing the Lesson Planning and Monitoring Tools that Jamie had submitted, Coach Jesse noted that Jamie had listed many strategies on the Monitoring Tool but very few assessing and advancing questions. Moreover, the advancing questions Jamie had created were not likely to move students toward the goal of the lesson. Therefore, Coach Jesse also chose to work on Challenge 7 (*Creating questions that move the students toward the goals of the lesson*) during the pre-lesson conference. In Analyzing Coaching 4.3, you will analyze the pre-lesson conference conversation between Jamie and Coach Jesse.

> ### ▶ Analyzing Coaching 4.3
> *Engaging in the Pre-Lesson Conference*
>
> The following transcript is an excerpt from the pre-lesson conference between Jamie and Coach Jesse. The pre-lesson conference began with a discussion of advancing questions (Challenge 7) since Coach Jesse wanted to make sure Jamie was prepared to ask questions that would move students toward the lesson goals. We join their pre-lesson conference as Jamie and Coach Jesse have moved on to Challenge 10 and are starting to discuss some ways to ***involve all members of a group***. As you read the transcript, consider these three questions, and record your responses in your journal:
>
> 1. What did Coach Jesse do to help Jamie address this challenge?
> 2. How might this conversation help Jamie involve all members of a group during the upcoming lesson?
> 3. Prior to the pre-lesson conference, Coach Jesse created a plan for the conference (see Appendix J). What do you notice about the plan? To what extent do you think it helped Coach Jesse during the actual conference?

Pre-Lesson Conference: Fractions of Fractions

1	Coach:	I noticed in your Teacher Challenges Tool, you highlighted the one about involving all
2		members of a group. I'm wondering, what are some ways that we can involve all
3		members of the group when they're working on the Fractions of Fractions task?
4	Jamie:	Well, it could be, as students are working, me directing an assessing or advancing
5		question toward a student that's quiet—let's call them Student A. Not necessarily to
6		single them out, but just to hold them accountable. Even though you're in a group, you
7		still need to know what's going on. Then, using that just as a conversation piece for the
8		whole group. Like, "Well, if Student A does not understand, it means that your group
9		hasn't worked together so that everyone is at the same point. So, it's important that
10		you're working together," so that everyone in the group can answer that assessing or
11		advancing question, depending on what it is.
12	Coach:	Yeah. So, it sounds like you'd go up to a group and, let's say they are working on the
13		first problem (*finding $\frac{1}{4}$ of the shaded area of a fraction bar where $\frac{1}{2}$ of the bar is*

		shaded), and they split both the shaded and unshaded parts of the fraction bar into 4ths and put stripes in one of the shaded 4ths. *(Coach points at the representation below)*
14		
15		
16		
17		
18		And you'd ask Student A, a quiet student in the group, an assessing question, "Could
19		you explain what your group did here? Why did you divide the fraction bar into 8
20		pieces?" What might we do if this student says, "I don't know" or "I'm not sure" or "I
21		didn't do it"?
22	Jamie:	So, it could be something like, "Well, if you're not sure, what's something that you
23		could do?" And this Student A might say, "I could ask someone else in the group to
24		explain why the fraction bar is divided into 8 pieces," or "I don't understand this. How
25		did we get 8 pieces?" Then, Student A will be an active participant, they are trying to
26		understand the solution strategy as well and not being afraid of asking for help. Like
27		knowing that it's okay to not understand, struggle can be good. So, if you need some
28		help, ask for help. That's why you're in a group, so that you guys can work together as
29		a team.
30	Coach:	Yeah. So, mentoring them to be able to advocate when they need help. This would also
31		allow them to see each other as a source of support when they are working together.
32		Then I'm wondering, too, so you ask this Student A, "Could you explain what you did
33		here?" and the student says, "I don't know." Then, as a group, they start to talk through
34		what they're going to do. What might your next step be?
35	Jamie:	When I ask that question to Student A and, as a group, they say what they're going to
36		do? It could be that I move away for a bit, give them some time, and then come back in
37		and check in after a little bit. But yeah, not just to stay there, but say something like,
38		"All right, I'm going to come back in three minutes and then I want for you to be able
39		to share with me, explain how you decided to divide the fraction bar into 8 pieces,"
40		for example.
41	Coach:	Yeah. So, as we try to involve all members of a group, we want them to serve each
42		other as resources. I think, even if they originally say, "I don't know," we can still get
43		them to work together when we ask them to explain to each other how they decided to
44		divide the fraction bar into 8 pieces. Like, "We're not just going to leave it, but I'm
45		going to come back and I want you to have something figured out."
46	Jamie:	Yeah. But I know that sometimes the confident students take the lead and the struggling
47		students stay quiet. Like I can imagine when a quiet student (Student A) says, "I don't
48		know," a confident student, let's say Student B, starts explaining they split each $\frac{1}{2}$ of
49		the whole into 4ths and got 8ths, without giving me a chance to keep the quiet student,
50		Student A, accountable.
51	Coach:	Yeah, that's definitely one way it could go. What can we do to know if all students in
52		the group are making sense of how they get 8ths? What kind of questions could we ask
53		or what kind of things could we do, do you think?
54	Jamie:	I think I can use one of those teacher moves, a retell. As I'm working with this group ...
55		*(Teacher points at the representation the coach brought up earlier)*
56		
57		
58		I ask the quiet Student A, "Could you retell in your own words and explain what
59		Student B just said?"

CHAPTER 4 | Preparing for and Engaging in the Pre-Lesson Conference   **55**

60	Coach:	Absolutely. I could see that, for a student who is struggling with understanding how to find a fraction of a fraction, when you're asking them to retell what they've heard so far, you can check for their understanding. So, then, that gives them a chance to be part of that discussion and know that their voice is important in that discussion. Again, if Student A says, "No, I can't," you could use those same questions that we discussed before, "Okay, well, I'm going to come back in a minute and I want you to be ready to explain how you decided to put stripes in that one part of the fraction bar."
67	Jamie:	Yeah, it makes sense.
68	Coach:	What do you think the benefit of asking a student to retell another student's explanation might be?
70	Jamie:	It just goes back to the students, having a mindset, knowing they're going to be held accountable. They're going to be checked in on to be able to check for understanding. They're not just going to be able to slide under the radar and just follow someone else's lead. They're going to be held accountable at some point.
74	Coach:	Yeah. Do you have other ideas about how we might involve all students? For example, when you go to another group that splits only the shaded part of the whole ... *(Coach points at the representation below)*

And you start with an assessing question, like the one from your Monitoring Tool, "Why is one of the pieces striped?" and one student, let's call them Student C, says "The problem said $\frac{1}{4}$ of the shaded part is striped. So we took the $\frac{1}{2}$ that was shaded and divided it into 4 equal pieces." Yeah?

83	Jamie:	Mm-hmm (affirmative).
84	Coach:	Then you continue with an advancing question and ask this group, "How much of the whole bar is striped?" and Student C answers $\frac{1}{5}$ but another student (Student D) says $\frac{1}{8}$. What can you do to engage the students in a discussion and come up with an agreed-upon answer?
88	Jamie:	So, it could be like a new assessing [question], asking each student to explain how they came up with their answers.
90	Coach:	Yeah, so that we would surface the thinking for Students C and D. But, you know, our goal is to involve all members of this group, so we need to make sure it is not just these two students talking but others are also listening.
93	Jamie:	Yeah, we want to keep everyone accountable. I mean, I can ask, "There are two different answers on the table. What does everyone think? Can you decide which answer is correct and be ready to explain why?" So, this would be an advancing question and then I would leave this group to discuss with each other and come up with an agreed-upon answer.
98	Coach:	Absolutely! You don't have to wait when they are working with an advancing question, you can leave the group with a question like, "Show me what the whole will look like, if we split the unshaded part into 4ths. What would the striped piece represent in relation to the whole?"
102	Jamie:	Sure. At that point, they should be able to see that $\frac{1}{4}$ of $\frac{1}{2}$ is $\frac{1}{8}$.
103	Coach:	Exactly! So what do you think about this challenge now, involving all members of a group? What teacher moves can you use to address this challenge?
105	Jamie:	Well, we talked about directing questions to quiet students in the group rather than posing a question to the group so that we make sure we hear from those quiet ones. And

107		if I get an "I don't know" kind of answer, I walk away to let them talk with each other
108		and be the resource rather than me. I mean, I really want to make sure they see each
109		other as resources.
110	Coach:	So, what behavior do you think we would hope to see if students realize that?
111	Jamie:	Just working collaboratively in groups, working together, staying focused and paying
112		attention, listening. So, asking questions if they don't understand, asking a partner, even
113		if I'm not there, I want them to say, "No, I need to understand this. I need to know how
114		this works. So can you explain what you did more just so I can understand?" type thing.
115	Coach:	Yeah. So really being more engaged with the lesson overall and the mathematical
116		thinking and content that comes with it. So, we're talking about having all group
117		members involved here. So why do you think if we're generalizing, if we're thinking
118		about it as a whole, what do you think the value is? Or why is it so important that we
119		get all kids involved and held accountable in those discussion times?
120	Jamie:	Because then we know we are able to better check for understanding. Students are
121		going to be more apt to actually understand the concept, just knowing that they're going
122		to be held accountable. They're not going to be able to slide by. They need to show that
123		they're able to understand why we're doing what we're doing, and knowing that if they
124		do not do that, then they need to ask a question. Because at some point someone's
125		going to ask a question whether it be the teacher, even a person they're working with,
126		assessing what they know.
127	Coach:	Yeah. I totally agree. The other piece I'm thinking about is then we're also hoping that
128		because of that, they're going to learn more, like really make sense of the mathematical
129		idea, right?
130	Jamie:	Oh, yeah. Which can, in the long run, can help with this confidence in math because
131		anxiety, when it comes to math, is a real deal, real thing.
132	Coach:	Yeah. I think if we switch into doing more of this type of accountability with groups,
133		you might see kids more anxious at the beginning, but they'll get used to it.
134	Jamie:	Oh, yeah.

Engaging in the Pre-Lesson Conference: Analysis

As you might have noticed, Coach Jesse did a variety of things to help Jamie address the challenge of involving all students in the group. Coach Jesse begins with an ***invitational*** move to get Jamie's thinking on the table: "I'm wondering, what are some ways that we can involve all members of the group when they're working on the Fractions of Fractions task?" (lines 2–3). Jamie responds by providing general things he might do (e.g., directing an assessing or advancing question toward a quiet student, getting everyone working together so that everyone in the group could answer the question teacher has posed; lines 4–11). The teacher seems to have an "idea" of what he might do, but his answer does not include any specific questions in response to any specific student thinking.

Next (starting on line 12), the coach takes the conversation to a more specific level by grounding Jamie's idea and engaging the teacher in a ***rehearsal***. In response to a specific assessing question, "Why did you divide the fraction bar into 8 pieces?" (lines 19–20), Coach Jesse poses something that a student might say: A student might say "I don't know" or "I'm not sure" or "I didn't do it" (lines 20–21). Then, Coach Jesse asks Jamie what he might do in such a case. Jamie notes that he could ask, "Well, if you're not sure, what's something that you could do?" to which the student may respond, "I could ask someone else in the group to explain why the fraction bar is divided into 8 pieces" (lines 23–24). Getting down to this deeper level of specificity can help the teacher operationalize some of the more general ideas they have generated thus far.

You might have noticed another *rehearsal* later in the transcript. When discussing the "directing questions to quiet students" as a teacher move to involve all members of a group, Jamie notes that the "confident students" can take over before the "quiet students" have a chance to participate (lines 46–50). Coach Jesse acknowledges this possibility and initiates a rehearsal to discuss what Jamie would do next (lines 51–53). Jamie shares that he could use "retell," a teacher move that asks one student to repeat what another has said (lines 54–59). Since Jamie's response includes a specific question to a specific student solution strategy, Coach Jesse agrees with this teacher move and emphasizes why it would work: "For a student who is struggling with understanding how to find a fraction of a fraction, when you're asking them to retell what they've heard so far, you can check for their understanding. So, then, that gives them a chance to be part of that discussion and know that their voice is important in that discussion" (lines 60–63). Coach Jesse also asks Jamie to explain the benefits of using "retell" (lines 68–69) to ensure Jamie's understanding, and we can see that Jamie is making sense of the importance of this teacher move in relation to student learning (lines 70–73).

So far, Jamie and Coach Jesse have considered two ways in which students might respond to the teacher's question as the teacher tries to involve all members of a group. First, a student might say "I don't know" or give no response. Second, another student might take over without giving a chance to the student who was expected to respond. Next, Jamie and Coach Jesse consider a third possibility. As Coach Jesse explains (lines 84–85), Jamie might get two different responses to the teacher's question "How much of the whole bar is striped?": Student C answers $\frac{1}{5}$ and Student D says $\frac{1}{8}$. Coach Jesse uses this possibility to engage Jamie in another *rehearsal* by asking, "What can you do to engage the students in a discussion and come up with an agreed-upon answer?" (lines 86–87). Jamie's initial response to this question is to check in on students C and D and have them explain how they got their answers. However, surfacing these two students' thinking is not enough to engage students in this group with each other. Thus, Coach Jesse reminds Jamie that his "goal is to involve all members of this group, so we need to make sure it is not just these two students talking but others are also listening" (lines 90–92). This reminder gets Jamie to rethink his answer and come up with a fleshed-out idea: "I can ask 'There are two different answers on the table. What does everyone think? Can you decide which answer is correct and be ready to explain why?'" (lines 93–95). This idea brings up *discussing disagreements* as another vehicle for involving all members of the group—one that calls for accountability *and* a mathematical critique of another student's—and one's own—thinking.

Overall, these rehearsals led to responses from Jamie that the coach found sufficient to address the challenge at hand, thereby eliminating the need for coach **suggestions**. Suggestions are warranted when conversations reach an *impasse*, meaning the teacher cannot generate ideas in response to a coach's question. The coach's **rehearsal** prompts drew responses from Jamie so that the coach doesn't need to make a suggestion in order to keep the discussion on track. At the same time, additional **invitational** moves ensured a productive coaching conversation (e.g., lines 86–87).

Toward the end of the conference (lines 118–119), Coach Jesse steps back from the specifics to push Jamie's thinking more broadly about the rationale for getting all students involved. The coach asks Jamie to think about why it is important to get all kids involved and held accountable during group discussions. Jamie notes that involving all students gives the teacher a better check for understanding. He also states that "Students are going to be more apt to actually understand the concept, just knowing that they're going to be held accountable" (lines 120–122). To this response, the coach adds that, because the teacher will be holding students accountable, students are going to learn more and make sense of the mathematical idea. Even though this part of the conference is critical to show Jamie's understanding of the importance of involving all members of a group during group discussions, we don't see any evidence of **generalization** of a practice that Jamie could use in future lessons. If Coach Jesse had asked Jamie, for example, "What will you do in future lessons to hold all members of a group accountable for participating in a discussion?", then Jamie could have extracted a general practice to use in the future (e.g., when creating assessing and advancing questions for anticipated solution strategies, preparing additional questions that will have students compare different strategies).

To summarize, Coach Jesse used the moves in the inquiry routine flexibly during the pre-lesson conference to engage Jamie in a thoughtful discussion of the challenge at hand so as to prepare him for the upcoming lesson. As discussed in Chapter 2, the inquiry routine helps to build the conversation on teacher thinking. By building coaching conversations on teacher thinking, you can support the teacher's meaningful learning of practices that they can use to address their challenges. In this case, Coach Jesse builds on Jamie's thinking by surfacing and responding to his initial thoughts regarding how to get more students involved. The rehearsals were notable in that they kept the discussions tied to the mathematical content of the task.

As a result of the conversation with Coach Jesse, Jamie now has several different strategies to use to involve all members of a group: directing questions to quiet students, asking one student to explain something when another student struggled to do so, leaving the group with a question to answer then returning to see what they came up with, retelling what another student has said, and discussing different answers and coming to consensus. But what Jamie gained was more than a set of abstract strategies. Through a series of rehearsals, Jamie had an opportunity to think through specific solutions that students might produce during the Fractions of Fractions lesson and to consider how he would respond to them.

When you look at Coach Jesse's pre-lesson conference plan, you may have noticed that what Coach Jesse planned was consistent with what happened during the conference. There are also many particulars you might have noticed about Coach Jesse's plan. In the first column of the plan, the coach listed Jamie's description of how the challenge plays out in his classroom, as well as a general approach she would take to help Jamie address this challenge: focusing on specific solutions and using assessing and advancing questions tied to specific solutions to stimulate conversation in the group. Coach Jesse used this strategy throughout the pre-lesson conference with Jamie to keep the discussion grounded in the Fractions of Fractions task. For example, early in the transcript, the coach took Jamie's idea about involving a quiet student in the group discussion (lines 4–11) and reframed Jamie's response in terms of a specific solution and provided a specific assessing question (lines 12–21).

In the second column of the plan, Coach Jesse indicated how she would use the inquiry routine (*Invite, Rehearse, Suggest,* and *Generalize*) to facilitate a conversation with Jamie that would elicit his thinking by specifying questions she could ask and suggestions she could offer, as needed, throughout the conference. For example, Coach Jesse launched the conference by stating Jamie's challenge and inviting him to identify ways to involve all members of the group (lines 1–3), precisely as planned. Coach Jesse engaged Jamie in three rehearsals, two of which she had planned. As we described, Coach Jesse did not use any suggestions in this conversation, although she was prepared to do so if need be. Finally, Coach Jesse also anticipated how she might push Jamie to generalize beyond the Fractions of Fractions lesson. Specifically, the coach anticipated asking, "What teacher moves are you going to use in the future to involve all members of a group?" and "Why is it important for all students to be involved in group work?" At the end of the conference, although she pressed Jamie to think more broadly about the rationale for getting all students involved (lines 118–119), she did not ask him to consider what this would mean for future lessons.

The pre-lesson conference plan arguably gave Coach Jesse a clear picture of what she wanted to accomplish during the pre-lesson conference, provided some concrete questions and suggestions to guide her, and helped her keep the conversation focused on the content of the upcoming lesson. The plan was not a rigid script to follow but a set of possible options to pursue flexibly, depending on Jamie's responses. A coach's planning for a conference (for both pre- and post-lesson) is similar to a teacher's planning for a lesson. If the coach can anticipate some of the things that are likely to happen, then every decision doesn't have to be made in the moment. As a result, the coach has freed up mental space to address things that come in the moment and were not anticipated.

Summary

Engaging in the pre-lesson conference is a critical point in the coaching cycle (Activity 3 in Figure 4.1). It is the first time the teacher and coach are meeting (preferably in person) to discuss one or more of the challenges the teacher is facing in the context of a specific lesson. What is discussed during the conference, and the understandings the teacher walks away with, can significantly impact the quality of the lesson the teacher is about to teach. Research shows that high-quality pre-lesson conferences improve teacher implementation of high-level tasks and facilitation of productive mathematics discussions (e.g., Russell et al., 2020; Witherspoon et al., 2021).

In this chapter, we have talked about how to determine the focus of the pre-lesson conference and have provided tools to aid you in your preparations. Here are a few additional tips for you to consider in preparing for the conference:

- Start the conference by asking the teacher to state their lesson goals. Although you and the teacher discussed the goals when preparing for the lesson (Activity 1 in Figure 4.1), having them clearly stated will ensure that neither you nor the teacher loses sight of the mathematical ideas that are the learning target for the lesson. You may even want to have the goals written out in a way that is shareable so that you can refer to them throughout the conference.

- Be familiar with the task the teacher has selected. Again, although you and the teacher have discussed the task, you need to be ready during the conference to suggest alternative strategies for solving the task, pose potential assessing and advancing questions to consider, and suggest possible ways to sequence solution strategies. This level of preparation will help you in making suggestions for the teacher to consider and in engaging the teacher in rehearsals.

- Be prepared to end the conference by asking the teacher to explicitly identify what they are working on in the lesson. If the teacher is not sure, you might suggest one of the challenges that were discussed during the conference. Agreeing on what the teacher is going to try to do during the lesson provides you with a lens through which to view the lesson and a potential starting point for a discussion in the post-lesson conference.

Looking Ahead

The pre-lesson conference is the last activity in the pre-lesson phase of the coaching cycle. The second phase of the coaching cycle is the lesson (see Figure 4.5). As the coach, you should make every effort to observe the lesson. Although the lesson will be video-recorded, being present for the lesson shows your support for the teacher and makes it clear that you are in this process together. In addition, if you are present for the lesson, you can assist with video recording as needed.

Figure 4.5 • Lesson phase of a coaching cycle

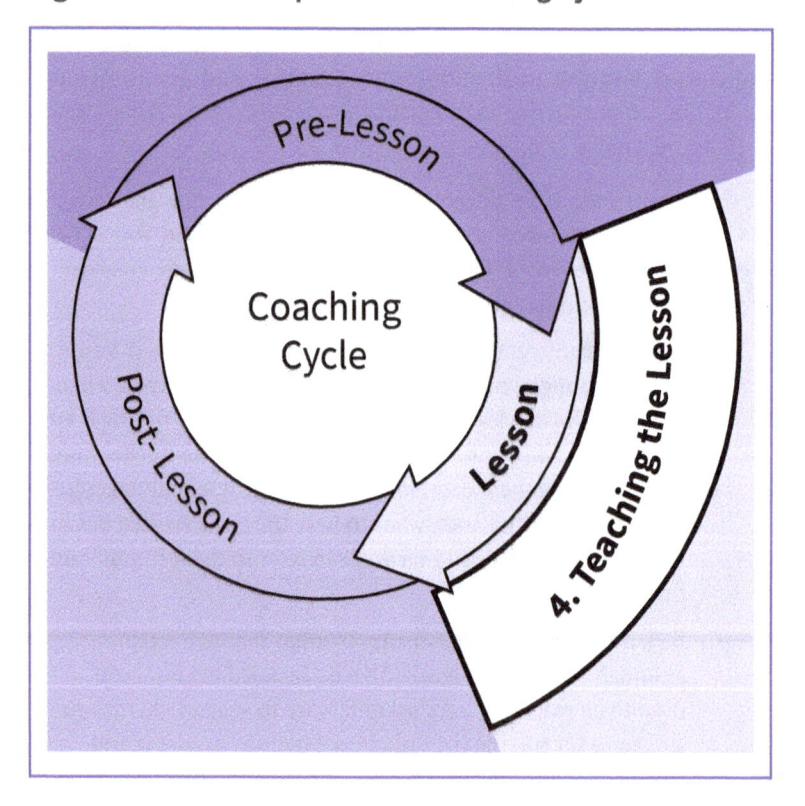

The focus of Chapter 5 is the final phase of the coaching cycle: Post-Lesson. This phase of the coaching cycle is about reflecting on the lesson that the teacher has taught. In Chapter 5, we discuss the activities that are involved in preparing for and engaging in the post-lesson conference and the tools that will support your work.

Putting into Practice

PLANNING FOR AND CONDUCTING A PRE-LESSON CONFERENCE

Ask a teacher with whom you work to engage with you in the pre-lesson phase of the coaching cycle.

1. As we discussed in Chapter 3, have the teacher complete the Teacher Challenges Tool (Appendix A), meet with you virtually or face to face to discuss the goal and task for the lesson, and complete the Lesson Planning (Appendix E) and Monitoring Tools (Appendix F).

2. Next, review the documents the teacher has completed and determine which challenges you should focus on during the pre-lesson conference. The four questions we outline in our discussion of Kyle's case should be helpful to you as you think through the focus of the conference.

3. Then, plan the pre-lesson conference, using the Pre-Lesson Conference Planning Tool (Appendix G), drawing on the Guide for Designing Conferences (Appendix B).

4. Finally, conduct the pre-lesson conference with the teacher.

After completing this pre-lesson conference, reflect on the conversation by writing down some notes in your journal. What did you learn about the teacher's understanding? What surprised you? To what extent could you use the inquiry routine? What do you expect to see in your observation of the lesson as a result of your conversation?

CHAPTER 5

Preparing for and Engaging in the Post-Lesson Conference

In this chapter, we move to the post-lesson phase of the coaching cycle (see Figure 5.1). Several activities comprise this phase, the most important of which is the post-lesson conference. In the sections that follow, we discuss what the coach must do to prepare for and conduct the post-lesson conference.

Figure 5.1 • Post-lesson phase of a coaching cycle

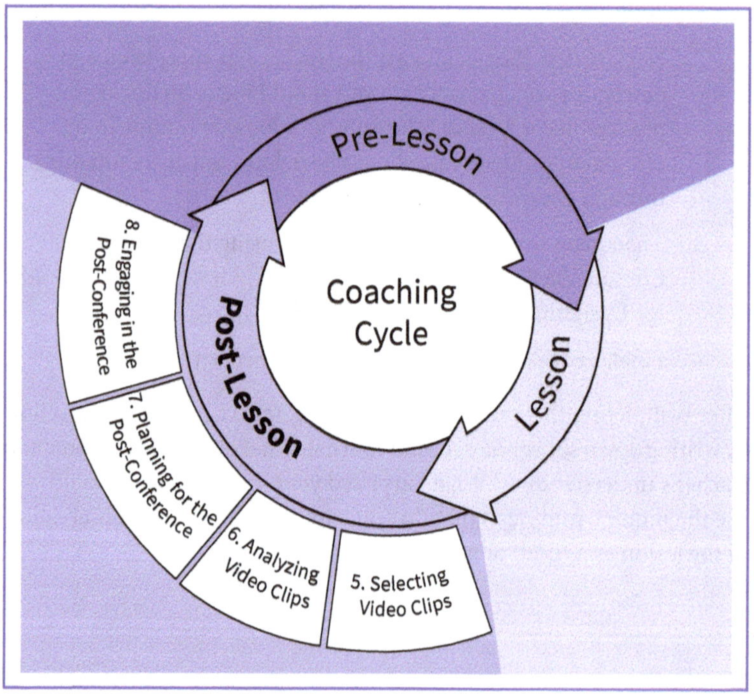

The purpose of the post-lesson conference is to support the teacher's reflection on a lesson they have recently taught, with a focus on what went well and what improvements could further enhance students' meaningful learning of mathematics. Through the post-lesson conference conversations, the coach helps the teacher consider specific events that occurred during the lesson and explore alternative ways of responding to them. The post-lesson conference also provides the coach a chance to acknowledge the progress the teacher has made with the challenges they aimed to address during the teaching of the lesson. As Coach Shawn explained:

> *I think the post-lesson conference is the most powerful vehicle for impacting teacher practice in the future. It gives the teacher a chance to thoughtfully reflect on the lesson's execution with their coach and make generalizations that will apply to future lessons.*

Preparing for the Post-Lesson Conference

Planning the post-lesson conference can be difficult. You need to consider all the information you have gathered during the pre-lesson phase (i.e., the teacher's documents you have reviewed and the pre-lesson conference you conducted) and the lesson you observed. Then, based on this information, you need to determine which parts of the lesson to reflect on during the post-lesson conference by selecting video clips that highlight the challenges you want to discuss. The video clips should have the greatest potential to result in the teacher's objective reflection on the lesson so that, as you engage in the post-lesson conference, you can support the teacher's learning. In the sections that follow, we provide some guidance regarding what it takes to plan the post-lesson conference, specifically what is involved in selecting and analyzing video clips and constructing a plan for the conference.

Selecting Video Clips

As we indicated in previous chapters, the lesson needs to be video-recorded and, if possible, observed live. The first step in the post-lesson conference planning is to watch the video recording of the entire lesson and identify two to three video clips (no more than five minutes each) to share with the teacher. These clips will be the focus of the discussion during the conference. The following criteria provide a lens through which to consider the selection of clips:

- Select clips that highlight a specific aspect of the 5 practices with which the teacher appeared to struggle (whether or not these are the challenges the teacher identified) and provide an opportunity:
  - To advance teacher learning (e.g., if the teacher is working on creating questions that move students toward the goal of the lesson yet asks a question not aligned with the

mathematical goal, then you may want to select a clip that highlights the teacher's question).

– For the teacher to consider if and how an alternative move may lead to different student outcomes (e.g., if the teacher is working on involving all members of a group yet interacts with only one group member, then you may want to select a clip of these one-on-one interactions).

• If possible, select one clip that shows teacher growth. The clip should relate to a challenge (whether or not discussed during the pre-lesson conference) that the teacher addressed appropriately during the lesson. For example, if the teacher identified *Keeping the entire class engaged* as a challenge and used appropriate talk moves during the whole-class discussion to keep students accountable, then you may want to select a clip that shows these talk moves.

In Analyzing Coaching 5.1, you will read an excerpt from a lesson taught by Nicki, an eighth-grade teacher. For this activity, taking on the role as Nicki's coach, you will select clips to discuss in the post-lesson conference. The goal and task that Nicki identified for this lesson are given in Figure 5.2. We encourage you to solve the task yourself if you are not already familiar with it. Thinking through the task before reading the lesson will make it easier to make sense of what Nicki's students do during the lesson.

Figure 5.2 • Nicki's goals and task

Goals

1. Linear functions grow at a constant rate.
2. There are different but equivalent ways of writing an explicit rule that defines the relationship between two variables.
3. The rate of change of a linear function can be highlighted in different representational forms: as the successive difference in a table of (x,y) values in which values for *x* increase by 1; the *m* value in the equation $y = mx + b$; and the slope of the function when graphed.

Tiling a Patio Task

Alfredo Gomez is designing patios. Each patio has a rectangular garden area in the center. Alfredo uses black tiles to represent the soil of the garden. Around each garden, he designs a border of white tiles. The pictures shown below show the three smallest patios that he can design with black tiles for the garden and white tiles for the border.

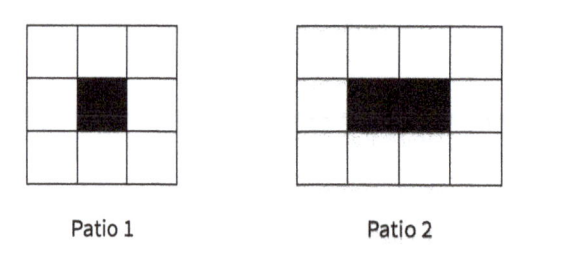

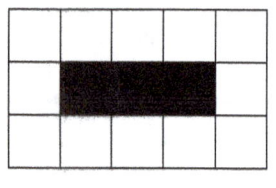

Patio 1   Patio 2   Patio 3

> a) Draw Patio 4 and Patio 5. How many white tiles are in Patio 4? Patio 5?
> b) Make some observations about the patios that could help you describe larger patios.
> c) Describe a method for finding the total number of white tiles needed for Patio 50 (without constructing it).
> d) Write a rule that could be used to determine the number of white tiles needed for any patio. Explain how your rule relates to the visual representation of the patio.
> e) Write a different rule that could be used to determine the number of white tiles needed for any patio. Explain how your rule relates to the visual representation of the patio.

Source: Adapted from *Navigating Through Algebra in Grades 3–5* by Cuevas and Yeatts (2005; as cited in Smith & Stein, 2018, p. 30, National Council of Teachers of Mathematics).

When completing the Teacher Challenges Tool (Appendix A), Nicki identified Challenges 5 (*Moving beyond the way you solved the problem*), 8 (*Trying to understand student thinking*), and 16 (*Keeping the entire class engaged and accountable during individual presentations*). During the pre-lesson conference, Nicki and Coach Alex talked about questions Nicki could ask to uncover what students were thinking. They also discussed specific moves Nicki could use to ensure that students were making sense of the explanations given by their peers. At the end of the conference, Coach Alex summarized what Nicki wanted to accomplish in the lesson: "*You want to find a way to connect the thinking of each of the different groups, while keeping all students engaged and participating*" and "*Instead of a show and tell between you and the presenting student, you want to find ways to keep the class engaged in those final discussions.*"

In Analyzing Coaching 5.1, you will read an excerpt from Nicki's lesson and consider what segments of the lesson you would focus on in the post-lesson conference if you were Nicki's coach.

Analyzing Coaching 5.1
Selecting Video Clips

The following transcript focuses on the whole-class discussion (about 20 minutes of a 50-minute class) in which Nicki asked the students to share and discuss three solution strategies for the Tiling a Patio Task. Students created posters (i.e., a sheet of 25" × 30" sticky poster paper) to represent their solution strategies. Nicki placed each poster in the front of the classroom as the strategies were discussed. Taking on the role as Nicki's coach, your task is to:

1. Review the lesson transcript.
2. Determine which part(s) of the whole-class discussion you would want to reflect on during the post-lesson conference.

> Note the line numbers in the transcript that correspond to no more than three lesson segments you have identified. The criteria for selecting video clips discussed earlier may help you in making your selections.
> 3. Explain why you selected the specific lesson segment.
> 4. Record your responses in your journal.

Lesson: Tiling a Patio

1	Teacher:	I am going to invite representatives from the groups that will be presenting to come up
2		and talk about their posters. Arden, can you come up here and just talk about what your
3		group wrote? *(Nicki hangs the poster that Arden's group created.)*
4	Arden:	We wrote that whenever there's, for example, one black tile, you add one white tile to
5		the top and the bottom, based on how many black tiles there are. So, we said if there are
6		50 black tiles, there are 100 white tiles because you add one to the top and bottom for
7		every black tile, and then you add 3 for each side, so it'd be 106 white tiles.
8	Teacher:	Can you show us what you mean on the picture with 3 on each side?
9	Arden:	*(Walking to their poster, Arden points to the following figure.)* So, for Patio 3, you have
10		3 black tiles, so you have one white tile on the top and one on the bottom for each black
11		tile *(shown in gray)*. So, to end it off, you have to add 3 on each side *(circled)*. It has a
12		border around it.
13		
14	Teacher:	Thank you, Arden. Can someone repeat or rephrase what Arden is saying? Go ahead,
15		Lindsey.
16	Lindsey:	For every black tile, there's one white tile on the top, one on the bottom, and then the
17		columns of 3 on the left and right.
18	Teacher:	Okay. So, how do we know how many black tiles there are? Sloan?
19	Sloan:	It's the patio number.
20	Teacher:	It is the patio number. So, if we know what patio we're finding, we automatically can
21		figure out how many black tiles we have. Right? Which means what, about our white
22		tiles? How do our white tiles compare to the black tiles? Go ahead, Arden.
23	Arden:	There are always two times more white tiles than there are black tiles.
24	Teacher:	Okay. There are always two times more white tiles than black tiles. But what else as
25		well? Go ahead, Peyton.
26	Peyton:	There are the columns with 3 [tiles] on each side.
27	Teacher:	There we go.
28	Peyton:	So, add the 6.
29	Teacher:	If I have 3 black tiles, there's two times as many white, but 3 on each side are always
30		there too. Okay? Kirby, come on up. Can you talk about your group's poster, please?
31		*(Nicki hangs the poster that Kirby's group created.)*

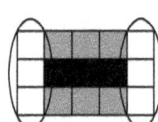

Coaching the 5 Practices

32	Kirby:	We said the rule is $y = 2x + 6$, where x equals the number of black tiles. Add two white
33		tiles for each black tile, then add three white tiles for each side. And then, I did a little
34		diagram for Patio 5 *(referring to the following figure)*.
35		

36		So, y equals 2 times x and instead of x we put in 5, so it is $2 \times 5 + 6$. Then we multiply
37		these; we got 10 plus 6 and then 16, and that is the patio basically. And we wanted to
38		show it would still work with a bigger patio, so we drew Patio 10. We have 10 black
39		tiles and a mystery number of white tiles. y equals 2 times x plus 6, and we multiply
40		that and that's 26 for the number of white tiles.
41	Teacher:	If we take a look at Kirby's rule, can someone connect that rule to what Arden was
42		saying? Go ahead, Marley. Thanks.
43	Marley:	Yeah. For every black tile ... Oh, wait. x would be the number of black tiles and then
44		you would just multiply that number of white tiles.
45	Teacher:	Okay. That's okay.
46	Arden:	Do you want me to try it?
47	Teacher:	Nope. I'm going to have somebody else do it. Thank you, though. Cameron?
48	Cameron:	The 2 represents the top and the bottom of the black tiles, so the white tiles on top then
49		the 6 is ...
50	Teacher:	Hang on one second. Can you actually point in Arden's diagram? Can you point to
51		what you mean by that?
52	Cameron:	This would be the 2 for the one of the black *(referring to the gray tiles)*, and then
53		those would be the two columns of 3 *(circled)*, which would be 6.
54		

55	Teacher:	Does everybody see that? Okay. Can someone repeat how that equation connects to one
56		of the pictures? Where is the number 2 and where is the number 6 showing up in those
57		pictures? Go ahead, Skyler.
58	Skyler:	The number 6 is the sides that bring the 3 from each column, and then the 2 is how
59		many times you multiply the black tile because there's going to be the same amount of
60		white tiles as black tiles, but just two times.
61	Teacher:	Awesome. So, Addison and her group created a different sort of rule. Addison, can you
62		explain how you got this? *(Nicki hangs the poster that Addison's group created.)*
63	Addison:	Okay, we had an equation too, but it was different from Kirby's. Like in Patio 5 *(shown*
64		*below)* the black tiles, or patio number, would be 5. There would be 5 white tiles on the
65		top and bottom *(shown in dark gray)*. But then we added 2 to the top and the bottom
66		rows *(shown in white)*. So instead of 5, the top and bottom row both had 7. So, the
67		length of the patio is 7 and the width of the patio is 3. So, you have three rows of 7
68		because the middle row has 2 white tiles next to the black ones on either side *(shown in*
69		*light gray)*. So, our equation was 3 times x plus 2, minus the patio number.

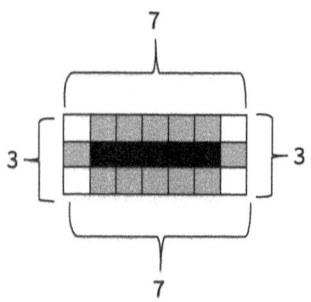

70			

[Diagram of patio: 7 tiles wide, 3 tiles tall, with black tiles in middle row and white tiles surrounding]

71	Teacher:	That was a lot to take in. Addison, could you repeat your explanation one more time?
72	Addison:	Okay, for Patio 5, there were 5 black tiles in the middle and 5 white tiles on the top and
73		the bottom. And we added 2 more white tiles to the top and the bottom, so it would be
74		7. So, it would be like two more than the patio number. So now you have three rows of
75		tiles, and each has 7 tiles in it. So, it is $3 \times 7 - 5$ which is $21 - 5$.
76	Teacher:	Where did they get the two extras from the patio number? Where do they represent
77		that? Hayden, what do you think?
78	Hayden:	It's the white ones on the corners in Addison's picture *(see arrows)*—two on the top
79		and two on the bottom.
80		

[Diagram of the same patio with arrows pointing to the four corner white tiles]

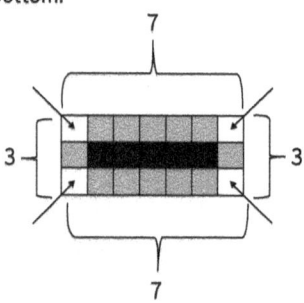

81	Teacher:	Addison, why did you subtract the 5 from 21?
82	Addison:	We found all the tiles including black and white, so we had to subtract the black ones
83		because they are not part of the patio.
84	Teacher:	Addison, I am wondering, can we rewrite your equation as $y = 3(x + 2) - x$?
85	Addison:	*(Addison hesitates for a few seconds)* Yes, you can. Because if you put in 5 for x you
86		get $3 \times 7 - 5$, which is what I did.
87	Teacher:	All right, Addison. Thank you. So, my last question is, how is Addison's equation
88		similar to Kirby's equation $y = 2x + 6$? Marley?
89	Marley:	It describes the same patio.
90	Teacher:	Okay. But can we have two different equations for the same thing?
91	Marley:	I guess.
92	Teacher:	How can I rearrange Addison's equation a little bit? What could we do to that? Jayden?
93	Jayden:	Combine like terms.
94	Teacher:	Combine like terms. What could we do? Jayden?
95	Jayden:	Distribute. Three times x and then 3 times 2. Which would be $3x + 6$. But then you have
96		to subtract the black tiles so it would be $3x + 6 - x$, which is $2x + 6$.
97	Teacher:	Is that the same equation our other group had?
98	Jayden:	Yeah.
99	Teacher:	So, these are equivalent, they just look different. What is the main difference between
100		Kirby's and Addison's approaches? Besides the actual numbers, what were they
101		thinking about differently?
102	Peyton:	Addison thought about all of the tiles first and got rid of the black tiles. Arden and
103		Kirby only worked with the white tiles.

104	Teacher:	All right? So, either way, we got the exact same equation; it's just written differently.
105		Okay, great job. What sort of equation is $y = 2x + 6$? Go ahead, Sloan.
106	Sloan:	Linear.
107	Teacher:	Linear equation. What do we know about linear relationships or patterns? Go ahead,
108		Marley.
109	Marley:	They form a straight line.
110	Teacher:	They do form a straight line if we graph them, absolutely. What else do we know about
111		linear? What else do we know about linear? Finley?
112	Finley:	It has x and y values.
113	Teacher:	Okay. x and y typically are a part of the equations. Yep.
114	Skyler:	I don't remember exactly but it has inputs and outputs.
115	Teacher:	Inputs and outputs. Okay. How are those related to each other with linear equations?
116		What sort of patterns are formed? Go ahead, Arden.
117	Arden:	It'll be hard for me to explain this, but when you multiply a black tile by 2 and you add
118		6, you basically do that each time. Yeah. It's hard to explain.
119	Teacher:	Awesome. Let's build on that. How can we add to Arden's explanation there that it's
120		each time we multiply by 2? What's another way to phrase that?
121	Jayden:	A slope.
121	Teacher:	What's special about slope? Go ahead.
122	Jayden:	It never changes each time.
123	Teacher:	It stays the same each time, so no matter how many black tiles we're adding, what do
124		we know about the number of white tiles? What'd you say?
125	Jayden:	It's going to be 2 times black tiles plus 6.
126	Teacher:	It'll always be 2 times and then plus 6, so we have this constant rate of change with
127		linear. If 2 is the slope or rate of change, what is the 6? Quinn?
128	Quinn:	It is the "b" in $y = mx + b$. It never changes no matter how many black tiles you have.
129	Teacher:	How would the "b" appear on a graph?
130	Quinn:	The y-intercept. Where the line crosses the y-axis.
131	Teacher:	What is the x value of the y-intercept?
132	Quinn:	Zero. *(Bell rings.)*
133	Teacher:	Awesome. Have a great weekend. We can pick this up on Monday.

Selecting Video Clips: Analysis

Many things occurred during the whole-class discussion at the end of this lesson that you could decide to focus on during the post-lesson conference. To give you several examples of segments you could select, we will discuss four lesson segments, all of which have the potential to engage the teacher in thoughtful reflection on the lesson.

Segment 1 (between lines 4 and 28): This segment could be selected for several reasons. First, the segment provides an example of Nicki's effort to address one of the challenges she identified (Challenge 16. *Keeping the entire class engaged and accountable during individual presentations*). Nicki invited three different students—Lindsey, Sloan, and Peyton—to iterate some or all of Arden's explanation. Hence, the segment provides an opportunity to acknowledge Nicki's growth in moving beyond "show and tell," one goal for the lesson identified by Coach Alex in her summary of the pre-lesson conference. Second, Nicki asks Arden to connect their verbal explanation to the patio diagram (line 8). In so doing, Nicki was aiming at clarifying Arden's explanation and providing students in the class with a visual representation of it. Although this was not an explicit goal, neither mathematically nor pedagogically, making connections between multiple representations is a move that supports students' conceptual understanding (Lesh et al., 1987). Acknowledging this important move could encourage Nicki to continue using it in future lessons. Finally, the segment also provides the opportunity to discuss alternative ways to keep the class engaged during a student presentation by inviting and surfacing the thinking of more students. For example, asking students to turn and talk to a partner about whether they agree or disagree with Arden and why, or asking students to try to apply Arden's strategy to another patio and see whether it works could be considered as different ways to engage students in the discussion of Arden's strategy.

Segment 2 (between lines 32 and 60): Following Kirby's explanation, Nicki asks students to connect Kirby's equation both to Arden's explanation and to one of the diagrams. Connecting the thinking of different groups was another thing that Nicki wanted to accomplish in the lesson. A few missed opportunities, however, could be explored. For example, Marley tried to connect Kirby's rule with Arden's strategy (lines 43–44) but could not provide a coherent explanation. This segment could also provide an opportunity to discuss one of the challenges that Nicki identified (Challenge 8. *Trying to understand student thinking*). Nicki and Coach Alex could use this segment to explore ways of further probing what Marley was thinking rather than just asking another student to respond to the question. In addition, since this was the first time in the lesson that a student used an explicit rule, it could be a chance for Nicki to consider what else could have been done to ensure that students understood Kirby's rule (e.g., ask students if the rule will always work or suggest that students try the rule on different patios to see whether they get the same answer they found using a different strategy).

Segment 3 (between lines 63 and 86): Following Addison's explanation of the rule their group created, Nicki poses a question to the class (lines 76–77), which is answered by Hayden. This is Nicki's only move to engage students in the class in making sense of Addison's solution. As a result, the segment provides the opportunity to explore with Nicki what she could have done to determine what other students understood about Addison's solution (e.g., ask students to repeat or rephrase what Addison said, write Addison's rule algebraically, or determine whether Addison's equation gives the same answers to the total number of tiles that they found with Kirby's equation).

Segment 4 (between lines 105 and 133): This portion of the lesson would be worth discussing because it is when the teacher has the opportunity to explicitly address two of the mathematical goals for the lesson: linear functions grow at a constant rate (goal 1) and the rate of change of a linear function can be highlighted in different representational forms—as the successive difference in a table of (x,y) values in which values for x increase by 1; the m value in the equation $y = mx + b$; and the slope of the function when graphed (goal 2). Although students identified the equation $y = 2x + 6$ as linear and provided a list of things they know about linear equations, none of the features students identified were explored. Discussing this segment would be an opportunity to explore alternative approaches to investigating linear equations in ways that would make the lesson goals transparent (e.g., ask students what the line would look like when graphed, to graph the line, and to relate the graph and the equation).

We discussed four segments in this analysis, which accounted for most of the transcript (and about 20 minutes of class time). When you are reviewing the video recording of a 45- to 60-minute lesson, you will have to be judicious about the segments you select. It would be too much for one conference to reflect on more than three segments, and you may find that one or two are sufficient. As Coach Robin's comments make salient, it can be difficult to select video clips for a post-lesson conference:

> *One large challenge for me is determining what will be most important to discuss during a debrief conversation. There are always so many events during the lesson and I find it challenging to pick a small number to focus on that align with the teacher's goal for growth and my own perceptions of what moments will be high-leverage to discuss.*

Therefore, when selecting video clips, you need to consider what issues you can reasonably address and what is likely to generalize to upcoming lessons. It isn't the number of segments you discuss that matters, but it is the depth of the conversation and the extent to which you can engage the teacher in thoughtful reflection.

> It isn't the number of segments you discuss that matters, but it is the depth of the conversation and the extent to which you can engage the teacher in thoughtful reflection.

Analyzing Video Clips

Once you have identified the video clips that will be discussed in the post-lesson conference, you and the teacher will analyze these video clips independently. By asking the teacher to analyze the clips before engaging in a post-lesson conference, you are providing them with the opportunity to reflect on what actually occurred during the lesson and to prepare for the discussion of specific classroom events. The teacher's analysis provides valuable insights into their thinking will help guide your planning the post-lesson conference plan.

Therefore, after selecting the video clips, you need to make these available to the teacher by providing specific time stamps for each clip (i.e., the minute and seconds [mm:ss–mm:ss] indicating the beginning and end of a clip). You and the teacher will review the selected clips separately and reflect on each clip using the Noticing and Wondering Tool (see Appendix K). The teacher will submit their completed Noticing and Wondering Tool to you prior to the post-lesson conference.

Noticing and Wondering (Smith, 2009) provides a non-threatening way to thoughtfully examine teaching practices and student thinking. Using sentence stems of "I notice" and "I wonder" can help teachers reflect on their own teaching practice, have deeper conversations about teaching and learning with others, and develop a critical stance towards teaching.

Noticings are factual statements based on what occurred during the lesson as evidenced by video recordings, student work, or other concrete artifacts. Noticings do not represent personal opinion or judgment and are not evaluative. For example, the teacher might notice:

- "Only one student at the table was engaged in the conversation."
- "I explained the student's thinking rather than asking them to explain."
- "I provided the student with a strategy to use."
- "All students were engaged in the task and were able to find a strategy to use to solve it."

Wonderings are statements that express curiosity about something that was noticed and may lead to exploring alternative actions that could result in a different outcome. For example:

- "I noticed that only one student at the table was engaged in the conversation."
- "I wonder what other students in the group were thinking and might have contributed during the conversation."
- "I noticed that I explained the student's thinking rather than asking them to explain."
- "I wonder how the student would have explained their own thinking and what I could have asked them to elicit it."
- "I noticed that I provided the student with a strategy to use."
- "I wonder what questions I could have asked to help the students develop their own strategy."
- "I noticed all students were engaged in the task and were able to find a strategy to use to solve it."
- "I wonder what about the task made it engaging and accessible."

The coaches who used our coaching model found noticing and wondering to be a productive way to discuss teaching practice without judgment or criticism. Coaches Drew and Shawn's reflections echo the benefits of this approach:

> *Since noticings are factual statements and not personal opinions, the conversation has the potential to remain non-threatening and non-judgmental. Starting the conversation with a factual statement allows the teacher and the coach to acknowledge a certain moment in time that opens up for further exploration. It becomes an opportunity to question, wonder, and learn from one another. These noticings and wonderings do not necessarily have to end in a right or wrong solution but often guide us to dig a little deeper into the instructional practice at play.* (Coach Drew)

> *Noticings and wonderings invite a spirit of inquiry and curiosity in a way that simply talking about the lesson's high and low points does not. Noticings and wonderings are also less shame-inducing than critiques. Wonderings open the door to thinking about future teacher practice that recapping the lesson does not.* (Coach Shawn)

Although our coaches felt that wonderings supported a stance of curiosity, they argued that the wonderings need to be authentic. As Coach Robin explained, "I feel that disingenuous wonderings can erode trust in the relationship. In other words, we as coaches must sincerely be curious and actually be wondering, not just using these words to sugar-coat direct suggestions."

Thus, before asking teachers to engage in analyzing video clips, you will need to explain what noticing and wondering is and what they need to do and, if possible, practice noticing and wondering using a video clip or transcript together. Noticing and wondering what matters most in terms of student learning is a skill that teachers (and coaches) can improve on over time.

> Noticing and wondering what matters most in terms of student learning is a skill that teachers (and coaches) can improve on over time.

Getting Ready to Plan a Post-Lesson Conference

The Noticing and Wondering Tool (Appendix K) and the video clips will provide the key resources for designing the post-lesson conference. Even though you may want to review other materials submitted by the teacher, such as the Teacher Challenges Tool (Appendix A), Lesson Planning Tool (Appendix E), Monitoring Tool (Appendix F), and the pre-lesson conference summary notes you created, they may be less directly useful than the noticing and wondering, since the aforementioned documents were used in the selection of the video clips.

The first step in planning a post-lesson conference is to review the Noticing and Wondering Tools you and the teacher completed, looking for similarities and differences between your and the teacher's reflections for each clip. You then select a noticing and wondering that best highlights the issue you want to discuss. If possible, select something that you and the teacher have both identified.

In Analyzing Coaching 5.2, you will have the opportunity to review the noticings and wonderings completed by Nicki and Coach Alex and determine which of them best highlights the issue(s) you think they should discuss in the post-lesson conference.

STOP AND CONSIDER

Before you engage in the activity that follows, review the transcript presented in Analyzing Coaching 5.1 and record what you notice and wonder about Segment 2 (lines 32–60) in your journal.

Analyzing Coaching 5.2
Identifying Focal Noticings and Wonderings

After reviewing the video clip that features Kirby's solution to the Tiling a Patio task (Segment 2, lines 32–60 of the lesson transcript in Analyzing Coaching 5.1), Nicki and Coach Alex completed noticings and wonderings about the clip as shown in Figure 5.3. Your task is to review their noticings and wonderings and determine what you think Coach Alex should focus on in

> the post-lesson conference and why. (You may want to review Nicki's task and goals [Figure 5.2] and what Nicki and Coach Alex discussed in the pre-lesson conference [immediately following Figure 5.2] before beginning this activity.)

Figure 5.3 • Nicki and Coach Alex's Noticings and Wonderings

		What I Noticed	What I Am Wondering About
Nicki	1.	I asked questions and didn't do any telling.	
	2.	I called on 3 different students after Kirby's presentations so it was not just me and Kirby.	I wonder if others were following our discussion.
	3.	When Marley couldn't answer I said "that's okay."	I wonder what Marley was thinking.
	4.	I asked students to connect Kirby's equation with Arden's diagram.	I wonder if everyone could see the connection. (One of my goals was to find a way to connect the thinking of each of the different groups.)
	5.	I noticed Arden wanted to answer, but I said no because Arden already shared their group's strategy.	I wonder if Arden would be able to connect their strategy to Kirby's equation.
Coach Alex	a.	Marley was not able to explain their thinking when asked.	I wonder what you could have asked Marley to help them articulate what they were thinking.
	b.	Two students (Cameron and Skyler) had a chance to make connections between the equation and the diagram.	I wonder what other students were thinking and what you could have done to include more students.
	c.	This was the first time an equation was presented in the lesson. Cameron and Skyler were able to connect the 2 and the 6 in the equation to the picture.	I wonder if it would have been helpful at this point to talk more about the equation—what the equation looks like when graphed, and how the 2 and the 6 impact the graph. Could this help you get at goals 1 and 3?

Identifying Focal Noticings and Wonderings: Analysis

You could have selected several different noticings and wonderings to focus on during the post-lesson conference. For example, Nicki's first two noticings ("I asked questions and didn't do any telling"; "I called on 3 different students after Kirby's presentation so it was not just me and Kirby") show that she recognizes the effort she was making to "engage students in the discussion," one of the goals stated by Coach Alex at the conclusion of the pre-lesson conference. Discussing these noticings would provide an opportunity to acknowledge both the progress Nicki has made and what else she could have done to engage more students.

Or you might focus on noticing 5 ("I noticed Arden wanted to answer, but I said no because Arden already shared their group's strategy"), which shows that Nicki was trying to involve more students to participate in the discussion. Since Cameron had not made a contribution, Nicki invited them to do so rather than have Arden respond again. This would provide an opportunity to talk about the importance of involving more students but also consider how Nicki could have assessed Arden's understanding of the connection between representations.

We think there are two noticings and wonderings that would best highlight the challenges Nicki and Coach Alex had discussed in the pre-lesson conference. These two noticings and wonderings are found on both Nicki's and Coach Alex's list: one related to Marley's struggle to answer a question (number 3 on Nicki's list and a on Coach Alex's list) and another one related to connecting the equation and the diagram (number 4 on Nicki's list and b on Coach Alex's list). Both noticings and wonderings would provide the opportunity to build a discussion around instances that were identified by the teacher (as well as the coach) and to link to the challenges that Nicki had identified and to the discussion in the pre-lesson conference.

In noticing 3, Nicki stated, "When Marley couldn't answer I said, 'that's okay'." One of the challenges Nicki identified was *Trying to understand student thinking* (Challenge 8), and during the pre-lesson conference, Nicki and Coach Alex talked about questions Nicki could ask to uncover what students were thinking. This noticing and the related wondering ("I wonder what Marley was thinking") would provide an opportunity to explore alternative ways of responding to Marley in particular but in general to students who can't answer a question.

In noticing 4, Nicki stated, "I asked students [Cameron and Skyler] to connect Kirby's equation with Arden's diagram." Another one of the challenges that Nicki identified was *Keeping the entire class engaged and accountable during individual presentations* (Challenge 16). During the pre-lesson conference, Nicki and Coach Alex discussed specific moves Nicki could make to ensure that students were making sense of the explanations given by their peers. Nicki also indicated that she wanted to connect the thinking of each group. This noticing and related wondering ("I wonder if everyone could see the connection") would provide an opportunity to acknowledge Nicki's effort to encourage students to connect Arden's diagram and Kirby's equation and to consider what Nicki could have done to determine if other students understood the connection. This would also be an opportunity to talk about how Cameron and Skyler's explanation of the "2" and the "6" in the equation and the picture could have also been connected to a graph (Coach Alex's wondering c) and ultimately surfaced the concept of linearity.

Constructing a Post-Lesson Conference Plan

Once you identify the noticings and wonderings you want to discuss, you can begin to plan a conversation for each video clip by using the Post-Lesson Conference Planning Tool (Appendix L). The first step in this process is to write down the time markers for the clip, the relevant practice and challenge being targeted, and why this clip was selected (i.e., What was the reason you picked this clip? What issues did you think it would raise? Why is this important?). Since the goal of our coaching model is to support teacher learning of ambitious teaching through addressing challenges with the 5 practices, you need to consider how reflecting on the video clips you selected will address specific teacher challenge(s).

The next step is to record the noticings and wonderings that will help you discuss the selected video clip. The goal is to ensure that you and the teacher have a shared understanding of the noticings and wonderings before you can start talking about what the teacher could have done differently in the lesson. To achieve this goal, you will consider what questions to ask. All of this will be recorded in the Identify the Challenge column of the Post-Lesson Conference Planning Tool.

Then, you will determine how you will discuss the clip so as to engage the teacher in thinking about a specific challenge more deeply—the Address the Challenge column. The inquiry routine—*Invite, Rehearse, Suggest,* and *Generalize*—could be useful in this process, and the Guide for Designing Conferences (Appendix B) can provide some suggestions in this regard. Although the guide is written in the future tense (e.g., what will you do if …), it can also be used to support the teacher in considering what they could have done and what they might have learned from doing something differently.

The last column (i.e., Guiding Rationale) is a place to articulate why the identified challenge is worth exploring both in general and for a particular teacher. Finally, the last cell on the bottom of the tool is for making note(s)—during the post-lesson conference—of things that the teacher understands they will do differently in the future and why it is important. Your notes in this cell can help you track a teacher's progress across coaching cycles.

Figure 5.4 provides an example of a completed Post-Lesson Conference Planning Tool, based on a lesson Joey taught that focused on the Max's Dog Food task (see Figure 1.2 in Chapter 1).

Figure 5.4 • Example of a completed post-lesson conference planning tool

Teacher: Joey Coach: Taylor Cycle: 1 Date:			Clip #: 1 Time Stamp: 15:05–19:00	Relevant Practice: Monitoring Focal Challenge: Trying to understand student thinking Why This Clip?: Although Joey indicated that he planned to work on assessing questions in this lesson, he ended up doing most of the explaining. In this clip, it wasn't clear what the student was thinking or what they understand about the task.	
T and/or C?	*Identify the Challenge*			*Address the Challenge*	*Guiding Rationale*
T	Noticing	I explained the student's thinking more than I asked about it from them. - Can you point to an example of where this occurred? (Review the clip together in order to ground the discussion) - What are the advantages and disadvantages of doing the explaining yourself?		Let's take the example we just discussed where you were interacting with Shonda about the number line strategy she used. Invite What do you think Shonda understands? What questions could you have asked that would have helped you learn more about her understanding? Rehearse You indicated that you would ask, "What did you do?" What will you ask as follow-up questions? I will play the student and you can be the teacher. T: What did you do? S: I made a number line. T: ??? What will you ask next? What is it you want to find out?	Questions are important because they help teachers to better understand what students are thinking. Noel has a tendency to take over the thinking of students, and therefore, it is really important that the teacher comes to see the importance of really understanding where students are and the types of questions that will help do that.

			Suggest	
			Let's look at some alternative ways of determining what Shonda understands and discuss whether they would be helpful:	
			Tell me about your number line.	
			What do the numbers on the top/bottom represent?	
			How did the number line help you find the answer?	
			Generalize	
	Wondering	I wonder what more I will learn about student understanding if I ask more guiding questions, rather than explaining the student's thinking for them. – What is it you want students to understand in this problem? – What do you mean by guiding questions?	What can you do in the future to gain more insight into what students understand?	

Notes *(i.e., commitment/focus for upcoming lesson, revisions to Teacher Goals/Challenges; evidence of growth in pedagogical reasoning)*: Teacher noted that they need to be sure to create assessing questions prior to the lesson and to have the questions with them as they are monitoring student work. Having easy access to these questions during the lesson will remind the teacher of the need to ask questions as well as what to ask.

In Analyzing Coaching 5.3, you will have the opportunity to work on a post-lesson conference plan that Coach Alex will use to discuss the Tiling a Patio lesson with Nicki.

> ### ▶ Analyzing Coaching 5.3
> *Constructing a Post-Lesson Conference Plan*
>
> Recall that, following the Tiling of the Patio lesson, Coach Alex selected Segment 2 (lines 32–60 in Activity 5.2) as the video clip to discuss in a post-lesson conference with Nicki. You are now going to complete the post-lesson conference plan that Coach Alex started (Figure 5.5). As you can see, Coach Alex has (a) completed the top portion of the tool; (b) indicated that both teacher "T" and coach "C" identified the same challenge; (c) listed the noticing and wondering about Marley using Nicki's wording; and (c) specified a "guiding rationale" for this discussion. Your task is to determine the questions Coach Alex should ask to clarify the noticing and wondering (if needed, see the Identify the Challenge column of Figure 5.5) and how she should help Nicki reflect on what occurred in the video clip and consider alternatives in moving forward (in the Address the Challenge column of Figure 5.5).

Figure 5.5 • Beginnings of Coach Alex's post-lesson conference plan

Teacher: Nicki Coach: Alex Cycle: 2 Date: 10/20/23	Clip #: 1 Time Stamp: 10:25-10:30	Relevant Practice: Monitoring Focal Challenge: 8–trying to understand student thinking; Why This Clip?: I picked this clip because although Nicki indicated that she wanted to uncover what students were thinking, there was a missed opportunity to do so with Marley.

T and/or C?	Identify the Challenge		Address the Challenge	Guiding Rationale
T+C	Noticing	Marley couldn't answer, I said, "That's okay." Clarifying Questions?	How will I help Nicki think about the issue?	Questions are the only tool we have to get at what students are thinking. If we don't know what they are thinking, we can't move them forward. Nicki has a tendency not to probe when the question she asks is met with an incomplete or incorrect answer or silence.
	Wondering	I wonder what Marley was thinking. Clarifying Questions?		

Notes (i.e., commitment/focus for upcoming lesson, revisions to Teacher Goals/Challenges; evidence of growth in pedagogical reasoning):

Constructing a Post-Lesson Conference Plan: Analysis

Coach Alex's plan could be completed in many different ways. Herein we will talk through one approach and explain what we are trying to accomplish with our suggestions. In Figure 5.6, we provide a plan for a conversation with Nicki on one event that occurred in Segment 2 (lines 32–60). The purpose of the set of questions in the Identify the Challenge column is to ensure that Nicki and Coach Alex have a shared understanding of what the teacher has noticed. For example, to surface whether the coach and the teacher have a shared understanding of the situation before exploring it further, Coach Alex could ask, "What question did you ask Marley?" and "What did Marley say?" These questions would also help Coach Alex make sure that the discussion is focused on what actually occurred rather than on subjective memory of events.

Figure 5.6 • Example of a post-lesson conference plan for Coach Alex

T and/or C?		_Identify the Challenge_	_Address the Challenge_	_Guiding Rationale_
T+C	Noticing	When Marley couldn't answer, I said, "That's okay." What question did you ask Marley? What were you hoping to hear?	You indicated that you wondered what Marley was thinking. Marley's response to your question was: For every black tile ... Oh, wait. x would be the number of black tiles and then you would just multiply that number of white tiles. Invite What do you think Marley understands about Kirby's rule or about the diagrams? What does Marley seem to be confused about? What questions could you ask Marley that might give you more insight into their current understanding? Rehearse Let's take that question you identified and do a role play. You play the teacher and I will play the students.	Questions are the only tool we have to get at what students are thinking. If we don't know what they are thinking, we can't move them forward. Nicki has a tendency not to probe when the question she asks is met with an incomplete or incorrect answer or silence.

			T: If x is the number of black tiles, how would you find the number of white tiles? S: There are the same number of white tiles on the top and bottom as there are black tiles. T:???? *Suggest* Let's talk about some alternative ways of supporting Marley and consider whether or how they might be helpful: Giving Marley and the other students a few minutes to turn and talk to a partner about the question and then asking them again to explain. Asking Marley to use one of the diagrams to explain how it relates to Kirby's rule. Coming back to Marley after Cameron and Skyler shared their explanations and giving them another chance to explain in their own words. *Generalize* What will you do when planning future lessons to make student thinking clear and visible? What is the benefit of continuing to work with a student who has not or cannot answer a question? What are the advantages to the teacher and the student?	
	Wondering	I wonder what Marley was thinking.		

CHAPTER 5 | Preparing for and Engaging in the Post-Lesson Conference

Regarding Nicki's wondering, it may or may not be necessary to ask a clarifying question. For example, Nicki's wondering (i.e., "I wonder what Marley was thinking") is pretty straightforward. Coach Alex might still ask about the understanding Nicki was targeting in the question (i.e., "If we take a look at Kirby's rule, can someone connect that rule to what Arden was saying?" lines 41–42) that Marley attempted to answer.

In the Addressing the Challenge column, Coach Alex can get to the specifics of the conversation regarding these noticings and wonderings that will help Nicki address the challenge (i.e., Challenge 8. *Understanding what students are thinking*). Using the moves from the inquiry routine (*Invite*, *Suggest*, *Rehearse*, and *Generalize*), Coach Alex can build the conversation on Nicki's thinking about the situation. For example, to engage Nicki in a conversation about the wondering they posed, Coach Alex can ask different **invitational** questions: "What do you think Marley understands about Kirby's rule or about the diagrams?" "What does Marley seem to be confused about?" "What questions could you ask Marley that might give you more insight into her current understanding?"

If Nicki identifies a question to ask Marley, then Coach Alex can engage her in a **rehearsal** to simulate what the conversation might look like. For example, if Nicki considers asking Marley, "*If x is the number of black tiles, how would you find the number of white tiles?*", then Nicki has to rehearse what Marley might say and how she might respond to Marley. By playing this out, Nicki has the opportunity to think about a series of questions that can elicit Marley's thinking.

If Nicki is having difficulty in coming up with ideas about questions to ask Marley, Coach Alex can make **suggestions** for Nicki to consider that provide alternative ways of determining what students understand: Giving Marley and the other student a few minutes to turn and talk to a partner about the question and then asking them again to explain; asking Marley to use one of the diagrams to explain how it relates to Kirby's rule; and coming back to Marley after Cameron and Skyler shared their explanations and giving them another chance to explain in their own words.

Finally, Coach Alex can plan **generalization** questions that are intended to help Nicki make explicit the teaching moves that would help her address the challenge of *Understanding what students are thinking* (Challenge 8) in future lessons. For example, Coach Alex can ask, "What will you do when planning future lessons to make student thinking clear and visible?" Moreover, Coach Alex can push Nicki to think about why it is important to access student thinking, whether it is an individual student like Marley or the majority of the class. Questions such as "What is the benefit of continuing to work with a student who has not or cannot answer a question?" and "What are the advantages to the teacher and the student?" can help Nicki understand the importance of uncovering student thinking in the current lesson under discussion and more generally.

STOP AND CONSIDER

Coach Alex went on to plan for a conversation with Nicki based on the other noticing and wondering they both identified in Analyzing Coaching 5.2—noticing that Nicki asked students to connect Kirby's equation to Arden's diagram and wondering if everyone was able to see the connection. Review Coach Alex's plan for this portion of the post-lesson conference (Figure 5.7), and record what you notice about the plan and what you are wondering about.

Figure 5.7 • Coach Alex's plan for the post-lesson conference

Teacher: Nicki Coach: Alex Cycle: 2 Date: 10/20/23	Clip #: 1 Time Stamp: 10:25–10:30	Relevant Practice: Connecting Focal Challenge: 16-keeping the entire class engaged and accountable during individual presentations Why This Clip?: Nicki is working on ensuring that students make sense of the explanations given by their peers. In this clip, this did occur with two students, but it isn't clear what others in the class understood.
T and/or C?		**Identify the Challenge**	**Address the Challenge**	**Guiding Rationale**
T+C	Noticing	I asked students to connect Kirby's equation with Arden's diagram. – Which students did you ask to do this? – What did the students say?	Asking Cameron and Skyler to connect Kirby's rule to Arden's diagram was an important move. It was related to a few things we talked about in the pre-lesson conference—connect the thinking of each of the different groups and keeping students engaged. You wondered if everyone could see the connection between the verbal description and diagram that Arden presented and the equation that Kirby described. *Invite* What do the students need to know or understand in order to make the connection? What could you do to determine whether students understood Kirby's rule? Arden's explanation? *Rehearse* You said you could ask students to try both Arden's explanation and Kirby's rule to find out the fencing for a different patio number. What would you do next, when they answer that question? How would you ensure that everyone understand that both strategies would give the same answer?	To learn from the whole-class discussion, students need to make sense of the material being presented. So as teachers we need to find ways to determine what they understand. Nicki is often satisfied to hear a correct answer from one or two students. She needs to think about how to check on understanding more widely.

			Suggest	
			Let's talk about some alternative ways of determining whether students understood Kirby's rule and consider whether or how they might be helpful: Asking a student to repeat or state Kirby's rule in their own words.	
			- Asking students to try Kirby's rule with different patio numbers and see if they got the same answers.	
			- Asking students to explain how they think the two strategies are connected to their elbow partners.	
			- Ask students to determine if the rule always works and why.	
			- Give students an exit slip and ask them each to explain Kirby's rule using Patio 4 and to draw a picture that shows their reasoning.	
			Generalize	
			If several students already gave complete and correct explanations, isn't that good enough? What is the benefit of checking in with more students about their understanding?	
	Wondering	I wonder if everyone could see the connection. What connection did you want students to see?		

CHAPTER 5 | Preparing for and Engaging in the Post-Lesson Conference

Coach Alex could create a workable plan to use in her conversation with Nicki in many different ways. The key is to make sure, as a coach, you are both interpreting the noticings and wonderings the same way as the teacher and that you use the inquiry routine to engage the teacher by first probing their thinking before rehearsing or providing suggestions, and pulling the conversation back to a generalization. Providing a rationale in the last column, as Coach Alex did, provides a reminder to the coach why this challenge is important in general and why this teacher needs to address this challenge in particular. The Guide for Designing Conferences (Appendix B) provides possible rationales for each challenge, but it is important for the coach to restate the rationale in a way that is meaningful to them and to the situation.

Engaging in the Post-Lesson Conference

Once you have a post-lesson conference plan, you are ready to put your plan into action and engage the teacher in reflecting on the lesson. In Analyzing Coaching 5.4, you will explore the conversation that took place between Jamie and Coach Jesse. Previously (in Chapter 4, Analyzing Coaching 4.3), we looked at the Fractions of Fractions lesson that Jamie was going to teach and joined the pre-lesson conference conversation between Jamie and Coach Jesse. Here, we will analyze their post-lesson conference conversation.

After Jamie taught the lesson, Coach Jesse identified three video clips to discuss in the post-lesson conference. In this activity, we will focus on the first clip. Coach Jesse selected this clip to address Challenge 10. *Involving all members of a group*, which was the challenge they worked on in the pre-lesson conference (Chapter 4, Analyzing Coaching 4.3). This clip starts as Jamie approaches a group of four students who are solving a problem in the Fractions of Fractions task (i.e., "If $\frac{1}{4}$ of the shaded part [$\frac{1}{2}$ of the whole fraction bar] is striped, how much of the bar is striped?"). There are four students in this group: Quinn, Casey, Charlie, and Sasha. First, Jamie asks Quinn to explain how they got $\frac{1}{8}$ as an answer to the problem. After listening to Quinn's response, Jamie asks the same question to Casey. Then, Jamie repeats Casey's response in his own words and moves on to another group.

For this clip, Jamie and Coach Jesse individually recorded their noticings and wonderings (see Appendix M for the Noticing and Wondering tools completed by Jamie and Coach Jesse). Jamie shared his noticing and wonderings about this clip with Coach Jesse. In preparation for the post-lesson conference, Coach Jesse reviewed the noticings and wonderings and created a post-lesson conference plan (Appendix N). In Analyzing Coaching 5.4, you will analyze the post-lesson conference conversation between Jamie and Coach Jesse.

> ## ▶ Analyzing Coaching 5.4
> *Engaging in the Post-Lesson Conference*
>
> The following transcript is an excerpt from the post-lesson conference between Jaime and Coach Jesse. As you read the transcript, consider these three questions, and record your responses in your journal:
>
> 1. What did Coach Jesse do to help Jamie address this challenge?
> 2. How might this conversation help Jamie involve all members of a group in the future?
> 3. Prior to the conference, Coach Jesse created a plan for the conference (Appendix N). What do you notice about the plan? To what extent do you think it helped Coach Jesse during the actual conference?

Post-Lesson Conference: Fractions of Fractions

1	Coach:	All right. I'm excited to talk about the group work part of this lesson. From my
2		perspective, most of the groups were working well together and I think the amount of
3		student participation in groups was a lot more equitable this time. This is what we
4		discussed in our pre-lesson conversation, involving all members of a group, and I saw
5		evidence that our conversation really seemed to pay off. You were directing questions to
6		specific students and especially to the ones that are usually silent, you were also using
7		retell when someone was just listening in their group.
8	Jamie:	Mm-hmm (affirmative). I think it went well overall. And our [pre-lesson conference]
9		conversation was helpful.
10	Coach:	Cool. So, now, let's talk about the first clip I sent you, that focuses on Quinn's group. In
11		your noticings, you wrote that they seemed to be working on their own and not really
12		talking too much. Could you start by just talking a little bit more about what you saw
13		happening with that group?
14	Jamie:	Yeah. So it just seemed like they were each doing their own thing. They all had the correct
15		answer, but they were not sharing their ideas. It didn't seem like they were collaborating at
16		all. I mean they were using different solution strategies.
17	Coach:	Why do you think this might have been the case?
18	Jamie:	I don't know, maybe because they were all on a correct path. It could have been due to
19		being certain of what to do. But at the same time, like we talked about using each other as
20		resources and maybe they didn't feel the need. Like they didn't need to ask another group
21		member for help.

22	Coach:	Yeah, it is possible that they didn't think they needed to work together because they had
23		their own ideas. But we certainly want them to communicate and discuss different ideas
24		because it is important for them to see how different solution strategies can get them to the
25		same answer.
26	Jamie:	That is why I asked them to explain their thinking.
27	Coach:	Yes, when you approached this group, you first asked Quinn, "How did you get $\frac{1}{8}$?" And
28		they were using this solution strategy you anticipated. (*Coach points at the*
29		*representation below.*) Do you remember what happened next?
30		
31	Jamie:	Yeah. So, Quinn explained they split the shaded part into $\frac{1}{4}$'s to find $\frac{1}{4}$ of $\frac{1}{2}$ and they
32		multiplied $\frac{1}{2}$ by $\frac{1}{4}$ and they got $\frac{1}{8}$. Then I turned to the group and asked, "So, $\frac{1}{4}$ times $\frac{1}{2}$ is
33		$\frac{1}{8}$, how did you get that?" And Casey answered.
34	Coach:	Yes. Did you notice that Casey was using a different solution strategy?
35	Jamie:	Yeah, Casey was using this one. (*Teacher points to the representation below.*)
36		
37	Coach:	Yeah. So Casey used the diagram to explain how they got the answer, but Quinn was
38		using multiplication to get the answer. And, Casey's diagram represents the situation, but
39		Quinn's multiplication got them the answer.
40	Jamie:	Yeah.
41	Coach:	Let's replay that part of the clip. (*Coach plays the clip as shown in lines 43–51.*)
42	Jamie:	Okay.
43	Casey:	So, there are two halves in the whole. One shaded, one not shaded. And one has fourths
44		because the problem asked us [to find $\frac{1}{4}$ of $\frac{1}{2}$] and put stripes in $\frac{1}{4}$. Then the other half also has
45		fourths. So altogether we have 8 pieces and $\frac{1}{8}$ striped.
46	Jamie:	So you striped $\frac{1}{4}$ of the shaded. So then to help you see how many equal parts there were in
47		the whole fraction bar, you did the unshaded part and broke into fourths as well. So then
48		you have 8 equal parts altogether, right?
49	Casey:	Mm-hmm (affirmative).
50	Jamie:	And you have 1 part striped, so then $\frac{1}{4}$ of $\frac{1}{2}$ is $\frac{1}{8}$.
51	Casey:	Yes. (*Clip ends.*)
52	Coach:	So after you had Quinn share their thinking, you continue with Casey. I wondered, in
53		that moment, what do you think we could have done in that exchange to bring other
54		members into the conversation?
55	Jamie:	I had this question in my Monitoring Tool. I could ask Quinn, "Could you explain what
56		Casey did here? Why did they divide the fraction bar into 8 pieces?" I mean this could
57		also be a retell, like, "Could you repeat what Casey said in your own words?"
58	Coach:	Yeah, certainly. And, again, you don't have to go back to Quinn, you could have asked
59		Charlie or Sasha.
60	Jamie:	Yeah. To see if these strategies make sense to them. Like, "Oh, okay. I got it. So I can see
61		that one fourth of one half, that would then become an eighth, because … " And be able to
62		defend or answer too, by showing on the fraction bar.
63	Coach:	Absolutely. But, like you said, Quinn and Casey both got the correct answer using
64		different strategies [the former using multiplication, the latter using a visual model] and

65		we want them to learn from each other. I wonder, how could we have them compare their
66		strategies? Or even have another student in the group to compare.
67	Jamie:	I guess an advancing question? I mean, I already asked the assessing question to get their
68		ideas, so comparing different strategies would be challenging. So, again, in my Monitoring
69		Tool, maybe I could ask, "Why did we end up dividing this into 8 pieces?" Or like, "Why
70		does Quinn have 4 pieces only here [in the shaded part] but Casey has 4 pieces here [in the
71		shaded] and 4 pieces there [in the unshaded part]?"
72	Coach:	Yeah, so if you just ask about the 8 pieces [in Casey's solution], then you might not get
73		them to compare. But probably the second question ["Why does Quinn have 4 pieces in
74		the shaded part but Casey has 4 pieces in the shaded and 4 pieces in the unshaded part?"]
75		would've brought their attention to the different strategies. Then, I wonder, what do you
76		think their answer would be?
77	Jamie:	Well, the first solution [Quinn] focuses on the shaded part only. Then they would say,
78		"Since we have two halves in the whole, Casey split each half into fourths. Quinn only
79		split the shaded part into fourths, but he could have split the unshaded part into fourths to
80		show that their striped piece is one of eight equal pieces."
81	Coach:	Yes, and we would know they understand how the different representations get to the
82		same answer.
83	Jamie:	Yeah, like, they would see Casey's model actually represents Quinn's multiplication.
84	Coach:	Exactly. So first we ask an assessing question to get different ideas on the table and
85		then do a retell to make sure everyone is making sense of these different solutions. We
86		can do this by asking Charlie or Sasha to explain what they heard. Then we ask an
87		advancing question to compare both strategies. Hopefully, we get an answer that will
88		show their understanding. But it is possible that someone might answer, "I don't know."
89	Jamie:	Yeah, we talked about this in the pre-lesson conference. Like, if Charlie cannot answer the
90		advancing question, I can have them ask questions to others, like to Quinn or Casey. So
91		they know they should be helping each other understand and work as a group.
92	Coach:	Exactly. And so, if we push a student, in this case, Charlie, to ask a question, then we're
93		still holding them accountable, right? And at that point, you can leave the group to talk
94		among themselves and tell them you will come back to hear from Charlie [the answer to
95		the advancing question of "Why does Quinn have 4 pieces in the shaded part but Casey
96		has 4 pieces in the shaded and 4 pieces in the unshaded part?"].
97	Jamie:	Yeah, I think that's a really good point of coming back to the same student [Charlie] after
98		I initially ask them the question and they are clearly feeling a little stuck. It's not like,
99		"Oh, I'm stuck. Again." And that's it. ... They have to be listening well enough to be able
100		to say, "I don't understand this part," and communicate that in some way.
101	Coach:	Why is that important?
102	Jamie:	Because then I'm making sure that students are understanding and aren't just "telling." So
103		when Quinn and Casey just shared their strategies, it is not like, "Well, okay. This is what
104		Quinn said" or "This is what Casey said, so I'm going to do the same." But holding the
105		other students accountable, making sure they understand why these two students solved it
106		the way they did.
107	Coach:	Right. So as you move forward, and thinking about how to keep all students engaged,
108		what are some things you want to take with you?
109	Jamie:	Looking now, just making sure that they are working together. And I should hear students
110		asking questions to each other, like, "Can you retell?" And having them see each other as
111		resources, whether for coming up with a solution strategy or sharing different solution
112		strategies to learn from each other.

113	Coach:	And how are you going to ensure that? I mean, that they share their thinking with the other
114		members of the group and help each other make sense of different strategies.
115	Jamie:	If they seem to struggle, I will ask them, "Well, what questions do you have? What don't
116		you get?"
117	Coach:	Yeah, so it sounds like there's a couple different ways. You're talking about how to
118		support the student who might be struggling and keep them engaged and part of that
119		conversation.
120	Jamie:	And when there are some students who already made progress with the task, like Quinn
121		and Casey in this clip, then ask advancing questions that will get everyone in the group to
122		compare different strategies and make connections [among different strategies]. And then
123		I can leave them to discuss within the group.
124	Coach:	Yeah, for sure. And what can we do together to help you prepare better in the future?
125	Jamie:	I mean, this is also time intensive and I think it's really hard to do it on the fly. You know
126		what I mean?
127	Coach:	Yeah, of course. And we will keep on working together. I think, in the future, when
128		planning for a lesson, I think we can consider specific advancing questions that get
129		at comparing different solution strategies. I mean, we talked about what to do when
130		student says, "I don't know," in a group and how we can engage them, and what to do
131		when one student had a correct answer and one didn't. But I guess this was different,
132		like having two different solution strategies that got the same answer.
133	Jamie:	Yeah, I guess in this group I was focused too much on the answers, not the engagement.
134		And I got to say, I would be the first to admit, I'm far from perfect. But this
135		conversation has just showed me areas that I can improve in.
136	Coach:	I think when we get going in day-to-day stuff, it can get hard to take time for reflection.
137		But you did a great job overall, like with other groups, they were really engaged with
138		each other. And we will keep working on this.

Engaging in the Post-Lesson Conference: Analysis

In this post-lesson conference, you might have noticed multiple things that Coach Jesse did to address Challenge 10. *Involving all members of a group*. First, Coach Jesse started by highlighting the progress Jamie made with this challenge in the lesson. In lines 1–7, Coach Jesse provides specific evidence of what Jamie did to address this challenge, which would encourage Jamie to use these moves in future lessons. Acknowledging the teacher's growth is also important because it motivates them to continue with their efforts to improve their practices.

Next, as Jamie and Coach Jesse were reflecting on the video clip, the coach facilitated a conversation that built on the teacher's thinking. Specifically, Coach Jesse was using the inquiry routine (*Invite, Rehearse, Suggest,* and *Generalize*). In lines 12–13, we see that Coach Jesse asked an **invitational** question to surface Jamie's thinking: "Could you start by just talking a little bit more about what you saw happening with that group?" Jamie's response to this question shows that he noticed the group of students in the clip were not engaged, although Jamie's goal was to ensure every student was involved in group work. To understand what Jamie thought the reason for the lack of interaction in this group was, Coach Jesse asked, "Why do you think this might have been the case?" (line 17). As we see in lines 18–21, Jamie thought the students in this group were all on a correct path and did not feel the need to discuss how they should move forward with the task. Compared with the pre-lesson conference when Jamie and Coach Jesse considered various reasons why some students might not be engaged in group work (e.g., students stay quiet, students don't know what to do), the group in this clip offers a new case of why students in a group aren't working together. That is, the students in a group might not feel the need to engage with each other if they can make progress with the task by themselves. Since something unexpected happened in this clip, Jamie probably did not know how to respond in ways that would address the challenge of involving all members of a group.

Once Coach Jesse confirmed that Jamie noticed the lack of interaction among the students in this group and recognized this could be because students were on "a correct path," Jamie and Coach Jesse could discuss what could have been done to ensure every student was involved in group work. As Coach Jesse specifies, we "certainly want [students in the group] to communicate and discuss different ideas because it is important for them to see how different solution strategies can get them to the same answer" (lines 23–25). In this way, Jamie would be equipped with moves to help him in similar situations in the future.

Note that, before discussing what Jamie could have done differently in the lesson, Coach Jesse wants to make sure the teacher remembers exactly what happened in the lesson (lines 27–51). To this end, the coach plays the clip as a reminder of the events. Instead of talking from memory, replaying the video clip that is under discussion is a critical step in establishing a shared understanding of classroom events. It helps with reflecting on the lesson more objectively.

> Instead of talking from memory, replaying the video clip that is under discussion is a critical step in establishing a shared understanding of classroom events. It helps with reflecting on the lesson more objectively.

Through the exchange between Jamie and Coach Jesse in lines 27–51, the coach establishes a shared understanding with the teacher that (a) there were two different solution strategies and they both got the same answer and (b) the teacher was retelling one student's (Casey's) explanation rather than engaging other students. Then, Coach Jesse poses a question to *invite* Jamie to think about alternative moves that could have been used to involve all members of the group in this clip (lines 52–54). In response, Jamie offers two alternative moves that he could have used (i.e., asking Quinn to explain Casey's strategy or asking Quinn to retell Casey's explanation, lines 55–57) and describe what this would have achieved: "To see if these strategies make sense to them. ... And be able to defend or answer too, by showing on the fraction bar." (lines 60–62).

Although Jamie's question could have helped students in this group to make sense of Casey's strategy, it would not get students to make connections between the strategies and, thus, understand "how different solution strategies can get them to the same answer" (lines 24–25). To engage Jamie in thinking about how he could have helped students make these connections, Coach Jesse asks another *invitational* question: "I wonder, how could we have them compare their strategies? Or even have another student in the group to compare" (lines 65–66). This question is more specific than the previous invite on lines 52–54 because the coach did not get a response from the teacher that would resolve the issue of having students connect the two strategies.

In response to Coach Jesse's question (lines 65–66), Jamie offers two alternative questions to ask students, acknowledging that these are advancing questions: "Why did we end up dividing this into eight pieces?" or "Why does Quinn have 4 pieces in the shaded part but Casey has 4 pieces in the shaded and 4 pieces in the unshaded part?" (lines 69–71). As Coach Jesse explained, the latter would achieve the goal of making connections between different strategies, unlike the former, which would not be helpful. Instead of telling Jamie that the former question would not be helpful, Coach Jesse could have engaged Jamie in rehearsal for both questions and had him decide whether or not these questions would support students in making connections between the two strategies.

With the question "What do you think their answer would be?" (lines 75–76), Coach Jesse engages Jamie in *rehearsal* with the question he could have asked ("Why does Quinn have 4 pieces in the shaded part but Casey has 4 pieces in the shaded and 4 pieces in the unshaded part?"). In response, Jamie explains that students could say, "Since we have two halves in the whole, Casey split each half into fourths. Quinn only split the shaded part into fourths, but he could have split the unshaded part into fourths to show that his striped piece is one of eight equal pieces." (lines 78–80). This type of student response, as both Jamie and Coach Jesse agreed, would show evidence for an understanding of the connection between the two strategies (lines 81–83).

We can also see that Coach Jesse engages Jamie in another *rehearsal* (line 88). This time the coach wants the teacher to consider a case in which the teacher's question ("Why does Quinn have 4 pieces in the shaded part but Casey has 4 pieces in the shaded and 4 pieces in the unshaded part?") would not get students to make the connection between Quinn's and Casey's strategies. Jamie says he could have students "ask questions to others, like to Quinn or Casey. So they know they should be helping each other understand and work as a group" (lines 90–91). Importantly, Jamie's response in reference to the pre-lesson conference ("Yeah, *we talked about this in the pre-lesson conference.* Like, if Charlie cannot answer the advancing question, I can have them ask questions to others, like to Quinn or Casey. So they know they should be helping each other understand and work as a group," lines 89–91) shows us evidence of teacher learning. We should also note that Coach Jesse asks Jamie to explain the benefits of having students ask questions to each other when they don't know what to do (line 101) to ensure Jamie's understanding. We can see that Jamie is making sense of the importance of this teacher move in relation to student learning (lines 102–106).

During the conversation, we also see Coach Jesse's use of **suggestion** (lines 58–59). As we discussed in Chapter 2, suggest is a move that coaches can use when the teacher is still struggling with the challenge without any progress toward resolution. By making a suggestion, coaches can provide teachers with specific ideas for consideration in resolving a challenge. In this post-lesson conference with Jamie, rather than introducing a new idea for the teacher to resolve the challenge, Coach Jesse's suggestion aims to improve the teacher's idea on lines 56–57. In this way, Coach Jesse shows us how suggestions can be used flexibly.

Starting at line 107, Coach Jesse asks Jamie to **generalize** what moves he could use in the future to keep all students engaged in a group discussion. Jamie notes that he would ensure students see each other as resources, whether they need help with solving the task or they are already making progress with the task. As Coach Jesse pushes Jamie to make explicit a practice to use when planning future lessons, Jamie explains that he would plan advancing questions to help students connect different solution strategies.

Overall, in this post-lesson conference, Coach Jesse used the inquiry routine to help Jamie reflect on the lesson by thinking deeply about what he did and what he could have done differently to involve students in a group discussion and, thus, support their learning. Through the inquiry routine, Coach Jesse was able to build the conversation on the teacher's thinking. Specifically, Coach Jesse could surface and respond to Jamie's ideas about ways to get more students involved even when students in a group are making progress. As a result, Coach Jesse was successfully supporting Jamie's meaningful learning of practices that he can use to address his challenge.

This post-lesson conference equipped Jamie with several different moves to use to involve all members of a group: having students retell another student's explanation (rather than the teacher doing it), asking advancing questions to help students compare different strategies and make connections between them, and pose questions directly to students other than the ones sharing their strategies. Through engaging in rehearsals, Jamie had an opportunity to consider whether and how each of these moves would help him address the challenge of *Involving all members in a group*. Thus, Jamie was able to develop a meaningful understanding of these moves and be prepared to use them effectively in future lessons.

You may also have noticed that Coach Jesse's post-lesson conference plan (Appendix N) was helpful in guiding the conversation during the actual conference. As you can see in the Address the Challenge column of the plan, Coach Jesse was prepared to use the inquiry routine to build the conversation on Jamie's thinking. Coach Jesse created specific questions to *invite* Jamie's thinking and *rehearse* the ideas Jamie could come up with, along with *suggestions* to make when needed. For example, Coach Jesse *invited* Jamie to describe what he "saw happening with that group" (lines 12–13) to surface his thinking, precisely as planned. Coach Jesse engaged Jamie in two rehearsals, both of which she had planned. Although Coach Jesse did not need the *suggestions* she prepared, her preparation of these possible suggestions helped her to make a suggestion to improve an idea Jamie came up with (lines 58–59). Finally, Coach Jesse also created questions to help Jamie make *generalizations* beyond the lesson he had taught. Specifically, the coach asked one of the questions she prepared: "As you move forward, what teacher moves are you going to use to involve all members of a group?" (lines 107–108).

To summarize, we could argue that the post-lesson conference plan provided Coach Jesse with a guide for engaging in a conversation that supported Jamie's learning. Coach Jesse's plan made explicit what she wanted to accomplish in this conference and how she could surface and respond to Jamie's thinking. The plan offered various routes to follow, depending on Jamie's responses. As we mentioned in Chapter 4, a coach's planning for a conference (for both pre- and post-lesson conferences) is similar to a teacher's planning for a lesson. As long as the coach is prepared for a conversation by anticipating what could happen, then they don't have to make decisions in the moment. This allows the coach to free up mental space to address things that were not anticipated.

Summary

One cornerstone of our coaching model, which we have highlighted throughout the preceding chapters, is the importance of planning. A teacher plans for a lesson, and a coach plans for the conferences that take place before and after a lesson. This advanced preparation limits the amount of in-the-moment decisions coaches have to make during the conferences (and teachers have to make in the classroom), which allows them time to listen more actively, question more thoughtfully, and respond in more tailored ways to teacher (or student) thinking.

Although planning for the post-lesson conference is critical to the success of the conference, it is not without its complexities. Here are a few tips that can provide additional guidance as you plan and conduct post-lesson conferences:

- Focus on at least one positive thing that occurred during the lesson—something that the teacher did well and that you want to make sure they continue to do.

- There may be many issues worthy of discussion in the lesson, but it is important to select just a few issues that are likely to yield the most traction. For example, failing to keep track of group progress may be less important than the fact that when students struggled with the task the teacher suggested they use a specific strategy.

- At the end of the conference, you should elicit from the teacher what they have taken away from the conference and how this will impact their next lesson.

- An additional tip comes from Coach Jesse:

    I think one of the biggest challenges is anticipating and preparing for where the conversation might lead with a teacher, and thinking through how to respond. Just like with students, as coaches, we try to think through what could happen and to prepare accordingly. Ultimately, we may not anticipate what actually occurs, but it is helpful to try to think of the possibilities regardless.

Coach Jesse highlights the importance of anticipating in advance of the conference what you think teachers will do and say and how you will respond to them. This is exactly what we are asking teachers to do in the practice of *Anticipating*. Although you will not be able to anticipate everything that will occur, thinking through what might happen will better position you to respond in the moment.

In closing, here is a final piece of advice from Coach Drew:

It is important to identify things done well and areas of growth, while also identifying areas for continued growth. Framing our work around the ideas of student learning, making students' thinking visible, and building on our practice of orchestrating a rich mathematical discussion with our students is key to all conversations including the post-lesson conference.

Putting into Practice

Planning for and Conducting a Post-Lesson Conference

Ask a teacher with whom you have been working to engage in a coaching cycle.

1. Have the teacher complete the Teacher Challenges Tool (Appendix A), meet with you virtually or face to face to discuss the goal and task for the lesson, and complete the Lesson Planning (Appendix E) and Monitoring Tools (Appendix F). (For details, you can refer back to Chapter 3.)
2. Start with reviewing the documents the teacher has completed and determine which challenges you should focus on during the pre-lesson conference. Next, plan for the pre-lesson conference, using the Pre-Lesson Conference Planning Tool (Appendix G), drawing on the Guide for Designing Conferences (Appendix B). Finally, conduct the pre-lesson conference and reflect on the conversation by writing down some notes in your journal. (For details, you can refer back to Chapter 4.)
3. Video-record the lesson taught by the teacher.

You are now ready to plan for and conduct the post-lesson conference.

1. Watch the video recording of the lesson and identify no more than three segments that you want to focus on during the post-lesson conference.
2. Ask the teacher to review the identified segments and to complete the Noticing and Wondering Tool (Appendix K) for each segment and then submit them to you. (Meanwhile, you will also write down your noticings and wonderings.)
3. Plan the post-lesson conference. Identify specific teacher challenge(s) you aim to address through discussing each clip. Review the noticing and wondering tools you and the teacher have completed and decide which noticings and wonderings will help you address the challenges. Complete the Post-Lesson Conference Planning Tool (Appendix L), drawing on the Guide for Designing Conferences (Appendix B).
4. Conduct the post-lesson conference. Reflect on the conversation by writing down some notes in your journal. What did you learn about the teacher's understanding? What surprised you? To what extent could you use the inquiry routine? What do you expect to see in your observation of the lesson as a result of your conversation?

CHAPTER 6
Looking Back and Looking Ahead

The goal of our coaching model is to support ambitious teaching by providing opportunities for teacher learning through teachers' one-on-one interactions with a coach. Specifically, our model focuses on the instructional challenges with which a teacher is grappling and provides tailor-made support to teachers for addressing their challenges. Through a set of eight activities that unfold over three phases of a coaching cycle (Figure 6.1),

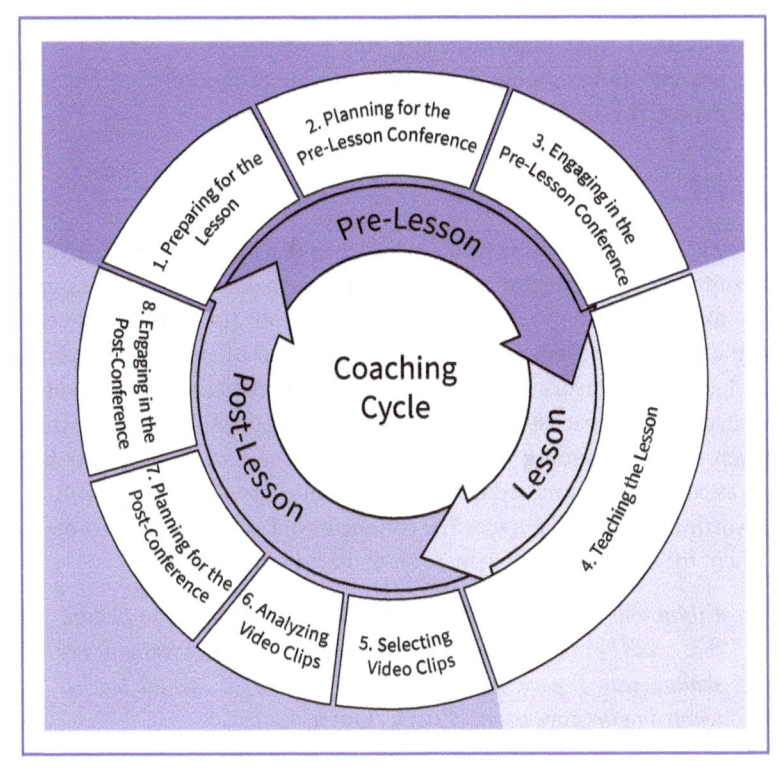

Figure 6.1 • Phases of a coaching cycle

coaches and teachers can carefully plan for and thoughtfully reflect on a lesson. In Chapters 2–5, we described these eight activities and their related tools. To support you in developing a deeper understanding of what each of these activities entails, we explored and analyzed examples of teacher and coach actions and interactions.

In this chapter, we attend to two questions: (1) Why should you use our coaching model? and (2) How can you begin to implement this model?

The Benefits of Our Coaching Model

There are lots of coaching models to choose from, so why choose this one? In her reflection on our coaching model, and her past practices as a coach, Coach Jordan provides her take on the model:

> *I love that more ownership of the process goes onto the teacher. I feel that, in my current practice as a teacher leader, I own too much of the process for myself and don't push enough of the thinking onto the teacher. Doing this work together has really shifted my mindset. I used to expect more out of my sixth-graders than my teachers. I realized that I need to shift my mindset and set higher expectations and have my teachers be a bigger part of the work.*

Coach Jordan's reflection highlights two features of our model that distinguish it from many others: giving teachers "more ownership of the process" and engaging the teacher in more of the thinking. We will discuss each of the features in the following sections.

Giving Teachers More Ownership

Asking teachers to identify specific challenges that they face when learning to support productive discussions gives them a major role in determining the focus of coach–teacher conversations in both pre- and post-lesson conferences. The challenges specify critical aspects of ambitious teaching and, therefore, ensure that coach–teacher conversations will be devoted to issues that impact student learning and engagement. Moreover, when given a voice regarding what to work on, teachers will more likely feel invested in and committed to instructional improvement as they identify a worthwhile issue to pursue. The comments of two of our coaches make salient the value of focusing on what matters to the teacher:

> *I think the teacher challenges really helped us focus on something that could be taken away from the lesson in a deep way versus a very shallow way. It gave us this laser focus for what it was the teacher wanted to improve upon.* (Coach Hunter)

> *I think the teacher challenges were a really important part because they pre-engaged the teacher before our coaching cycle started, to really think about which challenges they wanted to work on. And it gave me an entry point into the conversation that I didn't just make up. This is something that the teacher chose, so this is something we can talk about and I want to support them with their practice.* (Coach Jordan)

Engaging the Teacher in More of the Thinking

In terms of coaching, we argue that building coaching on teacher thinking is necessary for coach–teacher conferences to be effective. That is, to support teacher learning with understanding, coaches must elicit and respond to teacher thinking in ways that will help teachers connect new information to their existing knowledge. In our model, the inquiry routine (*Invite, Rehearse, Suggest*, and *Generalize*) provides a set of moves that coaches can use during their pre- and post-lesson conferences (or indeed any conversation) to build on teacher thinking. These moves can be used flexibly, adapting to the flow of the conversation. Although we argue that every conversation with teachers should begin with an **invite**, what happens next depends on how the teacher responds. For example, when you invite a teacher to share their ideas regarding what they would have done differently to address a challenge that they experienced in an enacted lesson, they might provide a well-reasoned alternative to sufficiently resolve the challenge. As a result, you might choose to move on to **generalize** to ensure that the teacher can extract a practice to be used in the future. In another scenario, the teacher's response might indicate that they have a vague or no alternative way of dealing with the situation. Then, you might need to engage them in a **rehearsal** to play out an alternative they proposed or move on to a **suggestion** for them to consider. The key is to use the routine fluidly to support the discussion and to ensure that the teacher's thinking is driving the conversation. Coach Jesse reflects on what she sees as the value of the inquiry routine:

> *First, it brings the teacher's voice into the conversation. I get the teacher's ideas out there, which is helpful for me because then I'm not making assumptions about what they understand or don't understand. Then, I think the rehearse [move] supports teachers in thinking about students. So, "What might we ask this student?" or "What might the student do, if we did this?" I think it gives teachers some practice. I think the suggest [move] is useful when the teacher's not sure, "Here are some things to try so you're not just struggling to figure it out." Then the generalization, I always think about that with mathematics anyways, but it makes sense with coaching and teaching, too. Just "Why is this important in general?" I think helps teachers carry a practice from lesson to lesson and not see it specific only to this particular lesson.*

The strength of our model is that the challenges provide a focus for coach–teacher conversations, the inquiry routine provides a set of moves for eliciting and responding to teaching thinking during those conversations, and the tools provide support for the planning of those conversations. The coach's comments about the model make clear the value they see in focus and structure:

> *This coaching model is so focused compared to what I used to do. I felt like it was more whack-a-mole, just trying to jump in and do what you need to do and run away. It doesn't have the structure that this coaching model did.* (Coach Hunter)

> *This coaching model really gave me some support and structure and kind of a routine to go through when working with teachers that I was really missing.* (Coach Jesse)

Beginning to Implement Our Coaching Model

Once you have decided to use our coaching model, you may be wondering about how to explain all that is involved in the model to the subset of teachers with whom you will be working. (Remember, you don't need to use this model with all of the teachers. In fact, you may want to begin with two or three teachers so that you can gain familiarity with this process before expanding to a larger number of teachers.) As we discussed in Chapter 1, you must establish a trusting relationship with the teachers you will be coaching before you introduce this coaching model to them (see the resources identified in Chapter 1 for support in building trust). Developing a trusting relationship with the teacher is critical because otherwise teachers might be uncomfortable that our model specifically targets the most challenging aspects of mathematics instruction and requires teachers to grapple with these challenges. Past research on coaching has found that teachers can feel vulnerable and be reluctant to talk about the challenging aspects of their practice (e.g., Heineke, 2013).

> You must establish a trusting relationship with the teachers you will be coaching before you introduce this coaching model to them.

You will need to communicate many aspects of our coaching model with teachers to ensure a shared understanding of the expectations and responsibilities. Here, we will provide some guidance on how to begin to implement the model.

Focusing on the 5 Practices

You might find that teachers who are familiar with the *5 Practices for Orchestrating Productive Mathematics Discussions* (Smith & Stein, 2011, 2018) will be more interested in engaging in this coaching model. Considering that you might be coaching teachers who are not familiar with the 5 practices, you might host a session to talk about the importance of orchestrating productive mathematics discussions and introduce the 5 practices. As teachers develop an interest (or already have an interest) in the 5 practices, it will be easier for you to discuss the goals of coaching the 5 practices.

With the teachers who are committed to using the 5 practices and learning more about orchestrating productive mathematics discussions, you can talk through what our coaching model can accomplish. Toward this end, you can start by sharing the challenges of facilitating high-quality mathematics discussions and then describe how our coaching model aims to support teachers in addressing these challenges. Since our coaching model is designed specifically with the 5 practices in mind, understanding the goal of our model is important for the teachers in setting their expectations.

Setting the Expectations

When you establish a shared understanding of the goals of our coaching model with the teachers you are going to coach, you should describe how a coaching cycle is going to work. You need to ensure that teachers know what is expected of them during a coaching cycle. You can walk through each of the coaching activities, along with the tools the teachers need to complete. You might also refer to completed examples of the tools we shared throughout the book (e.g., the Lesson Planning Tools completed by Emery and Kyle [Appendices H and I, respectively]; the Noticing and Wondering Tool completed by Nicki [Figure 5.3]). This could help teachers better understand the products they are expected to produce as a result of engaging in specific activities.

Be prepared to answer questions from the teachers! Since this will be a new coaching model for them, as much as it is for you, you need to allow teachers time to thoughtfully consider what they are being asked to do. You may want to hold a joint session with all the teachers you will be coaching rather than going through the same process with individual teachers. By talking with teachers as a group, you will also give them the opportunity to build comradery with their colleagues and benefit from the questions and concerns raised by their peers.

Video Recording Lessons

An important point to clarify to the teachers you are going to coach is that video recording each lesson is central to our coaching model. The use of video ensures that both parties are seeing exactly what occurred during the lesson and avoids the need to remember what happened. As reviews of research have found, video recordings make

> Video recordings make it easier to illustrate classroom events that might be difficult to describe otherwise and encourage teacher reflection on their practice.

it easier to illustrate classroom events that might be difficult to describe otherwise and encourage teacher reflection on their practice (Hollingsworth & Clarke, 2017; Santagata et al., 2021; van der Linden et al., 2022). Thus, by using video recordings of a lesson, you and the teacher can have deeper discussions about what actually happened during the lesson.

Although video recording is a valuable tool for analyzing what students are doing and learning during a lesson, the teacher might not be comfortable with being recorded. Coach Avery speaks to the benefits of using video and how she helped to relieve the teacher's anxiety about it:

> *It was super helpful for me using the video as kind of that third point.... It did up the anxiety at first because they were like, "Why are you recording in my room? I don't understand this." But then, afterwards, they were able to see that I'm not doing this to stress them out or to send it to anybody. I'm really doing it so that we can then look back on the lesson together.*

Therefore, to make the teachers feel comfortable with being recorded, it is important to establish with the teacher that the video will not be shared with anyone else. You can also assure the teachers that the video recordings can be erased after you both watch them and will not be used for evaluation purposes. You should also acknowledge that filming oneself can be uncomfortable. You could set up a camera in the classroom a few times without recording so that everyone in the classroom gets used to it. You can also offer to do it!

The best option to record a lesson is probably via Swivl, which is a recording tool that tracks the teacher as they walk around the room, captures student conversations in each group via individual voice recorders, and uploads all recordings to the cloud automatically. However, not every school is equipped with this tool, as it can be costly to purchase. Alternatively, if you can be present in the classroom with the teacher during the teaching of a lesson, you can use a handheld camera (e.g., a smartphone, tablet) to record the lesson as you follow the teacher. This would provide the best sound for teacher–student interactions during group work. You, or the teacher, can also use a stationary camera (e.g., laptop, camera attached to a tripod) to set up in the classroom at an angle that can capture all teacher moves as they walk around the classroom.

Timing of a Coaching Cycle

> The coaching cycle is time intensive.

Another important point to clarify to the teachers you are going to coach is that the coaching cycle is time intensive! Your first thought might be, "I don't have time for this." Many of the coaches we worked with had the same thought!

> It's time-consuming for teachers to be able to go through the coaching cycle. However, I think it's super impactful to teachers, they're going to walk away with something they're going to carry with them. (Coach Hunter)
>
> I think that [Coaching the 5 Practices] requires a lot of time. But that said, it felt very beneficial for both of the teachers that I worked with, and myself! I felt it was very helpful. (Coach Jesse)

Before engaging in a coaching cycle, you should also explain to the teachers the time that is needed to complete a cycle. A coaching cycle typically takes two–three weeks to complete (see Figure 6.2 for one possibility). The amount of time spent in a cycle depends to a great extent on the amount of support the teacher needs to prepare the lesson, specifically in setting a goal and selecting a task (Activity 1). As the teacher gains more experience with the planning process, you will be able to reduce the amount of time it takes to complete one cycle.

Figure 6.2 • Sample timeline for a coaching cycle

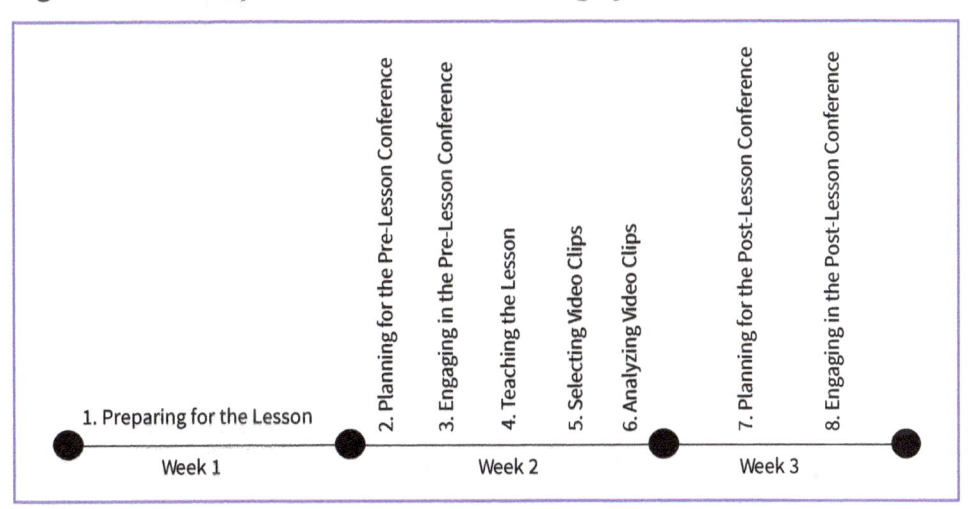

1. Preparing for the Lesson — Week 1
2. Planning for the Pre-Lesson Conference
3. Engaging in the Pre-Lesson Conference
4. Teaching the Lesson
5. Selecting Video Clips
6. Analyzing Video Clips — Week 2
7. Planning for the Post-Lesson Conference
8. Engaging in the Post-Lesson Conference — Week 3

The time allocated for a coaching cycle is necessary to reach the depth of a coach–teacher conversation that is likely to impact a teacher's practice. In our view, and the experiences of coaches, the investment of time should result in improved practices sooner. The coaching cycle encourages insightful reflection on current instruction, thoughtful planning in advance of the lesson, and deep reflection on what occurred during a lesson and its impact on students' learning. These activities are critical for long-term sustained improvement.

Considering the length of time a coaching cycle requires, you might wonder how many cycles you should aim to complete in an academic year. There is no magic number of coaching cycles that are necessary for improving teachers' learning and practice. In fact, a review of research on coaching concluded that there is a lack of evidence to suggest a "dosage effect," and thus, "the quality and focus of coaching may be more important than the actual number of contact hours" (Kraft et al., 2018, p. 565). However, the quality of coaching is as important as the sustained efforts that go into coaching. We encourage you to complete at least one coaching cycle each semester. As you and the teachers you coach get used to engaging in our coaching model, you will be able to increase the number of coaching cycles you complete!

Addressing Teacher Challenges

Another consideration regarding the cyclical work of coaching is related to the teacher's challenges. In each coaching cycle, you will help teachers address specific challenges with the 5 practices. The selection of what challenge(s) to focus on within a cycle or across cycles will depend on the progress the teacher has made and where they are struggling. For example, Jamie and Coach Jesse discussed Challenge 10. *Involving all members of a group* in the pre-lesson conference (Chapter 4). During the teaching of the lesson, Jamie was able to successfully implement the plan to address some aspects of this challenge (i.e., what to do and say when some students in the group were not participating), as Coach Jesse acknowledged at the beginning of the post-lesson conference (Chapter 5). However, during the lesson, Jamie also encountered a new aspect of this challenge that he was not prepared for (i.e., what to do when students in a group weren't talking with each other but had the correct solution). Thus, Coach Jesse planned a post-lesson conference conversation to address Challenge 10. *Involving all members of a group*, with this new perspective.

> The selection of what challenge(s) to focus on within a cycle or across cycles will depend on the progress the teacher has made and where they are struggling.

You might find yourself in a similar situation to Coach Jesse where you need to work on the same challenge within a cycle or even across multiple cycles. You might also feel confident that the teacher is prepared to move on to a new challenge. In that case, you can mark the teacher's progress, which will ensure that they will keep on implementing the practices they have learned, and then discuss a new challenge. The evidence you collect through the lesson video and the pre- and post-lesson conference conversations will inform you about the decision to work on a new challenge.

Online Coaching

Finally, we would like to note that our coaching model can be implemented both face to face and online. Scheduling meetings in person might be difficult at times, so you might feel the need to conduct pre- and post-lesson conferences online. The coaches who implemented our coaching model have engaged in both face-to-face and online coaching conversations. They reported no difference in the effects of coaching.

> Our coaching model can be implemented both face to face and online.

Similarly, other research on online coaching (e.g., Carson & Choppin, 2021) has found positive effects on teacher learning. However, it might be necessary to meet teachers in person if you are working with manipulatives or other tools that are difficult to view through screen sharing in an online meeting.

Conclusion

In this book, we introduced our coaching model for supporting ambitious teaching. Our emphasis throughout this book has been on what you, as the coach, need to do to provide opportunities for teacher learning within a coaching cycle. We have emphasized how to support teachers' lesson planning, engage them in thought-provoking discussions about upcoming lessons, and invite them to reflect on completed lessons and to consider not just specific cases but also more general implications for practice. Through these efforts, teachers will continue to refine their craft and become increasingly more skilled at implementing the 5 practices in ways that support the learning of each and every student.

We also argue that, as you implement our coaching model, you will have the opportunity to learn more about both teaching and coaching. Since reflection on practice is key in learning, we recommend you reflect on the coaching cycles you complete. Nearly a century ago, John Dewey argued that we don't learn from experience, we learn from reflecting on our experiences (1933). Following a pre- or post-lesson conference with a teacher, you should ask yourself whether you accomplished what you set out to do and look for evidence that the teacher learned (or is in the process of learning) what was intended. If you cannot find evidence of teacher learning, you need to determine what might account for this outcome and what you will do differently in the next cycle to better support teacher learning. This is similar to Artzt and Armour-Thomas's (2002) argument in *Becoming a Reflective Mathematics Teacher*:

> *Teachers must also be willing and able to acknowledge problems that may be revealed as a result of the reflective process. Moreover, they must explore the reason for the acknowledged problems, consider more plausible alternatives, and eventually change their thinking and subsequent action in the classroom.* (p. 7)

What Artzt and Armour-Thomas are saying applies to coaches too. Reflection can be supported by making audio or video recordings of conferences (with the teacher's permission, of course) or by keeping a journal. We have invited you throughout this book to record in your journal responses to the *Analyzing Coaching, Stop and Consider,* and *Putting into Practice* activities. You may find that extending this journal to include your ongoing practice may be particularly helpful. For example, before your next conversation with a teacher about identifying tasks and goals, you may want to review what occurred the first time you engaged a teacher in such a discussion (Putting into Practice at the end of Chapter 3) and consider what, if anything, you would do differently. As a coach, Woleck (2010) explained the value of using a journal as follows:

> *Journal writing can serve as a vehicle for revising and processing a coaching experience, looking objectively at the interaction, and reflecting on moves and decisions that were made; the writing is not an evaluative piece of writing but is undertaken in the spirit of self-reflection and growth.* (p. 147)

Coaching is not easy. What we are asking you to do will take some time to *get good at*, and it may require rethinking current practices. But through continued reflection and commitment, the journey can be a rewarding one. We close the book with a quote from Coach Jordan:

> *This coaching model has a focus and a framework. The focus was very clear. We were going after the 5 practices work. Now, there are a lot of things going on in that, but the overarching goal was to facilitate mathematical conversations in the classroom. So, I think that [this coaching model] helped me in my work to really be focused on what we were going to talk about.*

APPENDICES

APPENDIX A: Teacher Challenges Tool

Below is a list of challenges that teachers have reported facing when trying to implement ambitious teaching practices. Review the 19 challenges listed and identify up to 5 challenges that you struggle with. For each identified challenge briefly describe how the challenge plays out in your classroom.

	CHALLENGES	DESCRIPTION	THE CHALLENGE IN MY CLASSROOM
GOALS AND TASKS	1. Identifying learning goals	Goal needs to focus on what students will learn as a result of engaging in the task, not on what students will do. Clarity on goals sets the stage for everything else!	
	2. Identifying a doing-mathematics task	While doing-mathematics tasks provide the greatest opportunities for student learning, they are not readily available in some textbooks. Teachers may need to adapt an existing task, find a task in another resource, or create a task.	
	3. Ensuring alignment between task and goals	Even with learning goals specified, teachers may select a task that does not allow students to make progress on those particular goals.	
	4. Launching a task to ensure student access	Teachers need to provide access to the context and the mathematics in the launch but not so much that the mathematical demands are reduced and key ideas are given away.	

	CHALLENGES	DESCRIPTION	THE CHALLENGE IN MY CLASSROOM
ANTICIPATING	5. Moving beyond the way you solve a problem	Teachers often feel limited by their own experience. They know how to solve a task but may not have access to the array of strategies that students are likely to use.	
	6. Being prepared to help students who cannot get started on a task	Teachers need to be prepared to provide support to students who do not know how to begin work on the task so that they can make progress without being told exactly what to do and how.	
	7. Creating questions that move students toward the mathematical goals	The questions teachers ask need to be driven by the mathematical goals of the lesson. The focus needs to be on ensuring that students understand the key mathematical ideas, not just on producing a solution to the task.	
MONITORING	8. Trying to understand what students are thinking	Students do not always articulate their thinking clearly. It can be quite demanding for teachers, in the moment, to figure out what a student means or is trying to say. This requires teachers to listen carefully to what students are saying and to ask questions that help them better explain what they are thinking.	
	9. Keeping track of group progress—which groups you visited and what you left them to work on	As teachers are running from group to group, providing support, they need to be able to keep track of what each group is doing and what they left students to work on. Also, it is important for a teacher to return to a group in order to determine whether the advancing question given to them helped them make progress.	
	10. Involving all members of a group	All individuals in the group need to be challenged to answer assessing and advancing questions. For individuals to benefit from the thinking of their peers, they need to be held accountable for listening to and adding on, repeating and summarizing what others are saying.	

(Continued)

113

APPENDIX A (*Continued*)

CHALLENGES	DESCRIPTION	THE CHALLENGE IN MY CLASSROOM
11. Selecting only solutions that are most relevant to learning goals	Teachers need to select a limited number of solutions that will help achieve the mathematical goals of the lesson. Sharing solutions that are not directly relevant can take a discussion off track, and sharing too many solutions (even if they are relevant) can lead to student disengagement.	
12. Expanding beyond the usual student presenters	Teachers often select students who are articulate and on whom they can count for a coherent explanation. Teachers need to look for opportunities to position each and every student as a presenter and help students develop their ability to explain their thinking.	
13. Deciding what work to share when the majority of students were not able to solve the task and your initial goal no longer seems obtainable	Teachers may on occasion find that the task was too challenging for most students and that they were not able to engage as intended. This situation requires the teacher to modify her initial plan and determine how to focus the discussion so students can make progress.	
14. Moving forward when a key strategy is not produced by students	In planning the lesson, a teacher may determine that a particular strategy is critical to accomplishing the lesson goals. If the success of a lesson hinges on the availability of a particular strategy, then the teacher needs to be prepared to introduce the strategy through some means.	
15. Determining how to sequence incorrect and/or incomplete solutions	Teachers often choose not to share work that is not complete and correct for fear that students will remember incorrect methods. Sharing solutions that highlight key errors in a domain can provide all students with an opportunity to analyze why a particular approach does not work. Sharing incomplete or partial solutions can provide all students with the opportunity to consider how such work can be connected to more robust solutions.	

SELECTING & SEQUENCING

CHALLENGES	DESCRIPTION	THE CHALLENGE IN MY CLASSROOM
16. Keeping the entire class engaged and accountable during individual presentations	Often, the sharing of solutions turns into a show and tell or a dialogue between the teacher and the presenter. The rest of the class needs to be held accountable for understanding and making sense of the solutions that are presented.	
17. Ensuring key mathematical ideas are made public and remain the focus	It is possible to have students share and discuss a lot of interesting solutions and never get to the point of the lesson. It is critical that the key mathematical ideas that are being targeted in the lesson are explicitly discussed.	
18. Making sure that you do not take over the discussion and do the explaining	As students are presenting their solutions, the teacher needs to ask questions that engage the presenters and the rest of the class in explaining and making sense of the solutions. There is a temptation for the teacher to take over and tell the students what they need to know. When this happens, opportunities for learning are diminished. Remember whoever is doing the talking is doing the thinking!	
19. Running out of time	Teachers may not have enough time to conduct the whole class discussion the way they had planned it. In such cases it is important to come up with a Plan B that provides some closure to the lesson but does not turn into telling.	

CONNECTING

Source: From *The 5 Practices in Practice: Successfully Orchestrating Mathematics Discussions in Your Middle School Classroom* by M. S. Smith and M. G. Sherin, 2019, Corwin.

A downloadable version of this tool can be found at **https://qrs.ly/7jfti55**.

APPENDIX B: Guide for Designing Conferences

Identify the Challenge	Address the Challenge	Guiding Rationale

4. Launching a task to ensure student access.	i. Invite the teacher to explain how they plan to launch the task so that all students will be able to enter the task and understand what they are expected to do.
	• *You have selected the Max's Dog Food task as the basis for your lesson on the division of fractions. How will you present the task to your students? What will you do to ensure that students understand the context, the language, and the mathematics needed to begin work on the task?*
	
	ii. If the teacher is unsure about how to set-up or launch the task, make a suggestion about what they might do to ensure that students can access the task.
	• For each suggestion, consider what you could learn and how it would benefit your students.
	  – *Ask the students about having and feeding a dog (e.g., How many have a dog? Who is responsible for feeding the dog? Does anyone have a big bag of dog food? How do you decide how much the dog gets from the big bag each day?)*
	  – *Engage students in reading about Max's Dog Food (e.g., Can someone read the problem? What do we know about Max?)*
	  – *Consider language in the problem (e.g., what is "a serving"? How big is Max's serving?)*
	  – *Make sure students know what they are trying to figure out (e.g., What are we trying to find? If you were Max's owner, why would you want to know this?)*
	  – *Explain how students will work and what resources they will have available (e.g., you will work in your groups, there are materials in your buckets you can use as needed – paper, markers, fraction bars, rulers.)*
	
	iii. Push for generalization. Ask the teacher what they will do to plan a task launch in future lessons that will ensure student access and how this will support student learning and engagement.
		High-level tasks have multiple entry points that allow students to approach the task differently based on their prior knowledge and experiences. However, selecting a high-level task does not mean students will automatically make sense of the task and start working on it. Students need to understand what the task is asking of them.
		
		To ensure student access to the task, the teacher should plan a launch with 4 crucial aspects in mind:
		– Key contextual features of the task,
		– Key mathematical ideas of the task,
		– Development of a common language,
		– Maintenance of the cognitive demand of the task (Jackson et al., 2012[1]).
		
		By ensuring student access and maintaining cognitive demand during the launch, you will provide students with the opportunity to engage with the task, which will, in turn, increase student participation in the discussion about the task.
		
		--- 	
		[1] Jackson, K. J., Shahan, E. C., Gibbons, L. K., & Cobb, P. A. (2012). Launching complex tasks. *Mathematics Teaching in the Middle School, 22*(5), 304–307.

GOALS AND TASKS

Identify the Challenge	Address the Challenge	Guiding Rationale
5. Moving beyond the way they solved the problem.	i. Invite the teacher to consider strategies for solving the task beyond the one they produced. • I noticed that you solved the Max's Dog Food task using the division algorithm. Think about different representations that you might use—a diagram, a table, a number line. What would a solution strategy with each of these representations look like? Are these strategies that you think your students could produce? ii. If the teacher is unsure about how to use any of the representations mentioned to solve the task, make a suggestion about a few representations that students might use that will help advance the learning goal. • Let's focus on drawing a diagram. How could I represent each of the pounds of dog food? [Draw a rectangle to represent each pound and a half of the rectangle to represent a half of a pound.] Since a serving is $\frac{3}{4}$ of a pound, how could you show the number of servings in each pound? [Divide each pound into 4ths and shade in 3 of them.] How can you figure out how many servings there will be? [Determine how many $\frac{3}{4}$'s there are altogether. What will you do with the $\frac{1}{2}$ pound left over? Determine what fraction of a serving it is.] How could you use of this strategy help you achieve the lesson goals? • Let's take a look at the number line strategy (shown below). What thinking do you suspect is behind this strategy? Is this something you think your students would do? Why or why not? How could a solution using this strategy help you achieve the lesson goals? 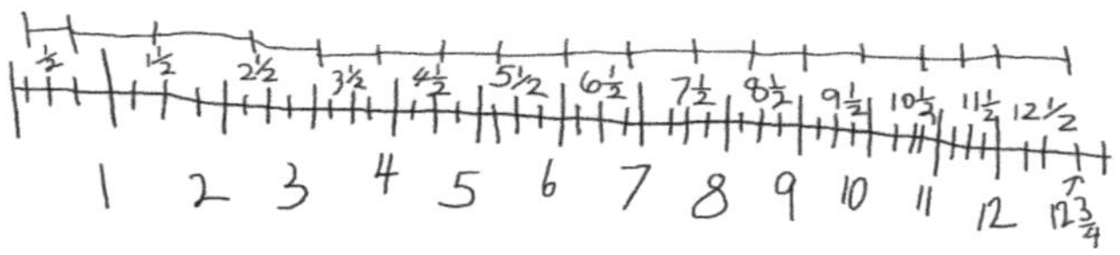 [number line from 1 to 12¾ with half markings: ¼, ½, 2¼, 3, 3¾, 4½, 5¼, 6, 6¾, 7½, 8¼, 9, 9¾, 10½, 11¼, 12, 12¾ above numbers 1–12¾]	Since students' prior knowledge and experiences are not the same as the teacher's, students are likely to approach tasks in ways that differ from the teacher's method—but it may be a valid method that makes sense to them. Anticipating student responses requires thinking about the variety of ways in which mathematical ideas can be represented, including ways that may be accessible to students based on their prior knowledge and experiences—visual (diagrams, graphs, and pictures), symbolic (numeric and algebraic), verbal, contextual, and physical (manipulatives and models). By anticipating the ways in which students might solve a task (both correctly or incorrectly) prior to a lesson, you will be better positioned to support student thinking during the lesson because you will be able to recognize specific strategies (and variations) and therefore be able to ask questions that clarify students' understandings and advance their thinking.

ANTICIPATING

(Continued)

APPENDIX B (*Continued*)

Identify the Challenge	Address the Challenge	Guiding Rationale
ANTICIPATING	• Let's look at a numeric strategy (shown below). What thinking do you suspect is behind this strategy? Is this something you think your students would do? Why or why not? How could use of this strategy help you achieve the lesson goals? [Goal 3 focuses on showing the connection between different representations. By sharing this strategy students can explore the relationship between the visual and numeric strategies and in so doing, show why the numeric strategy makes sense.] $$50 \div 3 = \frac{?}{4}$$ $$\begin{array}{r} 16\,r\,2 \\ 3\overline{)50} \\ \underline{3} \\ 20 \\ \underline{18} \\ 2 \end{array}$$ iii. Push for a generalization. Ask the teacher what they will do when planning future lessons to create different solution strategies and how this will help them prepare to support student learning during the lesson.	

Identify the Challenge	Address the Challenge	Guiding Rationale

6. Being prepared to help students who cannot get started on a task.	i. Invite the teacher to explain what they will do if a student does not begin to work on the task.
	
	• *What have you done in previous situations when students could not get started? Is there a similar task that students did previous work on? What strategies did they use in those tasks? Would those strategies be helpful here? What is a question you could ask that would help activate students' prior knowledge?*
	
	ii. Engage the teacher in rehearsing possible alternative teacher actions to help students enter the task without taking over their thinking. [Select a move or question that the teacher identified above and use the teacher-generated move or question as the starting point and go from there. If the teacher does not identify a move or question, then suggest a starting point and go from there.]
	
	• *You indicated that you would ask the student 'What do you know about the problem?' I will play the student and you can be the teacher.*
	
	T: *What do you know about the problem?*
	
	S: *It is about dog food.*
	
	T: *???*
	
	What will you ask next? What is it you want to find out?
	
	iii. If the teacher is unsure about what they should say or do if a student cannot get started, make a suggestion about what they might say or do.
	
	• For each suggestion listed below, consider what you could learn from a student's response and how the suggestion could help the student gain access to the task.
	  – *Invite the student to tell you what they know about Max's dog food.*
	  – *Ask the student to identify what the problem is about or what they are trying to figure out.*
	  – *Ask the student if they can draw a picture to represent the situation.*
	  – *Make available squares of paper and tell the students that a square represents a bag of dog food and invite the student to model the situation.*
	
	iv. Push for a generalization. Ask the teacher what they will do when planning for future lessons to help students who cannot get started on a task and how this will support students learning and engagement.
		Even after a successful launch, some students might still be unclear about what they are supposed to do. These students might not be connecting what they already know to what the task is asking from them. Such confusion can end up taking away from the time spent focusing on the core learning goals and math concepts of the lesson.
		
		To help students in getting started on the task, teachers should identify what students might struggle with and prepare a strategy to use (e.g., questions to ask, materials to use, model the problem). When deciding on how to support students' entry to the task, teachers should be careful to maintain the cognitive demand of the task.
		
		By being prepared to support students who struggle to get started, you will not have to react in the moment, which might cause you to remove the challenging aspects of the task. When you help students without taking over their thinking, students will be able to come up with their own strategies and have the opportunity to learn. This will also contribute to students' capacity to persevere in the face of struggle.

ANTICIPATING

(Continued)

119

APPENDIX B (Continued)

7. Creating questions that move students toward the goals of the lesson.

ANTICIPATING

Identify the Challenge	Address the Challenge	Guiding Rationale
7. Creating questions that move students toward the goals of the lesson.	i. Invite the teacher to explain how their advancing questions will move students toward the goals of the lesson. • You indicated that after you had the student explain the number line they had created, you would ask them if they could solve the problem another way. What is it you hope to learn from having a student produce a second solution strategy? How will this help you get to the key mathematical ideas you have targeted in the lesson? ii. Engage the teacher in rehearsing possible actions the teacher could take to move students toward the goals of the lesson. • You indicated that you had 3 goals for the lesson: – When you find "how many ___ are in ___?" you are doing division. That is, in $a \div b$ you are trying to find how many times b is contained in a. – When dividing by a fraction the remainder is expressed as a fraction of the divisor. – Division situations can be represented in different ways and connections can be made between symbolic, physical, pictorial, and contextual representations. Let's work on the second goal. What question(s) can you ask the students who produced the number line in order to focus on this goal? iii. If the teacher is unsure about what advancing question will move students toward the lesson goals, then make a suggestion about what they might say or do. • You want the students to understand that the $\frac{1}{2}$ pound that is left over needs to be represented as a fraction of a serving. Suppose I ask, "You had $2\frac{1}{2}$ lb. left after 16 servings. What part of a serving is this? Can you use your number line to investigate the relationship between pounds and servings?" What might you learn from asking this question? How is this different from the question you initially planned to ask? iv. Push for a generalization. Ask the teacher what they will do in future lessons to create questions that move students toward the goals of a lesson and how these questions will support student learning.	Engaging students with high-level tasks doesn't guarantee that they will learn the mathematics behind the task and achieve the learning goal. Successfully solving the task or making progress toward a "correct" solution doesn't mean that students understand what they are doing and why. To move students toward the goals of the lesson, teachers should create assessing and advancing questions that are guided by the goals of the lesson. Although assessing questions are used to surface student thinking and understand where students are, advancing questions move students from where they are toward the learning goal. When planning the lesson, teachers can create these questions for each of the correct and incorrect anticipated solution strategies. By creating assessing and advancing questions ahead of time, you will be prepared to respond to and support student thinking and, as a result, ensure that students don't just produce correct solutions to the task but also understand the key mathematical ideas you targeted.

MONITORING

Identify the Challenge	Address the Challenge	Guiding Rationale
8. Trying to understand what students are thinking.	i. Invite the teacher to explain what questions they will ask to determine how students are thinking about the problem and what it is students understand. • I noticed in your plan that when students have used an appropriate strategy and produced a correct answer, that you have not identified any questions to ask them beyond "How did you get that? Can you do it another way?" Imagine that a student produced the solution using this strategy: $$50 \div \frac{3}{4}$$ $$\frac{4}{4} \div \frac{3}{4}$$ $$\begin{array}{r} 16\,{}^{2}/{}_{3} \\ 3\overline{)50} \\ \underline{3} \\ 20 \\ \underline{18} \\ 2 \end{array}$$ – What does use of this strategy imply about what the student understands? – To what extent does the use of the strategy mean that the student understands the key ideas reflected in your goals? – What questions could you ask to determine what the student understands about fraction division? – How will these questions help you to support the student's learning?	During the lesson, teachers tend to make assumptions about student thinking by looking at student work and listening to student conversations. However, these observations provide limited information about student understanding. Whether or not students come up with a correct strategy to solve the task, if teachers fail to uncover student thinking, they cannot move students beyond where they currently are. To support student learning without telling them what to do and how, teachers should create assessing questions so students can explain their thinking. When creating these questions, teachers should focus on understanding what students are doing and why, rather than trying to guide students to the correct answer. By being equipped with questions to make students' thinking visible, you will be better positioned to understand what students are doing and why. A clear understanding of student thinking will then enable you to ask questions that will advance students toward the learning goal based on their own thinking.

(Continued)

APPENDIX B (Continued)

Identify the Challenge	Address the Challenge	Guiding Rationale
MONITORING	ii. Engage the teacher in rehearsing a possible sequence of questions that will illuminate students' thinking. • You indicated that you asked the student "How did you get that?" What will you ask as follow-up questions? I will play the student and you can be the teacher. T: How did you get that? S: I changed $12\frac{1}{2}$ to an improper fraction, found a common denominator, then divided the numerators. T: ??? What will you ask next? What is it you want to find out? iii. If the teacher is unsure about what question they will ask next, make a suggestion about possible follow-up questions. • Suppose you asked the student questions like: – What does $12\frac{1}{2}$ represent? What does $\frac{3}{4}$ represent? – Where did $\frac{50}{4}$ come from? What does it represent? – Why did you divide $\frac{50}{4}$ by $\frac{3}{4}$? What were you trying to find? – What does $16\frac{2}{3}$ represent? – Does this answer make sense? What might you learn from asking these questions? How will the information you gather help you in determining whether the students understand the mathematical ideas you were targeting? iv. Push for a generalization. Ask the teacher what they will do when planning future lessons to make student thinking clear and visible and how this will help the teacher support student learning.	

Identify the Challenge	Address the Challenge	Guiding Rationale
9. Considering ways to keep track of group progress.	i. Invite the teacher to explain how they plan to keep track of what they learn from visiting student groups as students work on the task, as well as the advancing question(s) they will leave students to work on. • You have anticipated different ways that students might solve the Max's Dog Food task and the strategies that will be most useful in achieving the goals of the lesson. How will you keep track of which students make a visual diagram, create a double number line, or use a common denominator so that you will be able to make decisions about who to have present during the whole-class discussion? How will you recall what you left the group to work on once you have moved on to work with another group? ii. Engage the teacher in rehearsing possible actions the teacher can take to keep track of groups' progress. • Suppose one group of students created the visual diagram below. What would you want to keep track of so that when you were preparing for the whole-class discussion you could decide whether or not this solution strategy would help you highlight the mathematical goals you have set? What question would you leave the group that used this strategy to work on and how will you recall that question when you return to the group? [hand-drawn visual diagram showing rows of boxes numbered 1–16 over 2–16, with "16/3" noted]	When students are working in groups, it is difficult to keep track of student progress. Teachers can forget to return to a group or skip a group while visiting others. It is also easy to forget which advancing questions a group was left to work on. To keep track of student progress, teachers should devise a way to record which groups they have visited, what they have done, and what advancing question they have left students to work on. Using the monitoring chart is one way to manage these issues. By developing a plan to keep track of group progress, you will be able to record which solution strategies students used and what aspects of certain solution strategies you might want to highlight during the whole-class discussion. Additionally, while more than one group may have used the same strategy, recording the names of which group members have shared previously can help you make sure that you are giving all students a chance to share their work.

(Continued)

APPENDIX B (*Continued*)

Identify the Challenge	Address the Challenge	Guiding Rationale
	iii. If the teacher is unsure about what what they should try to capture and/or how they can keep track of what they notice and asks, make a suggestion about what might be important to note and how to record it. • Could you use your monitoring chart to record which students are doing what? What are the noteworthy features of the solution strategy that you might want to capture? For example, in the who/what column for the visual diagram strategy, you might indicate the name of the students who were in the group who produced the strategy as well as noteworthy features of the strategy, such as "Represented 12 $\frac{1}{2}$ bags, divided bags into 4ths, grouped 3 $\frac{1}{4}$ 5, showed $\frac{1}{3}$ lb. as $\frac{2}{3}$rds, correct answer." You could keep track of the question you left the group to pursue by highlighting or underlining it if it is one you anticipated. Or, if you ask a different question, you could add it to your advancing questions as shown on the chart below. | Strategy	Assessing Questions	Advancing Questions	Who and What	Order
---	---	---	---	---
B- Visual Diagram E- Double Number Line Uses a visual model or a double number line to show 16 groups of $\frac{3}{4}$. Writes 16 $\frac{2}{3}$ as the answer.	• Can you tell me what you did? • Why did you divide your diagram/ number line into 4ths? • What does $\frac{1}{4}$th represent in the diagram/ number line?	• Where do you see 16 $\frac{2}{3}$ in your diagram/ number line? What does it mean? • What does the $\frac{2}{3}$ represent? • How much dog food is left over? • Why is the answer 16 $\frac{2}{3}$ and not 16 $\frac{1}{2}$?		| iv. Push for a generalization. Ask the teacher what they will do in future lessons to keep track of student thinking and how this will be useful to them as the lesson progresses.	

MONITORING

Identify the Challenge	Address the Challenge	Guiding Rationale
10. Involving all members of a group.	i. Invite the teacher to consider what they will do to involve all the members of a group in a discussion, in the event that one group member dominates the conversation. • Suppose a group has solved the problem using a visual diagram as you had anticipated. *(hand-drawn diagram of arrays of numbered squares labeled "Model")* • When you ask the group of 4 to explain what they did, one student in the group (S4) provides an explanation while the other members of the group remain silent. How will you know if the other students in the group understand what S4 is explaining? What can you do to involve other members of the groups? ii. Engage the teacher in rehearsing a possible sequence of questions that would provide them with insight regarding what the other members of the group understand about the strategy. • You indicated that you would involve other students in the group by asking "Do you agree with what S4 just said? What will you ask as follow-up questions? I will play the students and you can be the teacher.	Engaging students in group work doesn't necessarily mean that students will work together productively or that the work produced is understood by all members of the group. It is possible for one student in the group to take over and for the other students to go along. To involve all members of a group, teachers need to hold every student accountable for participating in the discussion and benefiting from each other's thinking. For example, teachers can pose questions to encourage participation (e.g., Can you repeat what X just said? Can you restate that in your own words? What do you think of that? Do you agree with X?). By involving all group members in the discussion, you will ensure that every student has the opportunity to think deeply about mathematics, rather than mindlessly following another student's thinking. Through their participation in group work, students will also have a chance to learn from each other and build on each other's thinking.

MONITORING

(Continued)

APPENDIX B (Continued)

Identify the Challenge	Address the Challenge	Guiding Rationale

MONITORING	T: Do you agree with what he just said?
	S1: YES
	S2: YES
	S3: YES
	T: ???
	What will you ask next and to whom? What is it you want to find out? Why is this important?
	
	iii. If the teacher is unsure about what questions they will ask next, make a suggestion about possible actions they can take.
	
	• Suppose that you asked a series of questions following S4's explanation and S1–3's agreement, targeting specific students (S1, S2 or S3), such as:
	  – Can you explain what S4 said in your own words?
	  – Why does this approach work?
	  – What does the answer $16\frac{2}{3}$ mean in this problem about Max's dog food?
	What could you learn from asking these questions? What message would it send to the group?
	
	• Suppose instead of waiting until S4 finished their explanation you interrupted them while they were explaining the strategy they used and asked another member of the group to continue the explanation or to recap what had been said. What would be the benefit of this approach? What message would it send to the group?
	
	iv. Push for a generalization. Ask the teacher what they will do in future lessons to hold all members of a group accountable for participating in a discussion and how this will support student learning and engagement.	

Identify the Challenge	Address the Challenge	Guiding Rationale

11. Selecting only solution strategies that are most relevant to learning goals.	i. Invite the teacher to explain why they think it is important to share every solution strategy produced by students during the whole-class discussion.
	
	• *I noticed that you plan to share all the correct solution strategies during the whole-class discussion. What do you see as the advantages and disadvantages of sharing all the strategies? Which solution strategies will best help you accomplish the goals for this lesson?*
	
	ii. If the teacher is unsure about why you would limit the number of solution strategies to be presented, make a suggestion about things they should consider in selecting student strategies.
	
	• *While sharing all the solution strategies that students produce gives all students a chance to share their thinking, acknowledges their effort, and motivates them to produce something, in deciding how many and which strategies to have shared, consider these factors:*
	
	    – *The amount of class time available for the discussion*
	    – *The attention span of students*
	    – *The extent to which a strategy has the potential to advance student learning toward the lesson goals*
	
	• *If your students produce all the strategies you have anticipated, will you have time to discuss them all? Will students stay engaged through all of presentations? Will a discussion of each and every strategy advance the goals of the lesson? (Review each strategy on the monitoring chart and consider it in terms of the goals—diagram, number line, ratio table, repeated addition, repeated subtraction, common denominator.)*
	
	iii. Push for a generalization. Ask the teacher what they will do in future lessons to select solution strategies that clearly embody the learning goals and how this will support student learning.
		Based on their prior knowledge and experiences, students approach a task in different ways. During whole-group discussion, sharing different solution strategies allows students to see the connections among different strategies and deepen their understanding. However, sharing every solution strategy is time consuming and can distract the discussion from the key mathematical idea.
		
		To achieve the goal of the lesson, teachers should purposefully select student solution strategies to be shared publicly. When selecting solution strategies, teachers should consider similarities and differences among various strategies and identify ones that are connected to the key mathematical idea. It is also important to select incorrect or incomplete responses if they can further students' understanding of the targeted mathematical ideas.
		
		By being purposeful about selecting only solution strategies that are relevant to the learning goal, the teacher can make the key mathematical ideas explicit. It will also help the teacher use class time efficiently and effectively. Moreover, selecting incorrect or incomplete solution strategies helps student understanding by showing why certain strategies do not work or engaging students in completing a strategy that started from someone else's reasoning.

SELECTING AND SEQUENCING

(Continued)

APPENDIX B (Continued)

Identify the Challenge	Address the Challenge	Guiding Rationale
12. Expanding beyond the usual presenters.	i. Invite the teacher to consider the costs and benefits of asking for volunteers to present solution strategies. • You indicated that when it is time for the whole-class discussion you will ask for volunteers to present their solution strategies. What do you think will happen? Who is likely to volunteer? What will you do if the presented work does not help you focus on the math you have targeted? Could you identify students to present rather than asking for volunteers? How could you do this? What might be the benefit in doing this? ii. If the teacher is unsure about how to identify presenters other than asking for volunteers, make a suggestion about strategies they could use. • Consider the following strategies for identifying specific students to present rather than asking for volunteers and the possible benefits of each strategy. Use a monitoring chart to list the strategies you anticipated and, as you monitor, keep track of which students use which strategies. – When you are ready to begin the discussion, invite students to present who have produced one of the desired strategies and, if possible, have not recently shared their thinking with the class. – Identify a student who has used one of the desired strategies but has not completed it, and use this as an opportunity to engage the entire class in a discussion and to involve a student who is not a usual presenter. – Identify one or more students who have good ideas about how to approach the problem but have not executed them yet. Ask these students to share their thoughts about how to get started early on as students work on the task (rough-draft talk). iii. Push for a generalization. Ask the teacher what they will do in future lessons to make sure they select specific students to share their thinking publicly and how this will broaden participation and contribute to students' learning and the development of mathematical identities.	A decision that is as important as selecting solution strategies is the decision of who to select to share their strategy. Teachers often tend to ask for volunteers or count on their "go to" students who they know will explain their thinking well. However, this approach limits other students' opportunity to learn how to express their thinking clearly and to be seen by their peers as mathematically competent. To give every student a chance to share their ideas over time, teachers should make deliberate decisions about choosing presenters. Teachers can ensure equal participation by keeping track of presenters over time and intentionally selecting students to present who have not recently had an opportunity to do so. Inviting students who do not have complete solution strategies can help teachers overcome the limitation of selecting only presenters with complete work. By expanding beyond usual presenters, you will provide all students with the opportunity to present their work in front of other students. This will help them develop skills to communicate their ideas and respond to other ideas by justifying their thinking. Moreover, you will be sending the message that each and every student is capable of doing mathematics, which will have a positive effect on students' identity development.

SELECTING AND SEQUENCING

Identify the Challenge	Address the Challenge	Guiding Rationale
13. Deciding what work to share when the majority of students were not able to solve the task and the initial goal is no longer attainable.	i. Invite the teacher to consider what they will do if the goals they have set do not appear to be obtainable. • You indicated that as a result of engaging in this lesson you wanted students to understand that: – When you find "how many ___ are in ___?" you are doing division. That is, in $a \div b$ you are trying to find how many times b is contained in a. – When dividing by a fraction, the remainder is expressed as a fraction of the divisor. – Division situations can be represented in different ways and connections can be made between symbolic, physical, pictorial, and contextual representations. What will you do if many students struggle to solve the problem (e.g., can't model the situation, use repeated addition or repeated subtraction unsuccessfully), making it difficult to accomplish what you set out to do? How will you identify what students are struggling with? Which solution strategies can you use to help other students move beyond these struggles and make progress toward the learning goal? ii. If the teacher is unsure about what to do if the task is too challenging and the original goal is not attainable, make a suggestion about strategies they could use. • If the majority of students are having difficulty coming up with a viable approach to solving the Max's Dog Food task, you need to consider what is challenging and how to move beyond the challenge. Consider what each of the following will accomplish in terms of the lesson goals: – Challenge: The students can't figure out how to represent the situation with a drawing. Possible option: Identify a student who has successfully drawn a diagram and ask them to share the drawing with the class. Give the students the opportunity to ask questions about the drawing. If needed, ask the class about the drawing—where is $12\frac{1}{2}$, why is it divided into fourths? How are halves and fourths related? How many fourths are there in the picture? What are you trying to figure out? Then let the class determine how to use the drawing to determine the solution.	At times a task might prove to be too challenging for students in the class. This may be due to a lack of prior knowledge or students may get sidetracked by aspects of the task that are not related to the key mathematical ideas targeted. As a result, student struggle might be unproductive, meaning that they might not be able to make progress toward the learning goal. To decide what work to share when the majority of students are not able to solve the task or the learning goal is not obtainable, teachers should consider an alternative way of continuing the lesson without reducing cognitive demand of the task. Prior to the lesson, teachers should anticipate aspects of the task that might be too challenging for the students. Then, teachers should consider how to select and sequence strategies that will help students clarify the aspects they are struggling with. By considering ahead of time what work to share to move students beyond their struggle, you will guarantee that task completion won't become the goal of the lesson. This will ensure that students will make progress toward the learning goal and their opportunity to learn won't be sacrificed.

SELECTING AND SEQUENCING

(Continued)

APPENDIX B (Continued)

Identify the Challenge	Address the Challenge	Guiding Rationale
	– Challenge: The students don't realize the equivalence of $12\frac{1}{2}$, $12\frac{2}{4}$, and $\frac{50}{4}$. Possible option: Pose the following situation—"One of my students in the other class said that $12\frac{1}{2}$ was the same as $\frac{25}{50}$ or $\frac{50}{4}$. Take a minute in your small groups to decide if you agree and why." Identify a student who figured this out and explain it to the class. Ask the class lots of questions about this equivalence. iii. Push for a generalization. Ask the teacher what they will do in future lessons to address student challenges, even if it means not accomplishing the lesson goals and how this will support student learning.	

14. Moving forward when a key strategy is not produced by students.	i. Invite the teacher to consider which solution strategies are critical to achieve the goals they have established for the lesson.
	• You indicated that as a result of engaging in this lesson that you wanted students to understand that:
	  – When you find "how many ____ are in ____?" you are doing division. That is, in $a \div b$ you are trying to find how many times b is contained in a.
	  – When dividing by a fraction, the remainder is expressed as a fraction of the divisor.
	  – Division situations can be represented in different ways and connections can be made between symbolic, physical, pictorial, and contextual representations.
	You anticipated that students would use several different strategies to solve the Max's Dog Food task (diagram, number line, common denominator, repeated addition, repeated subtraction, ratio table, keep-change-flip). Which strategies will most help you achieve your lesson goals? Why might it be helpful to identify such strategies in advance of the lesson?
	
	ii. If the teacher is unsure about what strategies will help them accomplish the lesson goals, make a suggestion about which strategies to consider and which ones to ignore.
		When planning the lesson, the teacher identifies key solution strategies that should be shared to achieve the learning goal. However, when these essential strategies are not produced by students, the teacher might try "saving the lesson" by "telling" the key strategy and, as a result, reduce the cognitive demand of the task.
		
		To move forward when a key strategy is not produced by the students, teachers should be prepared to introduce this strategy without taking over student thinking. First, teachers should determine, among the anticipated solution strategies, what strategies are essential to make the key mathematical ideas public. Then, for each essential strategy, teachers should either find or create a complete solution using the strategy that can be shared. Finally, teachers should share these strategies during the whole-class discussion in ways that engage students in thinking, reasoning, and sense-making.

SELECTING AND SEQUENCING

Identify the Challenge	Address the Challenge	Guiding Rationale
	- While there are many correct ways to solve the Max's Dog Food task, not all solution strategies will help you highlight the ideas you have targeted. For example, three strategies—creating a diagram, constructing a number line, and finding the common denominator—could collectively help you accomplish all three lesson goals. For each of these strategies, explain which goals could be targeted, and identify the questions you would need to ask to highlight the targeted ideas. - Are there other anticipated strategies that could help you achieve the goals? Which ones? What questions would you need to ask to highlight the targeted ideas? - Why might it be helpful to identify strategies that will help you accomplish the lesson goal in advance of the lesson? iii. Push for generalization. Ask the teacher what they will do in future lessons to be prepared to move forward in case a key strategy is not produced by students and how this will help them to support student learning.	By deciding how key solution strategies will be shared and discussed, you will be prepared to move the lesson forward when students don't produce a desired strategy. In this way, you will ensure that students will achieve the learning goal through their own efforts.
15. Determining how to sequence incorrect solution strategies.	i. Invite the teacher to consider whether having students share incomplete or incorrect work would enhance and/or advance student learning. - You indicated that students might get started on a productive strategy (e.g., making a diagram) but not be sure how to complete it. What could be the possible benefit of having a student share their initial work on a viable strategy? Under what conditions might it make sense to share incomplete work? [It might make sense to share incomplete work when the strategy is one the teacher wants to have shared, but no one has produced it or when the student who has produced the incomplete strategy is one who seldom gets a chance to present.] - You indicated that students might use a viable strategy but determine that the answer is $16\frac{1}{2}$, not $16\frac{2}{3}$. What could be the possible benefit of having a student share their work even when the final answer was not correct? Under what conditions might it make sense to share a wrong answer? When would you share it? [It might make sense to share a wrong answer when the strategy used is one the teacher wants to have shared, but no one has produced the correct answer using that strategy; when many students got the same wrong answer using the same or a different strategy; or when the wrong answer reflects a common misconception in the domain.]	When selecting solution strategies to share, teachers tend to focus on correct and complete solutions. Teachers might want to use these strategies as exemplars of "good work," or they might try not to confuse students with "wrong" answers. However, sharing only correct and complete work might limit students' opportunities to learn. To benefit from incorrect and incomplete student work, teachers should consider which strategies might be used to advance student thinking. For example, a computational error might not be worth sharing, whereas a common misconception might be critical to discuss. Also, teachers need to determine how these strategies would fit in the sequence of other strategies to share.

SELECTING AND SEQUENCING

(Continued)

APPENDIX B (Continued)

SELECTING AND SEQUENCING

Identify the Challenge	Address the Challenge	Guiding Rationale
	ii. If the teacher is unsure about when or why they would share incomplete or incorrect work, make a suggestion about conditions that might warrant sharing work that is not complete and/or not correct. • Having students present incomplete or incorrect work provides an opportunity for the entire class to engage in a level of analysis and discussion that completed correct work does not. Finding a correct answer using a viable strategy is one thing but determining why an answer does or does not make sense or how to finish a problem with a strategy that you had not used yourself requires a different level of understanding. What do you see as the potential benefit of each of the following? – No one in the class has found the answer using a number line, but several students have drawn number lines, labeling points 0 to 12 and dividing the distance between pounds into fourths. You decide to have one student share their work thus far and then engage the class in determining how to use the method to find the solution. – Several students determined that the answer was 16 $\frac{1}{2}$ servings, using different viable methods. You decide to start the discussion by having a student share their diagram—which was correct—and engage the class in discussing how to label the $\frac{1}{2}$ pound leftover in terms of servings. Is all incorrect or incomplete work worth sharing? Under what conditions might it make sense to share incorrect or incomplete work? iii. Push for generalization. Ask the teacher under what conditions they would share incorrect or incomplete solution strategies in future lessons and how this could advance the learning of the entire class.	By determining incorrect or incomplete solution strategies to include in the class discussion, you will increase students' opportunity to investigate why a strategy doesn't work or how to complete a strategy that someone else started. When presenting their incomplete/incorrect work, students will also get a chance to reflect on their thinking and revise or complete their strategy. Moreover, bringing incorrect work to the whole-class discussion will normalize making mistakes, which will help students take risks without worrying about being "ridiculed."

Identify the Challenge	Address the Challenge	Guiding Rationale
16. Keeping the entire class engaged and accountable during individual presentations.	i. Invite the teacher to explain what they will do to ensure that the explanations provided by students are clear, highlight the targeted ideas, and are understood by other students in the class. • *You selected 3 solution strategies to be presented in this order: (1) visual diagram; (2) number line; and (3) common denominator. What questions can you ask the presenters to ensure that their explanations are clear and that the ideas you have targeted are highlighted? What questions can you ask the class to ensure that students are engaged in making sense of the presented ideas?* ii. Engage the teacher in rehearsing a possible series of questions the teacher can ask to ensure that the explanation is clear, that targeted ideas are highlighted and understood by students. • *Consider the following: A student presents the visual diagram solution strategy to the class. The student explains: "I drew $12\frac{1}{2}$ boxes to show the pounds of dog food and then split each pound into fourths and then grouped three of the fourths together and got 16." What would you want to ask the student to make it clear what the student did and why and to highlight the key mathematical ideas you have targeted?* • *Suppose the following dialogue unfolds between you and student:* S: I drew $12\frac{1}{2}$ boxes to show the pounds of dog food and then split each pound into fourths and then grouped three of the fourths together and got 16. T: Why did you draw $12\frac{1}{2}$ boxes? S: Each box of the 12 whole boxes represents a pound of dog food. The $\frac{1}{2}$ box represents $\frac{1}{2}$ pound. T: Why did you split the boxes into fourths? S: Because serving size is $\frac{3}{4}$ of a pound and I wanted to see how many $\frac{3}{4}$'s there are. *Why might you ask these questions? What questions could you ask the class to ensure that they are making sense of the solution strategy being presented?*	Selecting and sequencing solution strategies to be shared doesn't guarantee that students will engage in meaningful discussions. Student presentations can turn into show and tell when a whole-class discussion of shared strategies is not actively facilitated. In such cases, the rest of the class may not be making sense of shared strategies, or be able to understand connections between different solution strategies and the learning goal. To engage students in a productive whole-class discussion, teachers should make decisions about ways to hold students accountable during individual presentations. First, teachers should determine what connections they expect students to make among selected solution strategies and between these solution strategies and the goal of the lesson. Then, they should prepare moves or questions to ensure that all students are thinking deeply about the solution strategies and building connections among them.

CONNECTING

(Continued)

APPENDIX B (Continued)

Identify the Challenge	Address the Challenge	Guiding Rationale

	iii. S: Because serving size is $\frac{3}{4}$ of a pound and I wanted to see how many $\frac{3}{4}$'s there are.
	
	Why might you ask these questions? What questions could you ask the class to ensure that they are making sense of the solution strategy being presented?
	
	iv. If the teacher is struggling to come up with questions they could ask or moves they could make to ensure that the explanation is clear and that targeted ideas are highlighted and understood by students, make a suggestion about what the teacher could do.
	
	• What could be gained by probing the presenter to make their thinking process transparent to others and to elicit justification for why they took a particular action? For example, how might a student respond to these questions: Why did you divide the pounds into fourths? Can you explain what you mean by 'grouping three of the fourths' together? What did you do with the $\frac{1}{2}$ pound box? How could that be $\frac{2}{3}$? These questions would highlight that you are trying to determine how many $\frac{3}{4}$'s there are in $12\frac{1}{2}$ pounds (goal 1) and $\frac{1}{2}$ pound that is left needs to be represented in terms of servings (the unit of the divisor) (goal 2).
	
	• Consider what could be gained by the following moves:
	  – Having a student repeat what the presenter said in their own words.
	  – Asking a student to add on to what the presenter said.
	  – Asking students to turn and talk to their elbow partner and decide if they agreed or disagreed with the answer the presenter found and why.
	  – Inviting another student to reason about what he thinks the presenter did.
	
	v. Push for a generalization. Ask the teacher what they will do in future lessons to hold students accountable for remaining engaged during individual presentations and how this will help student learning.
		By keeping the entire class engaged and accountable during individual presentations, you will help ensure that the connections are the focus of the whole-class discussion and make the key mathematical idea accessible to students who may not have solved the problem in the same way as the presenter. In this way, students will not only learn to express themselves clearly but also build their own understanding of different approaches and how they are all connected to the key mathematical idea.

CONNECTING

134

Identify the Challenge	Address the Challenge	Guiding Rationale

17. Ensuring key mathematical ideas are made public and remain the focus.	i. Invite the teacher to explain how they will use the strategies produced by students to highlight the key mathematical ideas that they have targeted.
	
	• *You selected 3 solution strategies to be presented and sequenced in this order: (1) visual diagram; (2) number line; and (3) common denominator. What questions can you ask that will highlight the mathematical ideas that you have targeted?*
	
	ii. Engage the teacher in rehearsing questions they could ask about the solution strategies that would highlight the key mathematical ideas.
	
	• *Suppose a student explained how they constructed the visual diagram (area model) and how they found the answer. Consider the questions you could ask to highlight any of the targeted ideas. I will play the student and you can play the teacher.*
	
	   S: *I drew $12\frac{1}{2}$ boxes to show the pounds of dog food and then split each pound into fourths and then grouped three of the fourths together and got $16\frac{2}{3}$.*
	   T: ???
	
	iii. If the teacher is struggling to come up with questions that would highlight the key mathematical ideas, make a suggestion about possible questions that could be asked.
	
	• *Suppose you asked the student who had created the visual diagram the following questions.*
	   – *Why did you draw $12\frac{1}{2}$ boxes? What does each box represent?*
	   – *Why did you split each box into fourths?*
	   – *Why did you group three of the fourths together? What were you trying to find? [directly relates to goal 1 – the number of $\frac{3}{4}$ in $12\frac{1}{2}$]*
	   – *Where does $\frac{2}{3}$ come from? What happened to the $\frac{1}{2}$? [directly relates to goal 2 – the remainder is written as a fraction of serving, the units of the divisor.]*
	
	What could each question illuminate and how does it relate to the lesson goals?
	
	iv. Push for a generalization. Ask the teacher what they will do in future lessons to ensure that the key mathematical ideas are public and how this will support student learning.
		Sharing different solution strategies doesn't automatically make the key mathematical idea transparent. Students might be engaged in a discussion of various strategies without connecting them to the key mathematical ideas.
		
		To achieve the learning goal of the lesson, teachers should determine how shared student solution strategies highlight the important mathematical ideas. Teachers should create questions to ask students during the discussion of the solution strategies. These questions should aim to go beyond clarification of student thinking and focus on mathematical meaning and relationships.
		
		By ensuring key mathematical ideas are made public and remain the focus of discussion, you will be able to facilitate productive discussions. Students will have the opportunity to make sense of the connections between different solution strategies and the mathematical idea. Class discussions that build on student ideas support meaningful learning of mathematics.

CONNECTING

(Continued)

APPENDIX B (Continued)

Identify the Challenge	Address the Challenge	Guiding Rationale
18. Making sure you do not take over the discussion and do the explaining.	i. Invite the teacher to describe what they will do to make sure that the students (and not them) are the ones who are doing the explaining during the discussion and that non-presenting students are making sense of the ideas being discussed. • You indicated that you plan to have students share three strategies for solving the task: (1) visual diagram; (2) number line; and (3) common denominator. What will you do to determine the extent to which students are grappling with the mathematical ideas that you have targeted during the lesson? Why is/or isn't this important? What do you see as the costs and benefits of telling students what you want them to know? ii. Engage the teacher in rehearsing possible actions they can take to ensure that students are the ones doing the explaining and sense-making. • Suppose a student has just finished presenting the common denominator strategy. S: I turned $12\frac{1}{2}$ into $\frac{25}{2}$ and then I made $\frac{25}{2}$ into $\frac{50}{4}$. Then I divided $\frac{50}{4}$ by $\frac{3}{4}$. So I divided the numerators (50 divided by 3 is $16\frac{2}{3}$) and the denominators (4 divided by 4 is 1). So the answer is $16\frac{2}{3}$. I will play the student and you play the teacher. What questions will you ask the student who used this strategy (and/or the other students in class) to determine what they understand about this solution strategy? [e.g., How did you get $\frac{25}{2}$ and $\frac{50}{4}$? Can you use either the visual diagram or the number line to show $\frac{25}{2}$ and $\frac{50}{4}$, how they relate to $12\frac{1}{2}$, and why all three are equivalent to each other? Where can you see $\frac{50}{4}$ divided by $\frac{3}{4}$ in the other two representations? Does it make sense to divide 50 by 3? Why? Can this be seen in either of the pictures?	Sometime during the whole-class discussion teachers end up telling students what it is they want them to know. Although telling is expedient in the short run, it deprives students the opportunity to make sense of the ideas and provides the teacher with no insight regarding what students understand. To help students build their own understanding, teachers should ensure that students have the opportunity to explain their thinking and make connections. Teachers should prepare questions in advance of the lesson that will engage all students in this process. By making sure you don't take over the discussion and do the explaining, you will hold students accountable for their learning. This will help them develop a better understanding of the key mathematical idea and learn meaningfully.

CONNECTING

136

Identify the Challenge	Address the Challenge	Guiding Rationale
	iii. If the teacher is unsure about what to do to ensure that students are the ones doing the explaining and sense-making, make a suggestion about questions the teacher can ask that will provide them with insights regarding students' thinking and understanding. • Here are some things that you can do to ensure that students are the ones doing the explaining and sense-making during the lesson. For each suggestion, consider what you could learn from using each move. — Create questions in advance of the discussion that will highlight the mathematical ideas you have targeted in the lesson (e.g., how is $12\frac{1}{2} \div \frac{3}{4}$ represented in the diagram and in the number line? Do those 2 representations show division? How?) and help students make sense of the strategies and how they are connected. — Probe the student presenting to provide more information about what they did and why they did it and make their thinking process transparent to the class (e.g., How did you get $\frac{25}{2}$ and then $\frac{50}{4}$ from $12\frac{1}{2}$? What does this mean in terms of dog food? Why did you divide $\frac{50}{4}$ by $\frac{3}{4}$? What are you trying to find? — Ask other students in the class to add on to what the presenter has said, to revoice what the presenter said in their own words, and/or to indicate whether they agree or disagree with the presenter's method and findings. iv. Push for a generalization. Ask the teacher what they will do in future lessons to ensure that students are engaged in making sense of the ideas being presented and how this will support student learning.	
19. Running out of time.	i. Invite the teacher to describe how much time they are planning to allot to each component of the lesson so that they do not run out of time. • You have indicated that you plan to launch the task, give students some private think time, have students work in groups, and finally engage the class in a whole-group discussion, with a series of student presenters. How much time do you have for the lesson? How much time do you plan to allocate to each of these components? Why is it worth considering the timing of lesson components?	Sometimes when implementing a lesson that will engage students in solving and discussing a challenging task, teachers run out of time. To use class time effectively and efficiently, teachers should decide how much time it will take to complete each component of the lesson. Even after careful planning, teachers may run out of time. Therefore, they need to consider an alternative way to conclude the lesson in the event that time becomes an issue.

(Continued)

CONNECTING

137

APPENDIX B (Continued)

Identify the Challenge	Address the Challenge	Guiding Rationale
CONNECTING	ii. If the teacher is unsure about how much time to allocate to different components of the lesson, make a suggestion about things they should consider doing to ensure that they can complete the lesson in the allotted time. • For each of these suggestions, describe how it could help complete the lesson as planned. – Allow less than 10 minutes for the launch. You don't want to spend so much time launching the task that students don't have sufficient time to engage with it. – Give students a short amount of private think time (less than 5 minutes)—enough time to get some initial ideas about the task that they can bring to a small group discussion. – Put a boundary on small group time. Set a timer and tell students how much time they have to work on the task. Consider how far students need to get in the task in order to benefit from the whole-group discussion—you don't have to wait until all students have completed the entire task (e.g., in the Max's Dog Food task, students may benefit from the discussion even if they started a diagram but couldn't complete it, got an answer of 16 $\frac{1}{2}$, started repeated addition but didn't arrive at an answer, etc.). – Select a small number of students to present during the discussion so that you can focus on getting key ideas on the table for discussion. Choose the smallest number of solution strategies that you need to make your point. iii. Push for generalization. Ask the teacher what they will do when planning for future lessons to ensure that class time is used effectively and efficiently and how timing the components of a lesson in advance will support students' learning during the lesson.	By being prepared to use class time effectively and equipped with an alternative conclusion, you will be better positioned to ensure that you will achieve the goal of the lesson without diminishing students' opportunities to learn and turning it into teacher telling.

APPENDIX C: Task Analysis Guide

Levels of Demands

Lower-level demands (memorization):

- Involve either reproducing previously learned facts, rules, formulas, or definitions or committing facts, rules, formulas or definitions to memory
- Cannot be solved using procedures because a procedure does not exist or because the time frame in which the task is being completed is too short to use a procedure
- Are not ambiguous. Such tasks involve the exact reproduction of previously seen material, and what is to be reproduced is clearly and directly stated.
- Have no connection to the concepts or meaning that underlie the facts, rules, formulas, or definitions being learned or reproduced

Lower-level demands (procedures without connections):

- Are algorithmic. Use of the procedure either is specifically called for or is evident from prior instruction, experience, or placement of the task.
- Require limited cognitive demand for successful completion. Little ambiguity exists about what needs to be done and how to do it.
- Have no connection to the concepts or meaning that underlie the procedure being used
- Are focused on producing correct answers instead of on developing mathematical understanding
- Require no explanations or explanations that focus solely on describing the procedure that was used

Higher-level demands (procedures with connections):

- Focus students' attention on the use of procedures for the purpose of developing deeper levels of understanding of mathematical concepts and ideas
- Suggest explicitly or implicitly pathways to follow that are broad general procedures that have close connections to underlying conceptual ideas as opposed to narrow algorithms that are opaque with respect to underlying concepts
- Usually are represented in multiple ways, such as visual diagrams, manipulatives, symbols, and problem situations. Making connections among multiple representations helps develop meaning.
- Require some degree of cognitive effort. Although general procedures may be followed, they cannot be followed mindlessly. Students need to engage with conceptual ideas that underlie the procedures to complete the task successfully and that develop understanding.

Higher-level demands (doing mathematics):

- Require complex and nonalgorithmic thinking—a predictable, well-rehearsed approach or pathway is not explicitly suggested by the task, task instructions, or a worked-out example.
- Require students to explore and understand the nature of mathematical concepts, processes, or relationships
- Demand self-monitoring or self-regulation of one's own cognitive processes
- Require students to access relevant knowledge and experiences and make appropriate use of them in working through the task
- Require students to analyze the task and actively examine task constraints that may limit possible solution strategies and solutions
- Require considerable cognitive effort and may involve some level of anxiety for the student because of the unpredictable nature of the solution process required

These characteristics are derived from the work of Doyle on academic tasks (1988) and Resnick on high-level-thinking skills (1987), the *Professional Standards for Teaching Mathematics* (NCTM 1991), and the examination and categorization of hundreds of tasks used in QUASAR classrooms (Stein, Grover, and Henningsen 1996; Stein, Lane, and Silver 1996).

Source: From "Selecting and Creating Mathematical Tasks: From Research to Practice" by M. S. Smith and M. K. Stein, 1998, *Mathematics Teaching in the Middle School*, 3(5), pp. 344–350.

APPENDIX D: Goal and Task Identification Guide

Identify the Challenge	Address the Challenge	Guiding Rationale

a. Selected a low-level task and a performance goal.	i. Invite the teacher to explain what she wants students to learn from engaging in the selected task.
	
	• You indicated that you wanted students to solve a division problem involving a mixed numeral and a fraction set in a context and you selected the pizza party task (given below). Using the features of the task analysis guide, how would you classify this task? [This would be a low-level task because no representational suggestions are provided; given the numbers in the task, students must have a procedure for solving it; there is no requirement to do anything but find the answer.]
	
	You ordered pizza for your birthday party. When the party was over, you still had $4\frac{1}{5}$ pizzas left over. Your mother decided to freeze the remaining pizza. She put $\frac{2}{3}$ of a pizza (one serving) in each freezer bag. How many servings would your mother be able to freeze?
	
	ii. If the teacher does not see that the task is low level, make a suggestion about features of the task that would make it high level.
	
	• Tell the teacher that tasks that are high level require more than application of a known rule and getting the correct answer. High-level tasks include features such as the following:
	   – The task requires students to think and reason
	   – There are multiple ways to enter the task and to show competence
	   – The task requires students to provide a justification or explanation
	
	Suggest that $4\frac{4}{5}$ be changed to $4\frac{5}{6}$ and the following instruction be added to the task: Draw a picture, construct a number line, or make a table to help explain your solution. Ask the teacher: How does this change the task? What features from the list above are now addressed? What opportunities does this task afford that the initial task did not?
		Learning goals for students set the stage for everything else. When a teacher knows what they want their students to learn, they are better equipped to make downstream decisions (e.g., deciding how to advance a student's thinking during small-group work; selecting which student responses to publicly share during the final phase of the lesson).
		
		Learning goals that are about what a teacher wants their students to understand are critical for the design of lessons in which students engage in high cognitive demand tasks. Performance goals, on the other hand, focus on procedures that lead to correct answers without providing insight into the underlying concepts or meaning.
		
		Student engagement with high-level tasks is a necessary condition for students' opportunity to develop thinking, reasoning, and problem-solving skills; to experience mathematics as something that is meaningful and that they can make sense of; and to build understanding of important mathematics ideas and concepts, including the learning goal of the lesson.
		
		Alignment matters! A high-level task without a learning goal often leads to lessons that fail to live up to their potential; a low-level task that is paired with a learning goal will not set into motion the kinds of thinking and reasoning that students must engage in to achieve the goal of the lesson.

Identify the Challenge	Address the Challenge	Guiding Rationale
	• Invite the teacher to consider how changing the task might change the opportunities for learning. Here are some things that students could learn from engaging in a task such as the Pizza Party. For each goal, consider how students' work on the task could help you accomplish the goal. – When you find "how many ___ are in ___?" you are doing division. That is, in $a \div b$ you are trying to find how many times b is contained in a. – When dividing by a fraction, the remainder is expressed as a fraction of the divisor. – Division situations can be represented in different ways and connections can be made between symbolic, physical, pictorial, and contextual representations. iii. Push for generalization. Ask the teacher to describe the characteristics of the revised task and to consider how these features of high level tasks can be helpful in selecting tasks for future lessons.	
b. Selected a low-level task and a learning goal.	i. Invite the teacher to explain how the selected task will help address the goals they established for the lesson. • How will the pizza task you have selected (shown below) help you accomplish the goals you have identified for the lesson (shown below)? Which goals could it help illuminate and which goals would be difficult to achieve? You ordered pizza for your birthday party. When the party was over you still had $4\frac{5}{4}$ pizzas left over. Your mother decided to freeze the remaining pizza. She put $\frac{2}{3}$ of a pizza (one serving) in each freezer bag. How many servings would your mother be able to freeze? – When you find "how many ___ are in ___?" you are doing division. That is, in $a \div b$ you are trying to find how many times b is contained in a. – When dividing by a fraction, the remainder is expressed as a fraction of the divisor. – Division situations can be represented in different ways and connections can be made between symbolic, physical, pictorial, and contextual representations.	

(Continued)

141

APPENDIX D (Continued)

Identify the Challenge	Address the Challenge	Guiding Rationale
	ii. If the teacher does not see the limitations of the task they have selected, make a suggestion about the features of the task they might take into consideration and how these features could be used to adapt the selected task or select a different task. • Does the task align with lesson goals? • Does the task require students to think and reason? • Are there multiple ways to enter the task and to show competence? • Does the task require students to provide a justification or explanation? Suggest that $4\frac{4}{5}$ be changed to $4\frac{5}{6}$ and the following instruction be added to the task: Draw a picture, construct a number line, or make a table to help explain your solution. Ask the teacher: How does this change the task? What features from the list above are now addressed? What opportunities does this task afford that the initial task did not? iii. Push for generalization. Ask the teacher to explain how high-level tasks, and the alignment of goals and tasks, can, in general, support student learning during a lesson.	
c. Selected a high-level task and a performance goal (or no goal).	i. Invite the teacher to explain what she wants students to learn about mathematics as a result of engaging in the lesson based on the task she has identified. • You indicated that you wanted students to solve a division problem involving a mixed numeral and a fraction set in a context and you selected Max's Dog Food as the task in which students would engage. What do you want students to understand about the fraction division through their work on the Max's Dog Food task? [e.g., a mixed numeral can be rewritten as an improper fraction; equivalent fractions can be created by multiplying the numerator and denominator of a fraction by the same number; in doing division $a \div b$ you are trying to determine how many copies of b are contained in the a; when there is a remainder, it must be expressed as a fraction of the divisor; division situations can be represented in different ways—with diagrams, number lines, tables, and symbols]	

142

Identify the Challenge	Address the Challenge	Guiding Rationale
	> Dog food is sold in a $12\frac{1}{2}$ pound bag. My dog, Max, eats $\frac{3}{4}$ of a pound of dog food every day. How many servings of dog food are in the bag? • Which of the identified understandings do students need to have prior to engaging with the task? [a mixed numeral can be rewritten as an improper fraction; equivalent fractions can be created by multiplying the numerator and denominator of a fraction by the same number.] ii. If the teacher is unsure about what students would learn from engaging in the task, make a suggestion regarding possible learning goals. • Here are some things that students could learn from engaging in the Max's Dog Food task. For each goal, consider how students' work on the task could help you accomplish the goal. — When you find "how many ____ are in ____?" you are doing division. That is, in $a ÷ b$ you are trying to find how many times b is contained in a. — When dividing by a fraction, the remainder is expressed as a fraction of the divisor. — Division situations can be represented in different ways and connections can be made between symbolic, physical, pictorial, and contextual representations. iii. Push for generalization. Ask the teacher to consider the characteristics of the revised goals and how these characteristics can support student learning in a lesson.	

(Continued)

APPENDIX D (Continued)

Identify the Challenge	Address the Challenge	Guiding Rationale
d. Identified a topic, unit, or standard but has not selected a task or established a learning goal.	i. Invite the teacher to consider a high-level task (or tasks) that would fit with the identified topic, unit, or standard and what students could learn from engaging in such a task. • You indicated that you wanted to use a task that involves the division of fractions, specifically a mixed number divided by a proper fraction. Here are two examples that you might consider: *Max's Dog Food* Dog food is sold in a $12\frac{1}{2}$ pound bag. My dog, Max, eats $\frac{3}{4}$ of a pound of dog food every day. How many servings of dog food are in the bag? Draw a picture, construct a number line, or make a table to help explain your solution. *The Pizza Party* You ordered pizza for your birthday party. When the party was over, you still had $4\frac{5}{6}$ pizzas left over. Your mother decided to freeze the remaining pizza. She put $\frac{2}{3}$ of a pizza (one serving) in each freezer bag. How many servings would your mother be able to freeze? Draw a picture, construct a number line, or make a table to help explain your solution. You could change the numbers and the context to what you think would work best for your students but think about the general structure of the problems. • How could students solve a problem of this type? • What prior knowledge would students need to solve a task like this? • What might students learn about fraction division from engaging in this task?	

Identify the Challenge	Address the Challenge	Guiding Rationale
	ii. If the teacher is unsure about what students would learn from engaging in such a task, make a suggestion regarding possible learning goals: • Here are some things that students could learn from engaging in a task such as Max's Dog Food or the Pizza Party. For each goal, consider how students' work on the task could help you accomplish each goal. – When you find "how many ___ are in ___?" you are doing division. That is, in a ÷ b you are trying to find how many times b is contained in a. – When dividing by a fraction, the remainder is expressed as a fraction of the divisor. – Division situations can be represented in different ways and connections can be made between symbolic, physical, pictorial, and contextual representations. iii. Push for generalization. Ask the teacher to explain how high-level tasks that are aligned with specific learning goals can support student learning during a lesson.	

APPENDIX E: Lesson Planning Tool

Learning Goals (Residue)	Evidence
What understandings will students take away from this lesson?	What will students say, do, or produce that will provide evidence of their understandings?

Task	Instructional Support—Tools, Resources, Materials
What is the main activity that students will be working on in this lesson?	What tools or resources will be made available to give students entry to—and help them reason through—the activity?

Prior Knowledge	Task Launch
What prior knowledge and experience will students draw on in their work on this task? **Essential Questions** What are the essential questions that I want students to be able to answer over the course of the lesson?	How will you introduce and set up the task to ensure that students understand the task and can begin productive work, without diminishing the cognitive demand of the task?

Anticipated Solution Strategies and Instructional Supports

What are the various ways that students might complete the activity? Be sure to include incorrect, correct, and incomplete solution strategies.

What questions might you ask students that will support their exploration of the activity and **bridge** between **what they did** and **what you want them to learn**? These questions should **assess** what a student currently knows and **advance** him or her toward the goals of the lesson. Be sure to consider questions that you will ask students who can't get started as well as students who finish quickly.

Use the **Monitoring Tool** to provide the details related to Anticipated Solution Strategies and Instructional Support.

Sharing and Discussing the Task

Selecting and Sequencing	Connecting Responses
Which solution strategies do you want students to share during the lesson? In what order? Why?	What specific questions will you ask so that students— – make sense of the mathematical ideas that you want them to learn – make connections among the different strategies that are presented?

Homework/Assessment
What will you ask students to do that will allow you to determine what they learned and what they understand?

Source: Adapted from "Thinking Through a Lesson Protocol: A Key from Successfully Implementing High-Level Tasks" by M. S. Smith, V. Bill, and E. Hughes, 2008, *Mathematics Teaching in the Middle School*, 14(3), (p. 132–138).

A downloadable version of this tool can be found at **https://qrs.ly/7jfli55**

APPENDIX F: Monitoring Tool

Anticipated Solutions Strategies	Instructional Supports			Who and What	Order
	Assessing Questions	Advancing Questions		
	•	•		
	•	•		
	•	•		
	•	•		
Other				

Source: From *5 Practices for Orchestrating Productive Mathematics Discussions* by M. S. Smith and M. K. Stein, 2018, National Council of Teachers of Mathematics. A downloadable version of this tool can be found at **https://qrs.ly/7jfli55**.

147

APPENDIX G: Pre-Lesson Conference Planning Tool

Teacher:
Coach:
Cycle:
Date:

Relevant Practice:
Focal Challenge(s):

Identify the Challenge	Address the Challenge	Guiding Rationale

Notes (i.e., commitment/focus for upcoming lesson, revisions to Teacher Goals/Challenges; evidence of growth in pedagogical reasoning):

online resources A downloadable version of this tool can be found at **https://qrs.ly/7jfti55**.

APPENDIX H: Kyle's Teacher Challenges, Lesson Planning, and Monitoring Tools

Kyle's Teacher Challenges Tool

Below is a list of challenges that teachers have reported facing when trying to implement ambitious teaching practices. Review the 19 challenges listed and identify up to 5 challenges that you struggle with. For each identified challenge briefly describe how the challenge plays out in your classroom.

	CHALLENGES	DESCRIPTION	The Challenge in My Classroom
GOALS AND TASKS	1. Identifying learning goals	Goal needs to focus on what students will learn as a result of engaging in the task, not on what students will do. Clarity on goals sets the stage for everything else!	
	2. Identifying a doing-mathematics task	While doing-mathematics tasks provide the greatest opportunities for student learning, they are not readily available in some textbooks. Teachers may need to adapt an existing task, find a task in another resource, or create a task.	
	3. Ensuring alignment between task and goals	Even with learning goals specified, teachers may select a task that does not allow students to make progress on those particular goals.	
	4. Launching a task to ensure student access	Teachers need to provide access to the context and the mathematics in the launch but not so much that the mathematical demands are reduced and key ideas are given away.	*I struggle making sure all students have access. I am not sure every student will understand this particular question and know how to work with more than one equivalent ratio.*

(Continued)

149

APPENDIX H (Continued)

CHALLENGES	DESCRIPTION	The Challenge in My Classroom
5. Moving beyond the way you solve a problem	Teachers often feel limited by their own experience. They know how to solve a task but may not have access to the array of strategies that students are likely to use.	
6. Being prepared to help students who cannot get started on a task	Teachers need to be prepared to provide support to students who do not know how to begin work on the task so that they can make progress without being told exactly what to do and how.	I have all of the Special Education students in my classes this year and they often struggle to get started on a problem.
7. Creating questions that move students toward the mathematical goals	The questions teachers ask need to be driven by the mathematical goals of the lesson. The focus needs to be on ensuring that students understand the key mathematical ideas, not just on producing a solution to the task.	

ANTICIPATING

8. Trying to understand what students are thinking	Students do not always articulate their thinking clearly. It can be quite demanding for teachers, in the moment, to figure out what a student means or is trying to say. This requires teachers to listen carefully to what students are saying and to ask questions that help them better explain what they are thinking.	
9. Keeping track of group progress—which groups you visited and what you left them to work on	As teachers are running from group to group, providing support, they need to be able to keep track of what each group is doing and what they left students to work on. Also, it is important for a teacher to return to a group in order to determine whether the advancing question given to them helped them make progress.	Many of my students will ask for help and I sometimes forget where I left off with a particular group in guiding them to a solution.
10. Involving all members of a group	All individuals in the group need to be challenged to answer assessing and advancing questions. For individuals to benefit from the thinking of their peers, they need to be held accountable for listening to and adding on, repeating and summarizing what others are saying.	I mix up my seating assignments daily and so this can make it difficult to have groups of all leveled students. There are times when all of the more savy students are together and the struggling students end up in a group together.

MONITORING

CHALLENGES	DESCRIPTION	The Challenge in My Classroom
11. Selecting only solutions that are most relevant to learning goals	Teachers need to select a limited number of solutions that will help achieve the mathematical goals of the lesson. Sharing solutions that are not directly relevant can take a discussion off track, and sharing too many solutions (even if they are relevant) can lead to student disengagement.	
12. Expanding beyond the usual student presenters	Teachers often select students who are articulate and on whom they can count for a coherent explanation. Teachers need to look for opportunities to position each and every student as a presenter and help students develop their ability to explain their thinking.	*This can be a challenge in my room because there are many times it is the same students who come up with the solution I am looking to highlight.*
13. Deciding what work to share when the majority of students were not able to solve the task and your initial goal no longer seems obtainable	Teachers may on occasion find that the task was too challenging for most students and that they were not able to engage as intended. This situation requires the teacher to modify her initial plan and determine how to focus the discussion so students can make progress.	
14. Moving forward when a key strategy is not produced by students	In planning the lesson, a teacher may determine that a particular strategy is critical to accomplishing the lesson goals. If the success of a lesson hinges on the availability of a particular strategy, then the teacher needs to be prepared to introduce the strategy through some means.	
15. Determining how to sequence incorrect and/or incomplete solutions	Teachers often choose not to share work that is not complete and correct for fear that students will remember incorrect methods. Sharing solutions that highlight key errors in a domain can provide all students with an opportunity to analyze why a particular approach does not work. Sharing incomplete or partial solutions can provide all students with the opportunity to consider how such work can be connected to more robust solutions.	

SELECTING & SEQUENCING

(Continued)

APPENDIX H (Continued)

	CHALLENGES	DESCRIPTION	The Challenge in My Classroom
CONNECTING	16. Keeping the entire class engaged and accountable during individual presentations	Often, the sharing of solutions turns into a show and tell or a dialogue between the teacher and the presenter. The rest of the class needs to be held accountable for understanding and making sense of the solutions that are presented.	
	17. Ensuring key mathematical ideas are made public and remain the focus	It is possible to have students share and discuss a lot of interesting solutions and never get to the point of the lesson. It is critical that the key mathematical ideas that are being targeted in the lesson are explicitly discussed.	
	18. Making sure that you do not take over the discussion and do the explaining	As students are presenting their solutions, the teacher needs to ask questions that engage the presenters and the rest of the class in explaining and making sense of the solutions. There is a temptation for the teacher to take over and tell the students what they need to know. When this happens, opportunities for learning are diminished. Remember whoever is doing the talking is doing the thinking!	
	19. Running out of time	Teachers may not have enough time to conduct the whole class discussion the way they had planned it. In such cases it is important to come up with a Plan B that provides some closure to the lesson but does not turn into telling.	

Kyle's Lesson Planning Tool

Learning Goals (Residue) **What understandings will students take away from this lesson?** • Students will understand that equivalent ratios represent mixtures with the same taste. • Students will understand that to compare different mixtures/ratios you need a common basis for comparison. • Students will understand that different strategies and models can be used to accurately compare the same set of ratios.	**Evidence** **What will students say, do, or produce that will provide evidence of their understandings?** Students will produce models and discuss how they came to the conclusion of which combination will be the most orangey.
Task **What is the main activity that students will be working on in this lesson?** Orange juice task	**Instructional Support—Tools, Resources, Materials** **What tools or resources will be made available to give students entry to—and help them reason through—the activity?** We have been working with double number lines and students will have rulers, calculators and a copy of the task.
Prior Knowledge **What prior knowledge and experience will students draw on in their work on this task?** My students have been working with double number lines and creating equivalent ratios. **Essential Questions** **What are the essential questions that I want students to be able to answer over the course of the lesson?** • How can you write a ratio to represent a situation, and what does that ratio mean? • How can you represent a relationship between two quantities? Can more than one ratio describe a situation?	**Task Launch** **How will you introduce and set up the task to ensure that students understand the task and can begin productive work, without diminishing the cognitive demand of the task?** I will introduce the task through a PowerPoint and give each student a handout with the task on it. I will give the students about 8 minutes of independent think time and then they will share answers in their groups. I will then circulate asking questions and selecting work from groups to share.

(Continued)

APPENDIX H (Continued)

Anticipated Solution Strategies and Instructional Supports

What are the various ways that students might complete the activity? Be sure to include incorrect, correct, and incomplete solution strategies.

I believe many students will use double number lines and find a common amount of batches. I also think there will be a few who may be able to find a unit rate. I also believe some students will incorrectly solve the task by determining the mixes with the most amount of water. I also believe a certain number of kids may choose to use a diagram to solve it.

What questions might you ask students that will support their exploration of the activity and bridge between what they did and what you want them to learn? These questions should assess what a student currently knows and advance him or her toward the goals of the lesson. Be sure to consider questions that you will ask students who can't get started as well as students who finish quickly.

Assessing questions:

- What does the 90 represent in your work? What does the numerator mean in your work? Why did you choose the one with the largest numerator? How do you know the shaded part is the most orangey?

- How do the cups of water added to the concentrate affect the taste of the mixed juice? What does it mean to have more water? You stated that Mix A and Mix C have the fewest cans of water—why does that tell you that they are the most orangey? How do you know which one is the most orangey? Why did you choose to make all the recipes use one cup of concentrate?

Advancing questions:

- Can you design a mix that is more orangey than Mix A? Why did you choose to use this strategy? Can you explain your thinking to me? What does it mean when you have more water? What about the concentrate? What would this look like if you were to use numbers instead of the picture? How can we keep adding cans of water without making the juice less orangey? What will happen to the concentrate if we keep adding water?

Sharing and Discussing the Task

Selecting and Sequencing	Connecting Responses
Which solution strategies do you want students to share during the lesson? In what order? Why? *I would start with the picture first, then the common denominator, and then the unit rate.* *The picture would go first because it is the most concrete solution and then I would move to the more abstract solution of equivalent ratios and finally the unit rate.*	**What specific questions will you ask so that students—** – make sense of the mathematical ideas that you want them to learn – make connections among the different strategies that are presented? *We have recently learned the word per and I would direct them to that word if anyone chooses to use unit rates. I would also focus on equivalent ratios and making sure to connect them to all of the work we have been doing in class.*

Homework/Assessment

What will you ask students to do that will allow you to determine what they learned and what they understand?

At the end of the unit I will ask them questions that determine their understanding of how quantities vary together and are able to see how the variation in one coincides with the variation in another. Recognizing ratios as distinct entities representing a relationship different from the quantities they compare.

Kyle's Monitoring Tool

Anticipated Solutions Strategies	Instructional Supports			Order
	Assessing Questions	Advancing Questions	Who and What	
Orange Juice task: Finding a common denominator	• What does the 90 represent in your work? • What does the numerator mean in your work? • Why did you choose the one with the largest numerator?	• How can we keep adding cans of water without making the juice less orangey? • What will happen to the concentrate if we keep adding water?		
Drawing a picture with a whole and shading in the amount of juice concentrate.	• How do you know the shaded part is the most orangey? • How do the cups of water added to the concentrate affect the taste of the mixed juice?	• What would this look like if you were to use numbers instead of the picture?		
Taking the amount of water and subtracting the concentrate.	• What does it mean to have more water? • You stated that Mix A and Mix C have the fewest cans of water—why does that tell you that they are the most orangey?	• Why did you choose to use this strategy? Can you explain your thinking to me? • What does it mean when you have more water? What about the concentrate?		
Finding a unit rate. Either getting the water or the juice concentrate to one.	• How do you know which one is the most orangey? • Why did you choose to make all the recipes use one cup of concentrate?	• Can you design a mix that is more orangey than Mix A?		
Other				

156

APPENDIX I: Emery's Teacher Challenges, Lesson Planning, and Monitoring Tools

Emery's Teacher Challenges Tool

Below is a list of challenges that teachers have reported facing when trying to implement ambitious teaching practices. Review the 19 challenges listed and identify up to 5 challenges that you struggle with. For each identified challenge briefly describe how the challenge plays out in your classroom.

	CHALLENGES	DESCRIPTION	The Challenge in My Classroom
GOALS AND TASKS	1. Identifying learning goals	Goal needs to focus on what students will learn as a result of engaging in the task, not on what students will do. Clarity on goals sets the stage for everything else!	
	2. Identifying a doing-mathematics task	While doing-mathematics tasks provide the greatest opportunities for student learning, they are not readily available in some textbooks. Teachers may need to adapt an existing task, find a task in another resource, or create a task.	
	3. Ensuring alignment between task and goals	Even with learning goals specified, teachers may select a task that does not allow students to make progress on those particular goals.	
	4. Launching a task to ensure student access	Teachers need to provide access to the context and the mathematics in the launch but not so much that the mathematical demands are reduced and key ideas are given away.	
ANTICIPATING	5. Moving beyond the way you solve a problem	Teachers often feel limited by their own experience. They know how to solve a task but may not have access to the array of strategies that students are likely to use.	*This is my second-year teaching 5th grade math. I am researching different strategies to solve fraction multiplication problems; however, I am struggling to find and fully understand said strategies in order to teach and have my students explore them.*
	6. Being prepared to help students who cannot get started on a task	Teachers need to be prepared to provide support to students who do not know how to begin work on the task so that they can make progress without being told exactly what to do and how.	
	7. Creating questions that move students toward the mathematical goals	The questions teachers ask need to be driven by the mathematical goals of the lesson. The focus needs to be on ensuring that students understand the key mathematical ideas, not just on producing a solution to the task.	

(Continued)

APPENDIX I (*Continued*)

	CHALLENGES	DESCRIPTION	The Challenge in My Classroom
MONITORING	8. Trying to understand what students are thinking	Students do not always articulate their thinking clearly. It can be quite demanding for teachers, in the moment, to figure out what a student means or is trying to say. This requires teachers to listen carefully to what students are saying and to ask questions that help them better explain what they are thinking.	
	9. Keeping track of group progress—which groups you visited and what you left them to work on	As teachers are running from group to group, providing support, they need to be able to keep track of what each group is doing and what they left students to work on. Also, it is important for a teacher to return to a group in order to determine whether the advancing question given to them helped them make progress.	
	10. Involving all members of a group	All individuals in the group need to be challenged to answer assessing and advancing questions. For individuals to benefit from the thinking of their peers, they need to be held accountable for listening to and adding on, repeating and summarizing what others are saying.	
SELECTING & SEQUENCING	11. Selecting only solutions that are most relevant to learning goals	Teachers need to select a limited number of solutions that will help achieve the mathematical goals of the lesson. Sharing solutions that are not directly relevant can take a discussion off track, and sharing too many solutions (even if they are relevant) can lead to student disengagement.	
	12. Expanding beyond the usual student presenters	Teachers often select students who are articulate and on whom they can count for a coherent explanation. Teachers need to look for opportunities to position each and every student as a presenter and help students develop their ability to explain their thinking.	
	13. Deciding what work to share when the majority of students were not able to solve the task and your initial goal no longer seems obtainable	Teachers may on occasion find that the task was too challenging for most students and that they were not able to engage as intended. This situation requires the teacher to modify her initial plan and determine how to focus the discussion so students can make progress.	

CHALLENGES	DESCRIPTION	The Challenge in My Classroom
14. Moving forward when a key strategy is not produced by students	In planning the lesson, a teacher may determine that a particular strategy is critical to accomplishing the lesson goals. If the success of a lesson hinges on the availability of a particular strategy, then the teacher needs to be prepared to introduce the strategy through some means.	
15. Determining how to sequence incorrect and/or incomplete solutions	Teachers often choose not to share work that is not complete and correct for fear that students will remember incorrect methods. Sharing solutions that highlight key errors in a domain can provide all students with an opportunity to analyze why a particular approach does not work. Sharing incomplete or partial solutions can provide all students with the opportunity to consider how such work can be connected to more robust solutions.	*I am still trying to figure out how to sequence solutions in a thoughtful way. Mostly I just decide which ones I want presented and they call on them.*
16. Keeping the entire class engaged and accountable during individual presentations	Often, the sharing of solutions turns into a show and tell or a dialogue between the teacher and the presenter. The rest of the class needs to be held accountable for understanding and making sense of the solutions that are presented.	*I would love ideas on how to help my students continue to be engaged when other students are sharing their solutions.*
17. Ensuring key mathematical ideas are made public and remain the focus	It is possible to have students share and discuss a lot of interesting solutions and never get to the point of the lesson. It is critical that the key mathematical ideas that are being targeted in the lesson are explicitly discussed.	
18. Making sure that you do not take over the discussion and do the explaining	As students are presenting their solutions, the teacher needs to ask questions that engage the presenters and the rest of the class in explaining and making sense of the solutions. There is a temptation for the teacher to take over and tell the students what they need to know. When this happens, opportunities for learning are diminished. Remember whoever is doing the talking is doing the thinking!	
19. Running out of time	Teachers may not have enough time to conduct the whole class discussion the way they had planned it. In such cases it is important to come up with a Plan B that provides some closure to the lesson but does not turn into telling.	*This year we have struggled to close class the way I would choose to close class. We have a time limit of an hour per class. I underestimate the time the task will take my students.*

CONNECTING

Emery's Lesson Planning Tool

Learning Goals (Residue) What understandings will students take away from this lesson? • I can use strategies that make sense to me to multiply whole numbers by a fraction by whole numbers. • I can decide when and how to use math tools, pictures, and models to help solve problems. • I can use strategies that make sense to me to solve real world problems using fractions and whole numbers.	**Evidence** What will students say, do, or produce that will provide evidence of their understandings? Students will produce a visual representation of multiplying a fraction by a whole number and write the equation.
Task What is the main activity that students will be working on in this lesson? The main activity students will be working on is multiplying a whole number by a fraction to gain knowledge on how to multiply a fraction by a whole number or mixed number.	**Instructional Support—Tools, Resources, Materials** What tools or resources will be made available to give students entry to—and help them reason through—the activity? Students will have access to virtual manipulatives and draw tools in order to manipulate this activity.
Prior Knowledge What prior knowledge and experience will students draw on in their work on this task? Students must understand the meaning of fractions and all operations with whole numbers as well as representing these with equations and visual representations. **Essential Questions** What are the essential questions that I want students to be able to answer over the course of the lesson? How can I model multiplication involving whole numbers and fractions?	**Task Launch** How will you introduce and set up the task to ensure that students understand the task and can begin productive work, without diminishing the cognitive demand of the task? To launch this lesson, we will begin by reviewing the objectives. We will discuss in depth what the expectation of each objective is before going into the task. Once into the task we will review expectations and students will investigate on multiplying fractions.

160

Anticipated Solution Strategies and Instructional Supports

What are the various ways that students might complete the activity? Be sure to include incorrect, correct, and incomplete solution strategies.

What questions might you ask students that will support their exploration of the activity and bridge between what they did and what you want them to learn? These questions should assess what a student currently knows and advance him or her toward the goals of the lesson. Be sure to consider questions that you will ask students who can't get started as well as students who finish quickly.

Assessing questions:
- *How does your picture represent your equation or how does your equation represent your picture?*
- *Explain to me how you went about answering this question.*
- *How did you know what to draw for your picture?*
- *Why did you use 2 cookies instead of 3? (Problem 3)*
- *How did you know how many cookies equaled _____ of a serving?*

Advancing questions:
- *Is there an alternate way/different strategy to find out your answer?*
- *Were you able to use your strategy for all problems involving multiplication of fractions?*
- *Can you write an explanation on how to use a picture to solve this problem?*

Sharing and Discussing the Task

Selecting and Sequencing	Connecting Responses
Which solution strategies do you want students to share during the lesson? In what order? Why? 1. *Models (Drawing Visual Representation)* 2. *Number Line* 3. *Repeated Addition with Like Fractions* 4. *Multiplication of Fractions*	What specific questions will you ask so that students— – make sense of the mathematical ideas that you want them to learn? – make connections among the different strategies that are presented?

Homework/Assessment

What will you ask students to do that will allow you to determine what they learned and what they understand?

Students will complete an exit ticket directly correlating to the task they completed.

161

Emery's Monitoring Tool

Anticipated Solutions Strategies	Instructional Supports		Who and What	Order
	Assessing Questions	Advancing Questions		
Models/Visual Representations	• How did you know what to draw for your model? • How do you know the answer to the question if your model is drawn that way?	• How does your picture represent an equation?		
Number Line	• How did you know how to split your number line? • Why are you jumping spaces like that?	• How does your number line represent an equation?		
Repeated Addition with Like Fractions		• Can you write an explanation on how to use a picture to solve this problem?		
Other				

APPENDIX J: Coach Jesse's Pre-Lesson Conference Plan

Teacher: Jamie
Coach: Jesse
Cycle: 3
Date:

Relevant Practice: Monitoring
Focal Challenge(s): Involving all members of a group

Identify the Challenge	Address the Challenge	Guiding Rationale
In the Teacher Challenges Tool, Jamie described: "There are always students who want to/will do most of the work. In addition, there are some students who will not immediately participate, possibly due to not having an entry into the task. I know that there are times where I can do better with making sure that everyone in a group is participating equally, and that everyone is held accountable for listening to, adding on, repeating, and summarizing what others in their group are saying." It looks like Jamie understands that he needs to do something to ensure that all students are engaged in group work and that they should be held accountable for their learning but doesn't have a clear idea about what specific teacher moves to use to make this happen. When we talk about this challenge, I will make sure we focus on specific solution strategies and how assessing/advancing questions tied to specific solutions can be used to stimulate conversations among group members. This will make the conversation more concrete for Jamie.	Invite: • What will you do to involve all members of a group when they're working on the Fractions task? (Possible responses: Reasoning, repeating) Rehearse: For reasoning: • Let's say the student who is always willing to do most of the work explains their solution strategy; you said you would use reasoning (e.g., "Do you agree with what (name) said?") and someone said they disagree. What would you do to engage all members with each other? For repeating: • You said you would ask students to repeat (e.g., "Can someone repeat what (name) said in their own words?"). What would you do next, if the student says, "I don't know"? Suggest: Consider what we could learn from students using some of the following questions: • Can you explain what (name) said in your own words? • Is this answer reasonable? How do you know?	All members of a group must be held accountable for engaging in the thinking and discussion of a task. Without this accountability, one or two students may complete most of the work for the group, while others may not feel the need to engage with the task. By holding all students accountable in the discussions, all students have the chance to interact with the mathematics of the lesson, learn from each other's thinking, and make connections with their own thinking. They may also realize misconceptions they hold and why they are misconceptions.

(Continued)

APPENDIX J (Continued)

Identify the Challenge	Address the Challenge	Guiding Rationale
	What could we learn from these questions? What message might this send to the students in the group? Consider what we could learn from the following actions: • Pausing the initial student explanation to ask another student to continue the explanation or to summarize what has been said so far. • Asking a different student to share each time you come to a group. • Giving students a few minutes to make sure all students understand and then coming back to ask for an explanation. What would be the benefit of this approach? What message might this send to the students in the group? Generalize: • What teacher moves are you going to use in the future to involve all members of a group? • Why is it important for all students to be involved in group work?	

Notes (i.e., commitment/focus for upcoming lesson, revisions to Teacher Goals/Challenges; evidence of growth in pedagogical reasoning):

APPENDIX K: Noticing and Wondering Tool

	What I Noticed	What I Am Wondering About
Clip 1		
Clip 2		
Clip 3		

A downloadable version of this tool can be found at **https://qrs.ly/7jfli55**.

APPENDIX L: Post-Lesson Conference Planning Tool

Teacher: Coach: Cycle: Date:	Clip # Time Stamp:		Relevant Practice: Focal Challenge: Why This Clip?:	
T and/or C?	*Identify the Challenge*		*Address the Challenge*	*Guiding Rationale*
	Noticing			
	Wondering			
	Noticing			
	Wondering			

Notes (i.e., commitment/focus for upcoming lesson, revisions to Teacher Goals/Challenges; evidence of growth in pedagogical reasoning):

A downloadable version of this tool can be found at https://qrs.ly/7jfti55.

APPENDIX M: Jamie and Coach Jesse's Noticing and Wondering Tool

Jamie's Noticing and Wondering Tool

	What I Noticed	What I Am Wondering About
Clip 1	Students were supposed to be working with their group members, but in this case, they seemed to be doing their own thing. They were not working together.	What can I do to improve the dialogue among group members? What can I do to make sure that all students are accountable as they work together?
	When Casey answered my question, I did a retell, instead of asking another student to retell.	What could I have done to include the other members of the group? Would asking another to retell help them engage?

Coach Jesse's Noticing and Wondering Tool

	What I Noticed	What I Am Wondering About
Clip 1	There were 4 students in this group, but they weren't talking much with each other. The teacher was talking mostly to Casey.	I wonder if asking another student to retell Casey's strategy would help them engage. What else could the teacher have done to ensure that each member is making sense of Quinn and Casey's answers?
	Both Quinn and Casey had correct answers, but their strategies were different.	I wonder if students realized there were two different solution strategies. What questions could the teacher have asked to help students understand there are different ways to solve this problem and how they are related?

APPENDIX N: Coach Jesse's Post-Lesson Conference Plan

Teacher: Jamie	Clip #: 1	Relevant Practice: Anticipating
Coach: Jesse	Time Stamp: 10:25–12:40	Focal Challenge: Involving all members of a group
Cycle: 3		Why This Clip?: With the other groups, the teacher did a good job engaging students, especially quiet ones. In this particular clip, the teacher talks mostly to Casey. This was probably because the students in this group were on the right track. I want the teacher to have an opportunity to reflect on what might have been done to bring other students into the conversation.
Date:		

T and/or C?		Identify the Challenge	Address the Challenge	Guiding Rationale
T	Noticing	When Casey answered my question, I did a retell, instead of asking another student to retell. • What is the benefit of doing the retell yourself or having someone else do it?	Invite: • Tell me a little bit more about what you saw happening with that group. (Possible responses: teacher retelling Casey's response, two solution strategies) Rehearse: For the teacher retelling Casey's response: • What would happen if you asked Charlie to retell Casey's answer? What would you expect to find out? For two solution strategies: • You said Quinn and Casey used different strategies and you would ask someone else to compare these strategies (specify advancing question). What do you think students would say? What would you do, if they said, "I don't know" or "They are the same answers"?	All members of a group must be held accountable for engaging with and discussing a task without this accountability, one or two students may complete most of the work for the group, while others may not feel the need to engage with the task. I want to make sure Jamie is equipped with tools to ensure that every group member is engaged with the group work. This is important even when students are on the right track. Sharing different solution strategies and understanding how they are related is important for students' conceptual understanding.
	Wondering	What could I have done to include the other members of the group? Would asking another to retell help them engage? • What would be the benefit of including other members of this group? What do you want them to learn from engaging with each other?		
T/C	Noticing	Students were supposed to be working with their group members, but in this case, they seemed to be doing their own thing. They were not working well together. • Why do you think this was the case? • What would be the benefit for the members of this group to work together?		

168

Wondering	What can I do to improve the dialogue among group members? What can I do to make sure that all students are accountable as they work together?	Suggest:
		Consider what we could learn from students using some of the following questions:
	• What do you want the members of this group to talk about? How would this help them achieve the goals of this lesson?	• Can you explain what Casey said in your own words?
		• What do you notice about Quinn's and Casey's models?
		What could we learn from these questions? What message might this send to the students in the group?
		Consider what we could learn from the following actions:
		• Pausing Casey's explanation to ask another student to continue the explanation or to summarize what has been said so far.
		• Giving students a few minutes to make sure all students understand both solution strategies and then coming back to ask for a comparison between strategies.
		What would be the benefit of this approach? What message might this send to the students in the group?
		Generalize:
		• As you move forward, what teacher moves are you going to use to involve all members of a group?
		• Why is it important for all students to be involved in group work?

Notes (i.e., commitment/focus for upcoming lesson, revisions to Teacher Goals/Challenges; evidence of growth in pedagogical reasoning):

References

Aguilar, E. (2020). *Coaching for equity: Conversations that change practice.* Jossey-Bass.

Aguirre, J., Herbel-Eisenmann, B., Celedón-Pattichis, S., Civil, M., Wilkerson, T., Stephan, M., Pape, S., & Clements, D. H. (2017). Equity within mathematics education research as a political act: Moving from choice to intentional collective professional responsibility. *Journal for Research in Mathematics Education, 48*(2), 124–147.

Aguirre, J., Mayfield-Ingram, K., & Martin, D. (2013). *The impact of identity in k–8 mathematics: Rethinking equity-based practices.* National Council of Teachers of Mathematics.

Artzt, A. F., & Armour-Thomas, E. (2002). *Becoming a reflective mathematics teacher.* Erlbaum.

Atteberry, A., & Bryk A. S. (2011). Analyzing teacher participation in literacy coaching activities. *The Elementary School Journal, 112*(2), 356–382.

Beisiegel, M., Mitchell, R., & Hill, H. C. (2018). The design of video-based professional development: An exploratory experiment intended to identify effective features. *Journal of Teacher Education, 69*(1), 69–89.

Boaler, J., & Staples, M. (2008). Creating mathematical futures through an equitable teaching approach: The case of Railside School. *Teachers College Record, 110*(3), 608–645.

Campbell, P. F., & Malkus, N. N. (2011). The impact of elementary mathematics coaches on student achievement. *The Elementary School Journal, 111*(3), 430–454.

Carson, C., & Choppin, J. (2021). Coaching from a distance: Exploring video-based coaching. *Online Learning, 25*(4), 104–124.

Chapin, S. (1994). Implementing reform in school mathematics. *Journal of Education, 176*(1), 67–76.

Coburn, C. E., & Russell, J. L. (2008). District policy and teachers' social networks. *Educational Evaluation and Policy Analysis, 30*(3), 203–235.

Cohen, D. K. (1990). A revolution in one classroom: The case of Mrs. Oublier. *Educational Evaluation and Policy Analysis, 12*(3), 311–329.

Costa, A. L., & Garmston, R. J. (2016). *Cognitive coaching: Developing self-directed leaders and learners.* Rowman & Littlefield.

Cuevas, G., & Yeatts, K. (2005). *Navigating through algebra in grades 3–5.* National Council of Teachers of Mathematics.

Darling-Hammond, L., Wei, R. C., Andree, A., Richardson, N., & Orphanos, S. (2009). *Professional learning in the learning profession: A status report on teacher development in the United States and abroad.* National Staff Development Council.

Dewey, J. (1933). *How we think: A restatement of the relation of reflective thinking to the educative process.* D. C. Health.

Heineke, S. F. (2013). Coaching discourse: Supporting teachers' professional learning. *The Elementary School Journal, 113*(3), 409–433.

Hiebert, J., & Carpenter, T. P. (1992). Learning and teaching with understanding. In D. A. Grouws (Ed.), *Handbook of research on mathematics teaching and learning* (pp. 65–97). Macmillan.

Hiebert, J., & Grouws, D. A. (2007). The effects of classroom mathematics teaching on students' learning. In F. K. Lester (Ed.), *Second handbook of research on mathematics teaching and learning* (pp. 371–404). Information Age.

Hiebert, J., Morris, A. K., Berk, D., & Jansen, A. (2007). Preparing teachers to learn from teaching. *Journal of Teacher Education, 58*(1), 47–61.

Hill, H. C., & Papay, J. R. (2022). *Building better PL: How to strengthen teacher learning.* Harvard University and Annenberg Institute at Brown University.

Hollingsworth, H., & Clarke, D. (2017). Video as a tool for focusing teacher self-reflection: Supporting and provoking teacher learning. *Journal of Mathematics Teacher Education, 20,* 457–475.

Hu, Y., & Veen, K. V. (2020). How features of the implementation process shape the success of an observation-based coaching program: Perspectives of teachers and coaches. *The Elementary School Journal, 121*(2), 283–310.

Ippolito, J. (2010). Three ways that literacy coaches balance responsive and directive relationships with teachers. *The Elementary School Journal, 111*(1), 164–190.

Institute for Learning. (2016). Max's dog food [Unpublished task]. University of Pittsburgh.

Jackson, K. J., Shahan, E. C., Gibbons, L. K., & Cobb, P. A. (2012). Launching complex tasks. *Mathematics Teaching in the Middle School, 22*(5), 304–307.

Knight, J. (2017). *Instructional coaching: A partnership approach to improving instruction.* Instructional Coaching Group.

Kochmanski, N., & Cobb, P. (2023). Identifying and negotiating productive instructional improvement goals in one-on-one mathematics coaching. *Journal of Teacher Education, 74*(5). 437–450.

Kraft, M. A., Blazar, D., & Hogan, D. (2018). The effect of teacher coaching on instruction and achievement: A meta-analysis of the causal evidence. *Review of Education Research, 88*(4), 547–588.

Kraft, M. A., & Hill, H. C. (2020). Developing ambitious mathematics instruction through web-based coaching: A randomized field trial. *American Educational Research Journal, 57*(6), 2378–2414.

Lappan, G., Fey, J., Fitzgerald, G., Friel, S., & Phillips, E. (2014). *Connected mathematics 3: Comparing and scaling.* Pearson.

Lesh, R., Post, T., & Behr, M. (1987). Representations and translations among representations in mathematics learning and problem solving. In C. Javier (Ed.), *Problems of representation in the teaching and learning of mathematics* (pp. 33–40). Erlbaum.

Martin, D. B., Gholson, M. L., & Leonard, J. (2010). Mathematics as gatekeeper: Power and privilege in the production of knowledge. *Journal of Urban Mathematics Education, 3*(2), 12–24.

McGatha, M. B., Bay-Williams, J. M., Kobett, B. M., & Wray, J. A. (2018). *Everything you need for mathematics coaching: Tools, plans, and a process that works for any instructional leader, grades K–12*. Corwin.

National Council of Teachers of Mathematics. (2014). *Principles to actions: Ensuring mathematical success for all*.

National Governors Association Center for Best Practices & Council of Chief State School Officers. (2010). *Common core state standards for mathematics*.

Nolan, E. C., Dixon, J. K., Roy, G. J., & Andreasen, J. (2016). *Making sense of mathematics for teaching grades 6–8: (Unifying topics for an understanding of functions, statistics, and probability)*. Solution Tree Press.

Olson, J., & Barrett, J. (2004). Coaching teachers to implement mathematics reform recommendations. *Mathematics Teacher Education and Development, 6*, 63–80.

Russell, J. L., Correnti, R., Stein, M. K., Thomas, A., Bill, V., & Speranzo, L. (2020). Mathematics coaching for conceptual understanding: Promising evidence regarding the Tennessee math coaching model. *Educational Evaluation and Policy Analysis, 42*(3), 439–466.

Saclarides, E. S., & Lubienski, S. T. (2020). The influence of administrative policies and expectations on coach-teacher interactions. *The Elementary School Journal, 120*(3), 528–554.

Santagata, R., König, J., Scheiner, T., Nguyen, H., Adleff, A. K., Yang, X., & Kaiser, G. (2021). Mathematics teacher learning to notice: A systematic review of studies of video-based programs. *ZDM Mathematics Education, 53*(1), 119–134.

Smith, M. S. (2009). Talking about teaching: A strategy for engaging teachers in conversations about their practice. In G. Zimmermann (Ed.), *Empowering the mentor of the experienced mathematics teacher* (pp. 35–36). National Council of Teachers of Mathematics.

Smith, M. S., Bill, V., & Hughes, E. K. (2008). Thinking through a lesson protocol: A key for successfully implementing high-level tasks. *Mathematics Teaching in the Middle School, 14*(3), 132–138.

Smith, M. S., Bill, V., & Sherin, M. G. (2020). *The 5 practices in practice: Successfully orchestrating mathematics discussions in your elementary school classroom*. Corwin.

Smith, M. S., & Sherin, M. G. (2019). *The 5 practices in practice: Successfully orchestrating mathematics discussions in your middle school classroom*. Corwin.

Smith, M. S., Steele, M. D., & Raith, M. L. (2017). *Taking action: Implementing effective mathematics teaching practices in Grades 6–8*. National Council of Teachers of Mathematics.

Smith, M. S., Steele, M. D., & Sherin, M. G. (2020). *The 5 practices in practice: Successfully orchestrating mathematics discussions in your high school classroom*. Corwin.

Smith, M. S., & Stein, M. K. (1998). Selecting and creating mathematical tasks: From research to practice. *Mathematics Teaching in the Middle School, 3*(5), 344–350.

Smith, M. S., & Stein, M. K. (2011). *5 practices for orchestrating productive mathematics discussions*. National Council of Teachers of Mathematics.

Smith, M. S., & Stein, M. K. (2018). *5 practices for orchestrating productive mathematics discussions* (2nd ed.). National Council of Teachers of Mathematics.

Stein, M. K., & Lane, S. (1996). Instructional tasks and the development of student capacity to think and reason: An analysis of the relationship between teaching and learning in a reform mathematics project. *Educational Research and Evaluation, 2*(1), 50–80.

Stigler, J. W., & Hiebert, J. (1999). *The teaching gap: Best ideas from the world's teachers for improving in the classroom.* The Free Press.

Stigler, J. W., & Hiebert, J. (2004). Improving mathematics teaching. *Educational Leadership, 61*(5), 12–17.

TERC. (2017). *Investigations 3: Grade 5, unit 7 races, arrays and grids.* Pearson.

Turner, E. E., & Celedón-Pattichis, S. (2011). Mathematical problem solving among Latina/o kindergartners: An analysis of opportunities to learn. *Journal of Latinos and Education, 10*(2), 146–169.

University of Chicago School Mathematics Project. (2007). *Everyday mathematics. Fifth grade: Teacher's resource package.* Wright Group/McGraw-Hill.

van der Linden, S., van der Meij, J., & McKenney, S. (2022). Teacher video coaching, from design features to student impacts: A systematic literature review. *Review of Educational Research, 92*(1), 114–165.

West, L., & Cameron, A. (2013). *Agents of change: How content coaching transforms teaching & learning.* Heinemann.

West, L., & Staub, F. (2003). *Content-focused coaching: Transforming mathematics lessons.* Heinemann.

Witherspoon, E. B., Ferrer, N. B., Correnti, R. R., Stein, M. K., & Schunn, C. D. (2021). Coaching that supports teachers' learning to enact ambitious instruction. *Instructional Science, 49*(6), 877–898.

Woleck, K. R. (2010). *Moments in mathematics coaching: Improving k-5 instruction.* Corwin.

Yurekli, B., & Stein, M. K. (in press). Research-based design of coaching for ambitious mathematics instruction. *Journal of Mathematics Teacher Education.*

Index

Area of right triangle, 37–39, 37 (figure)
Armour-Thomas, E., 109
Artzt, A. F., 109

Celebration Cakes task, 12 (figure), 13–15
Coaching cycle
  lesson phase, 62, 62 (figure)
  phases of, 10–11, 101–102
  post-lesson phase, 64, 64 (figure)
  pre-lesson phase, 25 (figure), 42 (figure)
  timing of, 106–108, 107 (figure)
Coaching for equity: Conversations that change practice (Aguilar), 1
Coaching model
  benefits, 102
  building, teacher thinking, 103–104
  5 practices, 104–105
  online coaching, 108–109
  online resources, 8
  ownership, teachers, 102–103
  setting expectations, 105
  teacher challenges, addressing, 108
  video recording lessons, 105–106
Coach–teacher conversations, 2, 5
  Celebration Cakes task, 11–15, 12 (figure)
  coaching cycle, phases, 10–11
  guide for designing conferences, 21–22, 22–23 (figure)
  inquiry routine, 17–20
  nature of, 12, 15–17
Cognitive Coaching: Developing Self-Directed Learners and Leaders (Costa & Garmston), 1
Common Core State Standards for Mathematics (CCSSM), 38

Dewey, J., 109

Emery
  challenges, 49–50
  goals and task, 48, 48 (figure)
  lesson planning tool, 160–161
  monitoring tool, 49, 162
  teacher challenges tool, 157–159
Everything You Need for Mathematics Coaching (McGatha), 1
5 Practices for Orchestrating Productive Mathematics Discussions (Smith & Stein), 2, 8, 104
Fractions of Fractions task, 52–53 (figure), 54–61, 90–94

Goals and tasks identification, 140–145
  analysis, 31–33
  area of right triangle, 37–39, 37 (figure)
  characteristics, 27
  Downloading Music task, 28 (figure), 29–31
  example, 34, 34–36 (figure)
  face-to-face communication, 28
  learning opportunities, 40–41
  Task Analysis Guide (TAG), 27, 33, 39, 139
Guide for designing conferences, 21–22, 22–23 (figure), 50, 116–138

Hiebert, J., 26, 40
High-level tasks, 26. *See also* Goals and tasks identification

Inquiry routine, coach–teacher conversations, 17–18
  generalization, 19–20, 24
  invitations, 18, 24
  rehearsals, 18–19, 24
  suggestions, 19, 24
Instructional Coaching: A Partnership Approach to Improving Instruction (Knight), 1

Jamie and Coach Jesse
  Fractions of Fractions task, 52–53 (figure), 54–61
  goals and task, 52–53 (figure)
  noticing and wondering tool, 167
  post-lesson conference plan, 168–169
  pre-lesson conference plan, 163–164

Kyle
  challenges, 44–47, 44 (figure)
  goals and task, 44 (figure)
  lesson planning tool, 153–155
  monitoring tool, 156
  teacher challenges tool, 149–152

Lesson planning tool, 39, 146, 153–155, 160–161
Levels of demands, 139
Logan and Coach Shawn
  Celebration Cakes task, 12 (figure), 13–15
  challenges, 15–17
  learning goals, 11–12
Low-level tasks, 26–27

Max's Dog Food task, 8 (figure), 22, 34, 79
Moments in Mathematics Coaching: Improving K–5 Instruction (Woleck), 9

Monitoring tool, 49, 147, 156, 162
Morgan and Coach Parker
   Downloading Music task, 28 (figure), 29–31
   goal and task, 28, 28 (figure), 31–33

Nicki and Coach Alex
   goals and task, 66, 66–67 (figure)
   noticings and wonderings, 76–79, 77 (figure)
   Patio task, 66–67 (figure), 68–73
   post-lesson conference plan, 83 (figure), 84–85 (figure), 88–89 (figure)
Noticing and wondering tool, 75–79, 77 (figure), 165, 167

Online coaching, 108–109
Online resources, 8

Patio task, 66–67 (figure), 68–73
Post-lesson conference
   constructing, 79–90
   engaging, 90–98
   Fractions of Fractions task, 90–94
   noticings and wonderings, 75–79, 77 (figure)
   planning tool, 166
   purpose of, 64–65
   tips for preparing, 99
   video clips, 65–75
Pre-lesson conference
   Celebration Cakes task, 12 (figure), 13–15
   constructing, 50–51
   Fractions of Fractions task, 52–60
   identifying challenges, 44–50
   planning tool, 148
   purpose of, 42–43
   tips for preparing, 61–62
Preparing for the lesson, 25–26
   goals and tasks identification, 27–38
   teacher's planning process, 26–27, 39–40

Sherin, M. G., 16
Smith, M. S., 16, 39
Stigler, J. W., 26

Task Analysis Guide (TAG), 27, 33, 39, 139
Teacher challenges tool, 26, 112–115
   addressing, 108
   advantages, 5–6
   coaching activities, 6–7
   Emery, 157–159
   5 practices, 2–4 (figure)
   Kyle, 149–152
   opportunity, 8–9
   organizing, 4–6
   ownership, 102–103
   purposes, 4–5

Video clips
   analysis, 73–75
   selection, 65–73
Video recordings, 105–106

Woleck, K. R., 9, 110

CORWIN Mathematics

Supporting TEACHERS | Empowering STUDENTS

PETER LILJEDAHL
14 optimal practices for thinking that create an ideal setting for deep mathematics learning to occur.
Grades K–12

CHASE ORTON
A guide that leads math teachers through a journey to cultivate a more equitable, inclusive, and cohesive culture of professionalism for themselves.
Grades K–12

KIMBERLY RIMBEY
Much-needed guidance on how to meet the diverse needs of students using small group math instruction.
Grades K–5

BETH MCCORD KOBETT, FRANCIS (SKIP) FENNELL, KAREN S. KARP, DELISE ANDREWS, LATRENDA KNIGHTEN, JEFF SHIH, DESIREE HARRISON, BARBARA ANN SWARTZ, SORSHA-MARIA T. MULROE
Detailed plans for helping elementary students experience deep mathematical learning.
Grades K–1, 2–3, 4–5

LOU EDWARD MATTHEWS, SHELLY M. JONES, YOLANDA A. PARKER
A resource for designing inspiring learning experiences driven by the kind of high-quality and culturally relevant mathematics tasks that connect students to their world.
Elementary, Middle and High School

JOHN J. SANGIOVANNI, SUSIE KATT, KEVIN J. DYKEMA
A guide for empowering students to embrace productive struggle to build essential skills for learning and living—both inside and outside the classroom.
Grades K–12

To order, visit corwin.com/math

**JENNIFER M. BAY-WILLIAMS,
JOHN J. SANGIOVANNI,
ROSALBA SERRANO,
SHERRI MARTINIE,
JENNIFER SUH, C. DAVID WALTERS**

Because fluency is so much more than basic facts and algorithms.
Grades K–8

**ROBERT Q. BERRY III, BASIL M. CONWAY IV,
BRIAN R. LAWLER, JOHN W. STALEY,
COURTNEY KOESTLER, JENNIFER WARD,
MARIA DEL ROSARIO ZAVALA,
TONYA GAU BARTELL, CATHERY YEH,
MATHEW FELTON-KOESTLER,
LATEEFAH ID-DEEN,
MARY CANDACE RAYGOZA,
AMANDA RUIZ, EVA THANHEISER**

Learn to plan instruction that engages students in mathematics explorations through age-appropriate and culturally relevant social justice topics.
Early Elementary, Upper Elementary, Middle School, High School

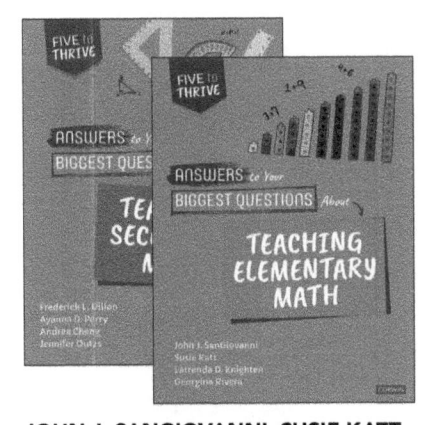

**JOHN J. SANGIOVANNI, SUSIE KATT,
LATRENDA D. KNIGHTEN,
GEORGINA RIVERA,
FREDERICK L. DILLON,
AYANNA D. PERRY,
ANDREA CHENG, JENNIFER OUTZS**

Actionable answers to your most pressing questions about teaching elementary and secondary math.
Elementary, Secondary

**SARA DELANO MOORE,
KIMBERLY RIMBEY**

A journey toward making manipulatives meaningful.
Grades K–3, 4–8

CM22153268

CORWIN

CORWIN
A Sage Company

Helping educators make the greatest impact

CORWIN HAS ONE MISSION: to enhance education through intentional professional learning.

We build long-term relationships with our authors, educators, clients, and associations who partner with us to develop and continuously improve the best evidence-based practices that establish and support lifelong learning.